PowerShel in 7 Days

Learn essential skills in scripting and automation using PowerShell

Liam Cleary

www.bpbonline.com

First Edition 2024

Copyright © BPB Publications, India

ISBN: 978-93-55518-910

All Rights Reserved. No part of this publication may be reproduced, distributed or transmitted in any form or by any means or stored in a database or retrieval system, without the prior written permission of the publisher with the exception to the program listings which may be entered, stored and executed in a computer system, but they can not be reproduced by the means of publication, photocopy, recording, or by any electronic and mechanical means.

LIMITS OF LIABILITY AND DISCLAIMER OF WARRANTY

The information contained in this book is true to correct and the best of author's and publisher's knowledge. The author has made every effort to ensure the accuracy of these publications, but publisher cannot be held responsible for any loss or damage arising from any information in this book.

All trademarks referred to in the book are acknowledged as properties of their respective owners but BPB Publications cannot guarantee the accuracy of this information.

To View Complete
BPB Publications Catalogue
Scan the QR Code:

www.bpbonline.com

Dedicated to

My beloved wife:
Lisa
and
My Children ***Bethan***, ***Joel***, ***Aidan*** *and* ***Noah***

About the Author

Liam Cleary has been deeply immersed in computer training, programming, and cybersecurity, discovering his passion for these fields early in his career. His professional journey led him to work extensively within core infrastructure and security services. He founded SharePlicity, a consultancy specializing in Microsoft 365 and Azure technologies, where he spearheads efforts to enhance collaboration, document management, and business process automation and implements robust security controls. A Microsoft MVP Alumni with 17 years of recognition and a Microsoft Certified Trainer, Liam excels in architecture, security, and bridging the gap to software development. His recent focus has been on security within Microsoft 365, Azure, and related platforms. As an educator, Liam develops online courses for platforms like Pluralsight, LinkedIn Learning, Cloud Academy, and Cybrary IT and teaches Microsoft Certification courses for Opsgility and Microsoft. Beyond professional pursuits, Liam is actively involved in community events, from user groups to conferences, sharing knowledge, coding with his kids, and engaging in various outdoor adventures.

About the Reviewer

Carole McNally is a tech industry veteran with an extensive 20-year journey. Rooted in the principles of neurodiversity and a staunch advocate for lifelong learning, Carole has dedicated her career to making technology accessible to all.

As an Integration Specialist, Carole excels in crafting seamless connections through a decade of expertise in multilanguage ETL. Her passion lies in innovating solutions that bridge the gap between technology and users.

Carole's proficiency shines in developing robust integration solutions, utilizing in-house products, APIs, and third-party tools. With a dynamic approach, she excels in configuring front-office products, expanding the Microsoft Bot Framework, and implementing Adaptive Cards to optimize user experiences and operational efficiency.

Within Techwitch Ltd, Carole has provided invaluable technical consultancy, achieving Cyber Essentials certification, troubleshooting complex issues, and overseeing successful migrations. Certified as a Conversational Designer, her skills extend to Azure Cognitive Services and API integrations, showcasing a commitment to staying at the forefront of industry advancements.

Acknowledgement

I want to express my deepest gratitude to my family and friends, especially my wife, Lisa, and my children, Bethan, Joel, Aidan, and Noah, for their unwavering support and encouragement throughout this book's writing.

I am also grateful to BPB Publications for their guidance and expertise in bringing this book to fruition. Writing this book was a long journey, with the valuable participation and collaboration of reviewers, technical experts, and editors.

I also want to acknowledge the valuable contributions of my colleagues and co-workers during many years working in the tech industry, who have taught me so much and provided valuable feedback on my work.

Finally, I thank all the readers who have taken an interest in my book and for their support in making it a reality. Your encouragement has been invaluable.

Preface

"PowerShell in 7 Days" is a comprehensive guide that aims to demystify the world of PowerShell scripting and automation. PowerShell is a must-have skill set for IT professionals and system administrators. This book guides you through PowerShell, making it an indispensable resource for newcomers and seasoned professionals aiming to refine their automation skills.

Throughout the book, you will embark on a structured journey that transforms you from a PowerShell novice to a proficient scripter. Starting from the very foundations of PowerShell, the book unravels its syntax and core functionalities. As you progress, you will delve into more advanced topics such as creating complex scripts, managing data locally and remotely, and effectively using PowerShell for problem-solving and system troubleshooting.

The book is for beginners and IT veterans looking to integrate PowerShell into their workflow. Through fundamental concepts and hands-on examples, you will learn to leverage PowerShell's capabilities to streamline your daily tasks, enhance system performance, and automate repetitive and complex operations. The focus is on the 'how' and the 'why,' providing a deep understanding of PowerShell's potential in various job roles.

By the end of "PowerShell in 7 Days," you will have gained a comprehensive understanding of PowerShell's capabilities and how to harness them effectively. The book is a learning tool and a reference guide that helps you in your professional journey. Whether automating a small task or tackling a large-scale enterprise operation, the insights and skills acquired here will be valuable to any professional toolkit. Welcome to the world of PowerShell – let's embark on this journey together.

Chapter 1: Introducing PowerShell – This chapter provides a comprehensive introduction for readers to understand and leverage PowerShell, Microsoft's task automation and configuration management framework. It includes essential information on the initial setup, guidance on the tools required for writing and executing scripts, and an explanation of PowerShell's powerful capabilities for automating a wide range of administrative tasks. The chapter also presents a historical perspective of PowerShell's evolution, its various versions, and the current landscape, setting the stage for why learning PowerShell is invaluable for IT professionals. Readers will also discover the diverse contexts in which

PowerShell can be applied, from basic system administration to complex automation scenarios.

Chapter 2: Setting Up PowerShell – This chapter provides a detailed guide to help readers install PowerShell on different platforms. It offers specific instructions for each installation method, including using the PowerShell Gallery for module management and direct installable packages for Windows users. The chapter also explains how to set up PowerShell on macOS and Linux. Additionally, the chapter includes a comparative overview of the various installation methods available. It helps readers make informed choices that suit their specific requirements and environment.

Chapter 3: Getting Started with Modules and Providers – This chapter provides a comprehensive understanding of the PowerShell environment, focusing on the critical roles of modules and providers. In this chapter, readers will learn how to use PowerShell modules in detail, including their purpose and how to leverage both built-in and external modules to enhance the shell's capabilities. The various types of providers and how to interact with different data stores within PowerShell are explained. The chapter also simplifies the help system, a valuable resource for mastering command syntax and functionality. Moreover, the chapter discusses the integration and use of WMI and CIM, demonstrating how to use these powerful tools for system management and information retrieval.

Chapter 4: Executing PowerShell Commands – This chapter provides readers with the necessary knowledge to execute PowerShell commands effectively in various environments. It explains the different types of cmdlets available and the appropriate way to use them within a Windows setting. The chapter also focuses on specific modules, teaching readers how to use specialized commands tailor-made for their scripting needs. Additionally, it emphasizes the importance of command outputs, allowing readers to interpret and use the data returned from their scripts. Furthermore, the chapter thoroughly explores the integration of PowerShell with Visual Studio Code, demonstrating how this powerful editor can enhance scripting efficiency. By the end of this chapter, readers will have acquired the skills to write and debug PowerShell scripts within Visual Studio Code, laying a solid foundation for advanced scripting and automation.

Chapter 5: Working with Variables and Pipelines – This chapter is about using variables and pipelines to manage data flow and storage in scripting. In this chapter, you will learn about the pipeline operator, a fundamental feature of PowerShell that allows for seamless output transfer between commands. The chapter covers the creation, manipulation, and management of variables, from basic data types to complex objects, giving readers the skills to handle data dynamically within their scripts. Additionally, it discusses the nuances of declaring and casting variable types to ensure data integrity and type safety. The chapter also covers advanced techniques for passing variables between commands, which enhances script modularity and reusability. Finally, readers will learn sophisticated strategies for filtering data within pipelines, allowing for refined and precise data operations. With practical examples and clear explanations, this chapter will give you a robust understanding of these core PowerShell concepts, ready to implement them in real-world scenarios.

Chapter 6: Deep Diving PowerShell Objects – This chapter provides detailed insights into PowerShell objects and their usage in scripting. It begins with the basics of PowerShell objects, which are crucial for utilizing the scripting language to its full potential. The chapter covers managing and creating string arrays, a fundamental skill for efficient data organization and handling. Further, it delves into the intricacies of object properties and methods, enabling the readers to manipulate custom data structures adeptly. The chapter also introduces the [PSCustomObject] data type, which offers a dynamic approach to object creation. Precisely defining data types within PowerShell variables is also emphasized as a critical practice for script accuracy. The chapter explores export and import cmdlets, which provide a pathway for maintaining data persistence. Lastly, the chapter concludes by demonstrating how PowerShell can be connected with .NET objects, expanding the reader's automation toolkit with the vast capabilities of the .NET framework.

Chapter 7: Using Functions and Parameters – This chapter aims to help readers learn how to create and use PowerShell functions, which will transform how they script and automate tasks. The chapter starts with the basics of crafting PowerShell functions, which will teach you how to encapsulate and modularize code for reusability and maintainability. After that, we move on to the critical aspect of determining the output of functions, which ensures that each function serves its intended purpose effectively. The journey continues by incorporating parameters into functions, significantly enhancing flexibility and adaptability for various use cases. The chapter further guides you through setting default values and defining data types for parameters, which is pivotal in maintaining data integrity and script reliability. The chapter also covers advanced features like parameter validation and input masks, offering methods to safeguard input and streamline function execution. Finally, the chapter culminates by demonstrating the integration of these elements into complex scripts, showcasing the power of tasks in creating sophisticated and efficient PowerShell tools.

Chapter 8: Flow Control, Looping, and Error Handling – This chapter provides comprehensive insights into the techniques of controlling script execution using loops and error handling, which are crucial for robust PowerShell scripting. The chapter starts with an overview of looping constructs within PowerShell, followed by an in-depth exploration of the ForEach-Object command and foreach loops, which are vital for iterating over collections. The chapter then delves into the Switch command, which streamlines decision-making in scripts based on conditional logic. The latter part of the chapter is dedicated to the foundational concepts of error handling in PowerShell, emphasizing its critical importance in scripting for preventing and managing runtime exceptions. Readers will learn to implement error-handling mechanisms that ensure scripts execute gracefully, even when encountering unforeseen issues. By the end of this chapter, readers will be equipped with the knowledge to manage the flow of their PowerShell scripts effectively, confidently address errors, and maintain control over script outcomes in various scenarios.

Chapter 9: Scripts for Multiple Output Paths – This chapter simplifies the process of managing the output of PowerShell scripts across different destinations. This chapter serves as a foundation for understanding PowerShell's output redirection, a valuable feature that allows you to route script results to the appropriate endpoints. It teaches you how to use output redirection operators precisely, directing outputs to files, consoles, or other processes. The chapter then covers the creation of commands capable of generating multiple output streams, enhancing script versatility. It also discusses techniques for piping output to various targets to ensure effective data distribution where needed. Additionally, the chapter presents the skill of splitting output into separate files, along with methods for appending data to existing files without overwriting valuable information. Finally, the chapter culminates with strategies for dynamically customizing output destinations using conditional logic and loops, tailoring the data handling to the script's context. The author provides practical examples to illustrate how these techniques come together, providing a template for scripts requiring complex output management.

Chapter 10: PowerShell Remoting, WinRM, and the Invoke-Comma – This chapter discusses using PowerShell Remoting, WinRM, and Invoke-Command for managing and scripting on remote computers using PowerShell. The chapter starts by introducing PowerShell remoting, which is an essential tool for remote management and automation. It explains Windows Remote Management (WinRM) and its role as the backbone of PowerShell remoting. The chapter also covers the different configurations, functionalities, and operational scope of WinRM. Furthermore, the chapter addresses the critical security aspect and highlights the best practices to ensure safe and secure remote operations. The readers are guided through the detailed steps to configure remoting in Windows and Linux environments, which will help them extend their administrative reach across different platforms. The chapter also explores the New-PSSession and Enter-PSSession cmdlets, allowing seamless remote connections to Windows and Linux systems. Finally, the chapter thoroughly examines the Invoke-Command cmdlet, which effectively executes commands on remote computers. By the end of this chapter, readers will have a comprehensive understanding of how to use PowerShell for remote management and automation tasks, regardless of the operating system.

Chapter 11: Managing On-premises Services – The chapter covers many topics, including an introduction to specialized PowerShell commands designed for on-premises administrative tasks. It then provides a detailed guide on configuring and managing Active Directory, simplifying the complexities involved in user and group management and highlighting the effectiveness of PowerShell in these critical areas. The chapter also delves into the management of domain controllers, providing insights into the nuances of this crucial aspect of network infrastructure. It covers essential network services such as the **Domain Name Service (DNS)** and **Dynamic Host Configuration Protocol (DHCP)**, demonstrating how PowerShell can be a powerful tool for managing them. Additionally, the chapter explains how to create and manage file shares, which is a crucial task in maintaining an organization's data accessibility and security. The chapter also explores managing certificates within Windows Server to ensure a comprehensive understanding of this vital security component. Finally, the chapter concludes by providing insights into managing various server roles and features, showcasing PowerShell's versatility in handling multiple server management tasks. This chapter aims to empower the reader with the knowledge and skills necessary to manage and optimize on-premises services using PowerShell, turning routine administrative tasks into streamlined processes.

Chapter 12: Troubleshooting Windows and Performance Optimization – This chapter starts by delving into system resource analysis, teaching readers how to scrutinize CPU, memory, disk, and network usage using PowerShell commands. This foundational knowledge is vital for identifying and addressing performance issues hindering system responsiveness and reliability. The chapter then transitions into the nuances of diagnosing and resolving performance bottlenecks, offering practical techniques to pinpoint and alleviate these critical issues. It teaches readers with PowerShell command expertise, such as utilizing ping, traceroute, DNS lookups, and firewall configurations, to diagnose and resolve network problems effectively. In the security realm, the chapter provides in-depth insights on identifying and remediating security vulnerabilities. Readers will learn to employ PowerShell for essential security tasks, including malware scanning, updating Windows Defender, and applying necessary security patches. The chapter also provides readers with the skills to analyze and filter event logs. By mastering these techniques, readers can extract critical information about errors, warnings, and events that could signify underlying system issues. Lastly, the chapter addresses common pitfalls and challenges of using PowerShell for Windows troubleshooting. It guides handling errors, exceptions, and permissions, ensuring readers are well-prepared to tackle real-world troubleshooting scenarios with confidence and expertise.

Chapter 13: Miscellaneous PowerShell Capabilities – The final chapter covers PowerShell security. It explains how to secure PowerShell environments, regulate script execution, and ensure a secure scripting environment. The chapter also discusses methods for maintaining computer and data security while using PowerShell and implementing AppLocker policies to turn off unauthorized PowerShell scripts. Additionally, it explains the importance of signing PowerShell scripts for script integrity and authenticity. Finally, the chapter offers valuable insights and guidance for IT administrators on the next steps in their journey with PowerShell.

Code Bundle and Coloured Images

Please follow the link to download the
Code Bundle and the *Coloured Images* of the book:

https://rebrand.ly/9faa44

The code bundle for the book is also hosted on GitHub at
https://github.com/bpbpublications/PowerShell-in-7-Days.
In case there's an update to the code, it will be updated on the existing GitHub repository.

We have code bundles from our rich catalogue of books and videos available at **https://github.com/bpbpublications**. Check them out!

Errata

We take immense pride in our work at BPB Publications and follow best practices to ensure the accuracy of our content to provide with an indulging reading experience to our subscribers. Our readers are our mirrors, and we use their inputs to reflect and improve upon human errors, if any, that may have occurred during the publishing processes involved. To let us maintain the quality and help us reach out to any readers who might be having difficulties due to any unforeseen errors, please write to us at :

errata@bpbonline.com

Your support, suggestions and feedbacks are highly appreciated by the BPB Publications' Family.

Did you know that BPB offers eBook versions of every book published, with PDF and ePub files available? You can upgrade to the eBook version at www.bpbonline.com and as a print book customer, you are entitled to a discount on the eBook copy. Get in touch with us at :

business@bpbonline.com for more details.

At **www.bpbonline.com**, you can also read a collection of free technical articles, sign up for a range of free newsletters, and receive exclusive discounts and offers on BPB books and eBooks.

Piracy

If you come across any illegal copies of our works in any form on the internet, we would be grateful if you would provide us with the location address or website name. Please contact us at **business@bpbonline.com** with a link to the material.

If you are interested in becoming an author

If there is a topic that you have expertise in, and you are interested in either writing or contributing to a book, please visit **www.bpbonline.com**. We have worked with thousands of developers and tech professionals, just like you, to help them share their insights with the global tech community. You can make a general application, apply for a specific hot topic that we are recruiting an author for, or submit your own idea.

Reviews

Please leave a review. Once you have read and used this book, why not leave a review on the site that you purchased it from? Potential readers can then see and use your unbiased opinion to make purchase decisions. We at BPB can understand what you think about our products, and our authors can see your feedback on their book. Thank you!

For more information about BPB, please visit **www.bpbonline.com**.

Join our book's Discord space

Join the book's Discord Workspace for Latest updates, Offers, Tech happenings around the world, New Release and Sessions with the Authors:

https://discord.bpbonline.com

Table of Contents

1. **Introducing PowerShell** 1
   Introduction 1
   Structure 1
   Objectives 1
   Introduction to PowerShell 2
   PowerShell versions and current state 2
   What is PowerShell? 3
   Who is PowerShell for? 4
   When should you use PowerShell? 4
   Conclusion 5

2. **Setting Up PowerShell** 7
   Introduction 7
   Structure 7
   Objectives 7
   Overview of the PowerShell installation options 8
   Installing using an installable package 10
   Installing on a non-Windows platform 13
   Using the PowerShell Gallery 15
   Conclusion 16

3. **Getting Started with Modules and Providers** 17
   Introduction 17
   Structure 17
   Objectives 18
   Introduction to PowerShell modules 18
   Purpose of PowerShell modules 18
   Understand the different types of providers 19
   Use the built-in PowerShell providers 21
   Find all PDF files in your documents folder 22

       Add a new value to the PATH environment variable 22

       Create a new registry entry 22

       Check the existence of a certificate and then import 23

   Import modules from the operating system 24

   Import external PowerShell modules 28

   How to use the help system 32

   Review WMI within PowerShell 36

   Review CIM within PowerShell 40

   Conclusion 42

4. **Executing PowerShell Commands** 45

   Introduction 45

   Structure 45

   Objectives 46

   Discovering commands to execute 46

   Understanding the different types of commands 55

       Cmdlets 55

       Functions 56

       Scripts 56

       Aliases 57

   Executing existing commands within a Windows computer 58

   Executing commands from specific modules 60

   Understanding the command return or response object 63

   Using PowerShell in Visual Studio Code 67

   Conclusion 69

5. **Working with Variables and Pipelines** 71

   Introduction 71

   Structure 71

   Objectives 72

   Understanding the pipeline operator 72

   Executing commands that flow into single and multiple pipelines 75

   Using variables in PowerShell 78

Creating and managing variables in PowerShell	80
Declaring and casting variable types	82
Passing variables between commands	87
Techniques for filtering data in the pipeline	89
Conclusion	93

6. Deep Diving PowerShell Objects 95
Introduction 95
Structure 95
Objectives 96
Understanding PowerShell objects 96
Creating and managing string arrays 98
Working with object properties and methods 100
Creating and managing custom objects 103
Using [PSCustomObject] data type 104
Setting specific data types within PowerShell variables 107
Using the Export and Import cmdlets 111
Understanding and working with .NET objects in PowerShell 114
Conclusion 118

7. Using Functions and Parameters 119
Introduction 119
Structure 119
Objectives 120
Creating PowerShell functions 120
Choosing the output of functions 123
Creating and using parameters in PowerShell functions 127
Using default values and data types in parameters 130
Advanced parameter features 132
Passing and returning values in PowerShell functions 137
Defining and calling PowerShell functions 140
Combining functions into complex scripts 142
Conclusion 146

8.	Flow Control, Looping, and Error Handling	147
	Introduction	147
	Structure	147
	Objectives	148
	Overview of looping within PowerShell	148
	Reviewing the ForEach-Object command	149
	Reviewing foreach loops	151
	Reviewing the switch command	154
	Looping capabilities	156
	Understanding error handling basics	158
	Implementing error handling to control the flow	159
	Conclusion	166
9.	Scripts for Multiple Output Paths	167
	Introduction	167
	Structure	167
	Objectives	168
	Introduction to PowerShell output redirection	168
	Using output redirection operators	168
	Creating commands that produce multiple outputs	170
	Piping output to multiple destinations	175
	Splitting output into different files	177
	Appending results to existing files	179
	Customizing output destinations with conditional statements and loops	180
	Examples of scripts with multiple output paths	183
	Conclusion	184
10.	PowerShell Remoting, WinRM, and the Invoke-Command	185
	Introduction	185
	Structure	185
	Objectives	186
	What is PowerShell remoting?	186
	Understanding WinRM and its role in PowerShell remoting	188

      Understanding the security implications of PowerShell remoting 189

      Configure remoting within Windows..191

      Configure remoting within Linux 193

      Creating and using a remote session with New-PSSession and
Enter-PSSession..196

      Remotely connecting to Windows and Linux using PowerShell.................199

      Using Invoke-Command to execute commands on remote computer 204

      Conclusion 208

11. Managing On-premises Services...209

      Introduction 209

      Structure 209

      Objectives 210

      Introduction to PowerShell for on-premises Management 210

      Configuring and managing Active Directory 211

      User and group management..216

      Managing domain controllers 222

      Managing DNS and DHCP services 226

      Creating and managing file shares..228

      Managing certificates...230

      Managing server roles and features 232

      Conclusion 234

12. Troubleshooting Windows and Performance Optimization...........................235

      Introduction 235

      Structure 235

      Objectives 236

      Analyzing system resources..236

      Diagnosing and resolving performance bottlenecks 242

      Troubleshooting network connectivity issues 247

      Identifying and remediating security vulnerabilities....................................252

      Analyzing and filtering event logs 255

      Challenges in using PowerShell for Windows troubleshooting 259

   Handling complex error messages 259
   Execution policy restrictions..260
   Misinterpretation of command outputs 260
   Overlooking security implications..260
  Conclusion 261

13. Miscellaneous PowerShell Capabilities **263**
  Introduction 263
  Structure 264
  Objectives 264
  Importance of securing PowerShell 264
  Understanding PowerShell Execution Policies 265
  Keeping computer and data secure...267
  Understanding PowerShell Constrained Mode 269
  Using AppLocker policies to disable PowerShell scripts..........................272
  Signing PowerShell scripts for reuse..273
  Next steps for the IT administrator 275
  Conclusion 276

Index.. **277-282**

CHAPTER 1
Introducing PowerShell

Introduction

This chapter will introduce you to PowerShell. We will start by reviewing the history of PowerShell, discussing versions and the current state of PowerShell, as well as providing an understanding of what PowerShell is and why you should consider using it.

Structure

In this chapter, we will cover the following topics:
- Introduction to PowerShell
- PowerShell versions and current state
- What is PowerShell?
- Who is PowerShell for?
- When should you use PowerShell?

Objectives

By the end of this chapter, you will understand PowerShell, its history, versions, current state, and rationale for usage.

Introduction to PowerShell

In November 2006, Microsoft released the first version of PowerShell, the initial release for Windows only, aiming to automate and simplify administrative tasks in Windows environments. Microsoft created PowerShell as a powerful scripting language and task automation framework to surpass the capabilities of the traditional command prompt.

In 2016 Microsoft released PowerShell Core, expanding the reach of the PowerShell scripting beyond Windows to include macOS and Linux platforms. It has evolved through multiple versions, with each iteration bringing new features, improvements, and cross-platform compatibility.

Today, PowerShell is an indispensable tool for system administrators and developers, offering a robust and flexible solution for managing and automating various tasks across diverse environments.

PowerShell versions and current state

The initial version of PowerShell was a Windows component only, known as Windows PowerShell. It only worked within Windows operating systems and provided a limited subset of capabilities for management. In August 2016, with the introduction of PowerShell Core, Microsoft made it open-source and cross-platform. The last version of Windows PowerShell is Windows PowerShell 5.1, and PowerShell 7+ is the successor to PowerShell Core 6+. The following table outlines the Windows PowerShell, PowerShell Core, and PowerShell versions and their respective release dates:

Type	Version	Release Date
Windows PowerShell	1.0	November 2006
Windows PowerShell	2.0	July 2009
Windows PowerShell	3.0	October 2012
Windows PowerShell	4.0	October 2013
Windows PowerShell	5.0	February 2016
Windows PowerShell	5.1	August 2016
PowerShell Core	6.0	January 2018
PowerShell Core	6.1	September 2018
PowerShell Core	6.2	March 2019
PowerShell	7.0	March 2020

Type	Version	Release Date
PowerShell	7.1	November 2020
PowerShell	7.2	November 2021
PowerShell	7.3	November 2022

Table 1.1: PowerShell versions and releases dates

PowerShell 6+ is installed side-by-side with earlier PowerShell releases. There are two editions of PowerShell 6+, the desktop and core versions. The desktop version runs on the .NET Framework, and the core version runs on .NET Core. PowerShell 7+, built on .NET Core 3.1, adds significant functionality compared to Windows PowerShell and aims to maintain full backward compatibility with Windows PowerShell.

The .NET Foundation and Microsoft develop and maintain PowerShell versions. They shifted the development focus to improve its capabilities, performance, cross-platform compatibility, and operability with different cloud platforms and services. The latest release supports Windows x64 / x86, Ubuntu, Debian, CentOS, Red Hat Enterprise Linux, OpenSUSE, Fedora, and macOS and supports multiple processor types. PowerShell 7+ is available for anyone to access and contribute, and it is available within the GitHub platform: **https://github.com/PowerShell**.

What is PowerShell?

PowerShell is a task-based command-line shell and scripting language built on the .NET and .NET Core Frameworks. Microsoft designed this tool to enable IT professionals to control and automate Windows administration. In contrast to traditional command-line interfaces, PowerShell revolves around objects. An object is a structure containing data and operations you can perform on this data.

PowerShell supports providers allowing access to data stores, such as the registry, certificate store, and file system. Commands, called cmdlets (pronounced "command-lets"), are single-function commands that manipulate objects in PowerShell. They are the native commands in the PowerShell stack. In cmdlet names, the verb indicates the action it performs, while the noun specifies the target of the action. A few example cmdlets are:

- This command lists the items, such as files or folders, in the current or specified directory:

    `Get-ChildItem`

- This command creates a new user in the active directory:

    `New-ADUser`

- This command removes specified capabilities from a Windows operating system image:

  `Remove-WindowsCapability`

- This command directly puts text or objects you specify into the clipboard:

  `Set-Clipboard`

The pipeline is a powerful feature in PowerShell, allowing you to pass objects, not just text, from one cmdlet to another. It enables you to perform complex multiple operations with a single line of code.

Lastly, PowerShell allows you to write scripts and functions to automate tasks. A script is a plain text file containing one or more PowerShell commands, while a function is a list of statements with a name you assign. IT professionals can also distribute written scripts, making it an excellent solution for consistently managing deployments and configuration.

Who is PowerShell for?

Primarily, PowerShell serves IT professionals, system administrators, and developers who manage Windows-based systems, but its reach is much more comprehensive. Network engineers frequently use PowerShell for network-related tasks, from configuration to automation. **Database Administrators (DBAs)** often employ it in SQL Server environments, benefiting from its seamless database management capabilities. In the era of DevOps, the tool's scripting and automation proficiency prove indispensable for DevOps teams. Security experts also leverage PowerShell's robust features for system hardening and security audits. Cloud professionals, particularly those engaged with Azure, find its cmdlets helpful in managing cloud resources. PowerShell is widely used in various IT roles for its scripting, automation, and administrative capabilities, particularly in Microsoft environments.

When should you use PowerShell?

PowerShell is a powerful tool for automating administrative tasks and managing systems, whether those systems are in the cloud or on-premises. Some of the main reasons to use PowerShell are:

- **Automation:** PowerShell automates repetitive tasks, reducing manual effort and errors, particularly in large setups.
- **Consistency:** Scripting ensures tasks consistently perform similarly, minimizing errors.
- **Efficiency**: Automation allows swift completion of complex tasks, freeing time for other duties.

- **Compatibility:** Being a Microsoft product, PowerShell works well with other Microsoft products like Windows Server, Exchange Server, and more.
- **Cross-platform:** PowerShell Core (version 6+) can run on Linux, macOS, and Windows, broadening its utility.
- **Object-based:** PowerShell works with complex data structures, not just text, making it more powerful than many scripting languages.
- **Community support:** With a large active community, finding scripts, solutions, and best practices becomes easy.
- **Built-in security:** PowerShell incorporates features like execution policy to run scripts securely.
- **Integration with .NET:** Being built on .NET, PowerShell can access .NET classes and objects, opening additional functionality.

Conclusion

In conclusion, PowerShell has emerged as a crucial tool for automating tasks and managing systems. Since its inception in 2006, PowerShell has made significant strides in evolving its capabilities and extending its reach to various platforms. From being a Windows-specific component, it has transitioned to being cross-platform and open-source, encapsulating enhancements in its functionality and performance. The strength of PowerShell lies in its object-based operations, integration with .NET, compatibility with Microsoft products, and vast community support. With a range of features such as automation, efficiency, and built-in security, PowerShell is an indispensable tool for IT professionals in managing administrative tasks. As we continue this book, we will delve deeper into its functionalities, exploring PowerShell's immense potential in transforming system administration and task automation.

In the next chapter, we will review the installation of PowerShell, focusing on the various installation approaches and installing it in a non-Windows environment.

Join our book's Discord space

Join the book's Discord Workspace for Latest updates, Offers, Tech happenings around the world, New Release and Sessions with the Authors:

https://discord.bpbonline.com

CHAPTER 2
Setting Up PowerShell

Introduction

This chapter guides you through installing PowerShell from various options like the PowerShell Gallery, installable packages, and on non-Windows platforms such as macOS and Linux. It provides an overview of these options, detailed instructions for each method, and considerations for non-Windows installations.

Structure

In this chapter, we will cover the following topics:
- Overview of the PowerShell installation options
- Using the PowerShell Gallery
- Installing using an installable package
- Installing on a non-Windows platform

Objectives

By the end of this chapter, you will understand the various options for installing PowerShell, including the PowerShell Gallery, installable packages, and alternatives for non-Windows platforms like macOS and Linux. You will follow instructions for each method and consider the specific needs of non-Windows installations. This knowledge will enable you to install and use PowerShell in your chosen environment.

Overview of the PowerShell installation options

Several options exist for installing PowerShell, depending on the platform and version you wish to install:

- **Windows PowerShell:** Windows PowerShell 5.1 comes pre-installed on most modern Windows operating systems, including Windows 10 and Windows Server 2016/2019.
- **PowerShell 7+ (Latest version):** PowerShell 7+, the successor to PowerShell Core 6+, is cross-platform and works on Windows, Linux, and macOS.
- **Windows Package Manager (Winget):** For newer Windows 10 and 11 versions, you can install the Windows Package Manager (Winget) to install PowerShell.
- **Docker:** If you want a completely isolated environment, you can use Docker to run PowerShell in a container.
- **Azure Cloud Shell:** If you are working with Azure, PowerShell is available in the Azure Cloud Shell. No installation is required.
- **Direct installation from a Linux terminal:** For Linux distributions, PowerShell can be installed directly from the terminal using specific commands.

Understanding what gets installed is critical to PowerShell installation. The primary component is the Windows PowerShell engine, and this core component enables the execution of PowerShell scripts and commands. It is responsible for various fundamental aspects of PowerShell's functionality, such as parsing commands, managing objects, controlling the pipeline, and invoking cmdlets.

The Windows PowerShell Engine has crucial components that make it work. The Command Parser interprets command inputs and prepares them for execution, working with cmdlets, functions, script blocks, and control structures. Unlike other shells that only handle text, PowerShell uses an object pipeline to pass objects between cmdlets quickly. Based on the parsed instructions, the engine activates these cmdlets, whether compiled commands, PowerShell functions, or scripts. This process occurs within the scripting host and interacts with the session state, including variables, functions, aliases, and more. Providers, or groups of cmdlets, provide a consistent interface to manage diverse data stores, with the engine facilitating access to data and storage types such as the registry, certificate store, and file system.

Microsoft Windows has pre-installed Windows PowerShell in every version since Windows 7 and Server 2008. The installed version of PowerShell is different depending on the operating system. The list below displays which versions of PowerShell are compatible with various Windows operating systems:

- **Windows Vista:** PowerShell 1.0
- **Windows 7:** PowerShell 2.0
- **Windows 8:** PowerShell 3.0
- **Windows 8.1:** PowerShell 4.0
- **Windows Server 2008/2008 R2:** PowerShell 2.0
- **Windows Server 2012:** PowerShell 4.0
- **Windows Server 2012 R2:** PowerShell 5.0
- **Windows Server 2016:** PowerShell 5.1
- **Windows Server 2019:** PowerShell 5.1
- **Windows 10:** PowerShell 5.1
- **Windows 11:** PowerShell 5.1

PowerShell 6+, or PowerShell Core, is cross-platform, enabling installation on various operating systems, and is the predecessor to PowerShell 7. However, unlike Windows PowerShell 5.1 and earlier versions, it does not come pre-installed with any operating system. Even the latest versions of Windows do not include the latest PowerShell; instead, they come with PowerShell 5.1.

> **Note: Older versions of Windows operating systems (2008 R2 SP1, 2012, and 2012 R2) must have the Windows Management Framework 5.1 installed to support Windows PowerShell 5.**

Before installing PowerShell, it is essential to have specific prerequisites in place for your operating systems, such as Windows, Linux, macOS, Arm, or Docker. The list below outlines these essential requirements:

- **Windows**: When installing PowerShell on Windows operating systems, Winget is recommended for Windows clients, while an MSI package is best for Windows Servers and enterprise deployment. Despite its limitations, the Microsoft Store package is a more straightforward installation option, especially for casual PowerShell users. To install multiple versions or 'side load,' use the ZIP package method, which also works for Windows Nano Server, Windows IoT, and Arm-based systems. .NET developers may prefer the .NET Global tool as another viable option.

- **Linux**: Different Linux distributions support PowerShell installation. Most Linux platforms and distributions release a yearly update, including a package manager for installing PowerShell. Each version of Linux may require a different command for installation. There are alternate ways of installing PowerShell using the Snap Package manager, binary archives, or the .NET Global tool.
- **macOS**: Installing PowerShell on macOS requires 10.13 or higher. The preferred package manager for macOS, Homebrew, offers one such method. Alternatively, you can directly download PowerShell or install it from binary archives. Choose the method that best suits your needs.
- **Arm**: PowerShell's support for Arm processors aligns with the support policy of its underlying .NET version. Although .NET supports a wide range of operating systems, PowerShell's Arm support remains limited.
- **Docker**: Microsoft provides Docker images with PowerShell pre-installed. You need Docker 17.05 or later to run the released images. Additionally, you should be able to operate Docker without needing sudo privileges or local administrative rights.

You must choose the correct installation option for your operating system selected.

Installing using an installable package

To install PowerShell on Windows, you have two options available for download from GitHub: **https://github.com/PowerShell/PowerShell/releases**:

- **MSI Package** is the easiest method and involves downloading a file with a name like **PowerShell-x.x.x-win-x64.msi** (for 64-bit systems) or **PowerShell-x.x.x-win-x86.msi** (for 32-bit systems), where **x.x.x** is the version number. Once downloaded, simply double-click the file to launch the Windows installation wizard.
- **ZIP Package** is useful if you prefer a portable version or don't have administrative rights to install software. The ZIP file will have a name like the MSI but with .zip at the end. After downloading, extract the files to a folder of your choice and run PowerShell directly from there.

There are four steps to install PowerShell:

1. **Download the MSI file**: Navigate to the releases page and download the appropriate MSI file based on your system architecture (64-bit or 32-bit).

2. **Run the installer**: Double-click the downloaded MSI file to start the installation process. You will be greeted with a setup wizard.
3. **Follow the setup wizard**: The wizard will guide you through the installation process. You can choose the installation directory and customize other settings, or simply go with the default options.
4. **Complete the installation**: Once the installation is complete, you can launch PowerShell from the Start menu.

As a beginner, the MSI installation method is recommended for its simplicity. The ZIP method is more advanced and is generally used in scenarios where an installation is not feasible or when you need a portable version of PowerShell.

Before installing PowerShell, you can check the current version by executing the following command:

$PSVersionTable

After executing the command, you will see the PowerShell version, the operating system, the platform, and the supported PowerShell versions. The following figure displays the default PowerShell version properties within a Windows 10 workstation:

```
PS C:\Users\Trainer> $PSVersionTable

Name                           Value
----                           -----
PSVersion                      5.1.22000.653
PSEdition                      Desktop
PSCompatibleVersions           {1.0, 2.0, 3.0, 4.0...}
BuildVersion                   10.0.22000.653
CLRVersion                     4.0.30319.42000
WSManStackVersion              3.0
PSRemotingProtocolVersion      2.3
SerializationVersion           1.1.0.1
```

Figure 2.1: Default Windows 10 PowerShell Properties

To install the software, double-click the installer file after downloading it and follow the prompts on your screen. Refer to the following figure:

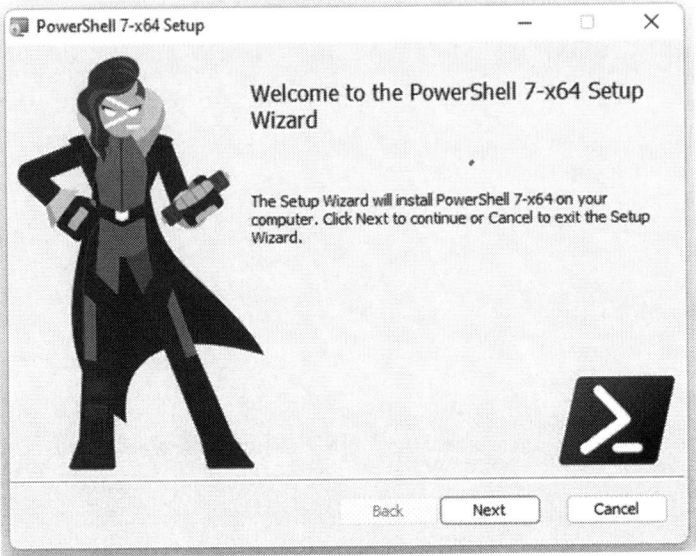

Figure 2.2: Beginning screen the PowerShell Installer

PowerShell 7+ installs into a new directory at **$env:ProgramFiles\PowerShell\7**, allowing it to run side-by-side with Windows PowerShell 5.1. The installation process adds this new directory to **$env:PATH** and removes directories from previous releases. The installation also replaces PowerShell versions 7.0 and below. You can modify the default installation location if needed during the setup process. Refer to the following figure:

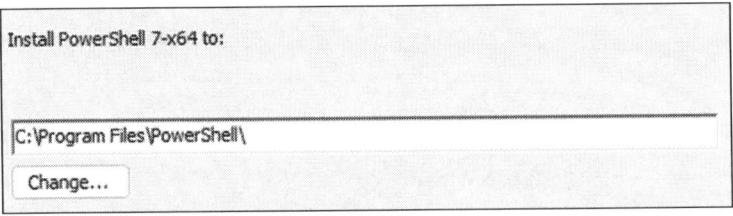

Figure 2.3: The default installation path for PowerShell 7

When prompted, check the **Add PowerShell to Path Environment Variable** options and **Register Windows Event Logging Manifest**. You also can check either or all of the following options. Refer to the following figure:

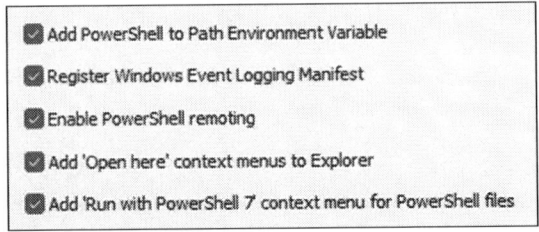

Figure 2.4: Configuration options within the PowerShell 7 Installer

PowerShell 7 supports updating using **Microsoft Update** or **Windows Server Update Services (WSUS)**. If you require this, ensure you check the options when prompted, as shown in the following figure:

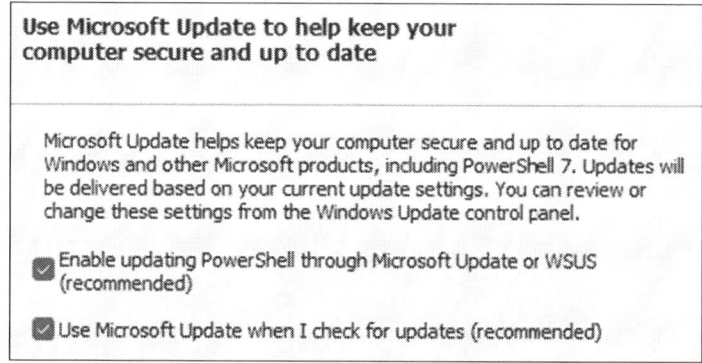

Figure 2.5: PowerShell 7 Windows update options

Once installed, launch PowerShell through the **Start** menu, or run `$env:ProgramFiles\PowerShell<version>\pwsh.exe`. After completing the installation and launching PowerShell 7, rerunning the `$PSVerionTable` command will display the updated version details:

```
PS C:\Users\Trainer> $PSVersionTable

Name                           Value
----                           -----
PSVersion                      7.3.4
PSEdition                      Core
GitCommitId                    7.3.4
OS                             Microsoft Windows 10.0.22000
Platform                       Win32NT
PSCompatibleVersions           {1.0, 2.0, 3.0, 4.0...}
PSRemotingProtocolVersion      2.3
SerializationVersion           1.1.0.1
WSManStackVersion              3.0
```

Figure 2.6: PowerShell 7 Windows update options

Installing on a non-Windows platform

Installing and updating PowerShell on Linux is simple through package repositories. If installing into Ubuntu Linux, you can download the required version by accessing the GitHub releases site and choosing the `.deb` version. The latest version now includes a universal package for easier installation:

https://github.com/PowerShell/PowerShell/releases/download/<Version>/power-shell_<Version>-1.deb_amd64.deb

Once the file downloads, you need to launch a terminal and issue the installation command:

`sudo dpkg -i powershell-lts_7.3.4-1.deb_amd64.deb`

After installing PowerShell, you should execute a general installation command to resolve any missing dependencies and finish the installation. This step may only sometimes be required, but ensuring all is working as expected is helpful.

`sudo apt-get install -f`

After the installation, you can execute **pwsh** within the terminal, and PowerShell will load:

```
trainer@UBUNTU: $ pwsh
PowerShell 7.3.4
PS /home/trainer>
```

Figure 2.7: Launching PowerShell 7 within Ubuntu Linux

Executing **$PSVersionTable** displays the exact details as Windows, albeit specifically for the Linux environment:

```
Name                           Value
----                           -----
PSVersion                      7.3.4
PSEdition                      Core
GitCommitId                    7.3.4
OS                             Linux 5.19.0-42-generic #43~22.04.1-Ubuntu
Platform                       Unix
PSCompatibleVersions           {1.0, 2.0, 3.0, 4.0…}
PSRemotingProtocolVersion      2.3
SerializationVersion           1.1.0.1
WSManStackVersion              3.0
```

Figure 2.8: PowerShell 7 version table within Ubuntu Linux

Installing within a macOS environment is similar to the Linux platform. You have several options to install PowerShell on macOS. You could choose to install it using Homebrew, which is the preferred package manager for macOS. Alternatively, you could opt for a direct download of PowerShell or install it from binary archives. To install using Homebrew, you must first install it; then, you can execute the installation command:

`brew install powershell/tap/powershell`

After the installation, you can execute **pwsh** within the terminal, and the PowerShell will load, as shown in the following figure:

```
trainer@Mac-mini ~ % pwsh
PowerShell 7.3.4
PS /Users/trainer>
```

Figure 2.9: Launching PowerShell 7 within macOS

Executing **$PSVersionTable** displays the exact details of Windows and Linux, albeit specifically for the macOS environment. The following figure displays the updated PowerShell version properties within the macOS workstation:

```
PS /Users/trainer> $PSVersionTable

Name                           Value
----                           -----
PSVersion                      7.3.4
PSEdition                      Core
GitCommitId                    7.3.4
OS                             Darwin 21.5.0 Darwin Kernel
Platform                       Unix
PSCompatibleVersions           {1.0, 2.0, 3.0, 4.0…}
PSRemotingProtocolVersion      2.3
SerializationVersion           1.1.0.1
WSManStackVersion              3.0
```

Figure 2.10: Launching PowerShell 7 within macOS

Using the PowerShell Gallery

The PowerShell Gallery is a hub for PowerShell content, hosting scripts, modules, cmdlets, and **Desired State Configuration** (DSC) resources authored by Microsoft and the PowerShell community. You utilize the **PowerShellGet** module to discover, install, update, and publish packages from the gallery. You can use the following command to install the latest version of the **PowerShellGet** module, which will update the existing version:

`Install-Module PowerShellGet -Force -AllowClobber`

Once the module is installed, you can download and install PowerShell modules and packages from the PowerShell Gallery.

PowerShell Gallery packages can contain artifacts such as modules, DSC resources, role capabilities, and scripts. You must first find the required package to install a package from the PowerShell gallery. You can narrow down your search results by using various parameters. These include filtering by the package's name, version history, minimum or required version, and associated tag and finding packages containing specific components. You can also search for DSC resources, role-specific packages, and packages containing required commands. You can also filter by using a custom search string.

There are many PowerShell modules available within the gallery. To manage **Internet Information Services** (**IIS**), you can search for the direct name or filter using the filter parameter. The figure below shows all the PowerShell modules that have **IIS** in their name:

```
PS C:\Users\Trainer> Find-Module -Filter 'IIS'

Version        Name                          Repository
-------        ----                          ----------
1.1.0.0        IISAdministration             PSGallery
2.13.0         Carbon                        PSGallery
0.9.3.334      ACMESharp.Providers.IIS       PSGallery
0.1.8          TaskModuleIISManageUtility    PSGallery
1.5.1          CPolydorou.IIS                PSGallery
2.0.0          Az.ApplicationMonitor         PSGallery
1.2.0.0        xWebDeploy                    PSGallery
1.0.0          cAspNetIisRegistration        PSGallery
```

Figure 2.11: Finding the IIS PowerShell Module within Windows

You can retrieve the properties using the `Get-Member` command to view more details about the module:

`Find-Module -Name 'IISAdministration' | Get-Member`

The module has been identified and can be installed using the full name with the use of the `Install-Module` command:

`Install-Module -Name 'IISAdministration'`

After installing the module, you can verify its functionality by utilizing the `Get-Module` command:

`Get-Module -Name 'IISAdministration'`

The PowerShell gallery offers multiple benefits, making it a valuable resource for IT professionals and developers. It simplifies package management by providing a seamless way to discover, install, update, and publish packages. It also promotes time efficiency, code reuse, and standardization. It fosters community collaboration by enabling users to share their packages. Furthermore, its integration with the `PowerShellGet` module increases usability and productivity by offering a consistent package management interface.

Conclusion

In conclusion, understanding and effectively implementing the installation of PowerShell on various platforms like Windows, Linux, and macOS is a crucial step toward leveraging its robust functionality. We have explored multiple methods of installation tailored to different scenarios, demonstrating the flexibility and cross-platform nature of PowerShell. Remember to choose the best installation method for your unique requirements and environments. Be it Homebrew for macOS, various packages for Windows, or package managers for other Linux distributions, PowerShell's adaptability is excellent. As you progress, do not forget to explore the PowerShell Gallery, a valuable resource for scripts, modules, and more.

In the next chapter will review how to use PowerShell modules and providers.

CHAPTER 3
Getting Started with Modules and Providers

Introduction

This chapter will explore PowerShell modules and providers, including their differences and functionalities. We will cover when to use them, the differences between built-in and external providers, and how to import and utilize them. Additionally, we will discuss the PowerShell help system to assist with finding the correct syntax for commands available with built-in and external modules. Lastly, we will delve into the **Windows Management Instrumentation (WMI)** and the **Common Information Model (CIM)** commands.

Structure

In this chapter, we will cover the following topics:
- Introduction to PowerShell modules
- Purpose of PowerShell modules
- Understand the different types of providers
- Use the built-in PowerShell providers
- Import modules from the operating system
- Import external PowerShell modules

- How to use the help system
- Review WMI within PowerShell
- Review CIM within PowerShell

Objectives

By the end of this chapter, you will have a firm grasp of the essentials of PowerShell modules. You will understand the different types of providers and learn how to utilize the built-in PowerShell providers effectively. You will also know how to import local modules from your operating system and external PowerShell modules, giving you the power to adapt and expand PowerShell. You will become very familiar with the help system in PowerShell, which will make it easy for you to navigate and solve problems within the platform. You will learn about WMI and CIM in PowerShell, which will help you manage your system more efficiently. This knowledge will give you the confidence to use PowerShell modules and providers effectively in your environment.

Introduction to PowerShell modules

PowerShell modules are fundamental building blocks. Modules are containers for related components and are a way of distributing scripts and functions. A module contains PowerShell members, such as cmdlets, providers, functions, and variables.

Knowing PowerShell modules is crucial since they expand the capabilities of PowerShell beyond its built-in features. They are an essential tool in tasks involving automation, system administration, and other IT roles. These modules can be shared and reused, which promotes efficient and collaborative scripting practices.

There are three types of modules: script, binary, and manifest. Script modules end with a .psm1 extension and contain script files. Binary modules are compiled DLL files written in a .NET language. Manifest modules are .psd1 files and provide metadata for other modules. You can easily import and remove modules, providing their functionality only when necessary. It keeps the scripting environment clean and efficient without using up unnecessary resources.

You can take a considerable step towards mastering PowerShell and its advantages by proficiently using PowerShell modules.

Purpose of PowerShell modules

PowerShell modules serve many essential purposes in a system administration and scripting context. They act as containers for related functionalities, which help organize and distribute scripts and functions. Bundling related commands into a single, reusable unit simplifies the scripting process and fosters code reusability. They are helpful add-ons that enhance the functionality of built-in commands. They provide specialized and complex operations that are unavailable by default in PowerShell. You can unlock these additional capabilities and expand your scripting potential by importing a module.

Modules facilitate collaboration and sharing between various users and teams. If you have developed a function or script that can benefit others, you can package it into a module and share it. This approach improves productivity across teams and enables the effective reuse of code. They also enhance the efficiency of the PowerShell environment by controlling the availability of their contained functionalities. PowerShell loads modules on demand rather than all scripts and functions at start-up, which can consume resources. It ensures that the functionalities provided by a module are available only when necessary, leading to more efficient resource utilization.

Using modules encourages modular programming, which splits code into independent, interchangeable modules. This approach makes code easier to understand and maintain and reduces the chance of errors. PowerShell modules can help standardize scripting across multiple administrators or teams in an enterprise setting. They allow for consistently using functions and scripts, ensuring everyone uses the same code for everyday tasks. It helps maintain a uniform environment and reduces the possibility of conflicts or inconsistencies.

PowerShell modules are pivotal in extending PowerShell's capabilities, enhancing efficiency, promoting best practices, and standardizing scripting. Understanding and leveraging the purpose of PowerShell modules is a vital step in mastering PowerShell.

Understand the different types of providers

PowerShell providers are critical components of the PowerShell environment that allow access to data stores, like how file system drives give access to files and directories. Different PowerShell providers let you interact with data from varied sources and formats, presenting them in a consistent, hierarchical structure. A few typical providers that are essential to PowerShell are:

- Filesystem provider
- Registry provider
- Environment provider
- Certificate provider
- Function provider
- Alias provider
- Variable provider

Understanding what each of these PowerShell providers do and why you would use them is essential. The most commonly available providers are:

- With the **FileSystem** provider, you can easily access and manage files and directories on your system. It presents data in a directory tree format, making it simple to navigate and perform tasks such as adding, deleting, and modifying files and folders using familiar commands.
- The **Registry** provider is a tool that provides access to Windows Registry keys and values. This tool can be beneficial for tasks that involve reading or modifying registry values. Using it simplifies interacting with the registry, allowing you to manipulate it as if it were a file and directory structure.
- The **Environment** provider grants access to the system's environment variables, which can be easily modified and read through this feature. It simplifies tasks that involve environmental configuration.
- There is also the **Certificate** provider, which enables access to the digital certificates on a machine, presenting them in a hierarchical structure.
- The **Function** provider lets you view the functions currently loaded in your PowerShell session. It also enables you to examine, add, modify, or delete functions like files in a drive.
- The **Alias** provider allows users to access aliases within their session. It provides an easy way to view, create, modify, or delete these aliases.
- The **Variable** provider allows you to access the variables in your PowerShell session as if they were drive and file-like objects.

There are more specialized providers, such as the Active Directory, SQL Server provider, and more, each serving a unique purpose. To view the available PowerShell providers within your environment, such as the Windows operating system, you can execute **Get-PSProvider**. Refer to the following figure:

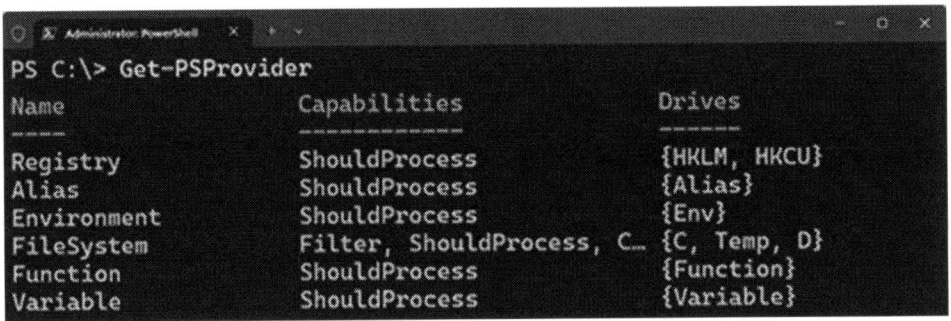

Figure 3.1: *List of default PowerShell Providers within Windows*

Understanding these different PowerShell providers is crucial, as they allow you to seamlessly interface with various data sources. Each provider, with its unique capabilities, enhances the versatility and efficiency of PowerShell.

Use the built-in PowerShell providers

The built-in PowerShell providers allow access to various data stores and types, seamlessly integrating them into the PowerShell environment. For example, you can use the **FileSystem** provider to interact with files and directories on your system. The following command lists all the items within the C drive as if you were navigating through a file explorer:

```
Get-ChildItem -Path C:\
```

You can use the registry provider to manipulate Windows Registry keys and values. For instance, to list all the software installed under the current user in the registry, you execute the following command:

```
Get-ChildItem -Path HKCU:\Software
```

The environment provider offers access to system environment variables. Running the following command allows you to see all the environment variables currently set on the system:

```
Get-ChildItem -Path Env:\
```

Similarly, the **Certificate** provider allows for interaction with digital certificates on your machine. The command below lists all certificates for the current user:

```
Get-ChildItem -Path Cert:\CurrentUser\My\
```

On the other hand, the **Function**, **Alias**, and **Variable** providers provide access to functions, aliases, and variables in your current PowerShell session. For example, these commands will return all functions, aliases, and variables:

```
Get-ChildItem -Path Function:\
```

```
Get-ChildItem -Path Alias:\
```

```
Get-ChildItem -Path Variable:\
```

Understanding and utilizing these built-in PowerShell providers enables you to navigate and manipulate various data types and sources from your PowerShell console. It is essential to understand the real benefits of using PowerShell providers. To do this, we have four use cases:

- Find all **.pdf** files in your Documents folder.

- Add a new value to the **PATH** environment variable.
- Create a **New Registry Entry**.
- Check the existence of a certificate and then import.

Find all PDF files in your documents folder

The FileSystem provider makes it possible to identify files within folder structures:

> Note: You will need to update the "Path" property to your desired path

```
$params = @{
    Path = 'C:\Users\User\Documents'
    Filter = '*.pdf'
    Recurse = $true
}
Get-ChildItem @params
```

The above command will recursively search for all "pdf" files in the Documents directory and its subdirectories.

Add a new value to the PATH environment variable

If you have installed new software that requires access through the command line, you may need to add its path to the **PATH** environment variable. To add a custom installation directory for Python, you execute this command:

```
$env:PATH += ";C:\Python"
```

Create a new registry entry

To add a registry key to turn off the lock screen on Windows. First, create a new registry key, **Personalization**, under **HKLM:\Software\Policies\Microsoft\Windows**. Then, you add a **DWORD** value **NoLockScreen** and set it to **1**, which turns off the lock screen:

```
New-Item `
-Path 'HKLM:\Software\Policies\Microsoft\Windows\Personalization'
```

```
New-ItemProperty `
-Path 'HKLM:\Software\Policies\Microsoft\Windows\Personalization' `
-Name 'NoLockScreen' `
-Value 1 `
-PropertyType DWORD
```

Check the existence of a certificate and then import

The provider can find certificates with a specific thumbprint in the local machine store. It imports the certificate from the **"pfx"** file if it does not find one:

```
$thumbprint = "3472543GR87347T8T43H8FR2897E2"
$certificatePath = "C:\Certificates\certificate.pfx"
$certificatePassword = ConvertTo-SecureString `
-String "Password" `
-Force -AsPlainText

$certificate = Get-ChildItem `
-Path Cert:\LocalMachine\My | Where-Object { $_.Thumbprint -eq $thumbprint }

if ($null -eq $certificate) {
Import-PfxCertificate `
-FilePath $certificatePath `
-CertStoreLocation Cert:\LocalMachine\My `
-Password $certificatePassword
}
```

Each of these examples highlights the versatility of PowerShell, showcasing its capabilities as a vital tool for system administration and scripting.

Import modules from the operating system

You can import local modules to enhance PowerShell's functionalities. These modules group together related cmdlets, making it easier to perform complex tasks and reuse previously written code. By importing a module, you can access its cmdlets, providers, and functions in your current session.

PowerShell usually auto-loads modules when you invoke a cmdlet from that module for the first time. This auto-loading feature enhances the user experience by eliminating the need for manual module loading in most situations. However, you might need to import a module explicitly when you require a specific module version or when the system has auto-loading disabled.

Importing a PowerShell module does not affect the performance because the cmdlets are only loaded when needed. This approach is known as loading a module on demand, which contributes to the efficient use of resources.

PowerShell uses system and environment variables in scripts to gather information about system configuration, manage the execution environment, and load modules or resources. Below are some of the commonly used variables for loading resources:

- The `$env:PSModulePath` environment variable in PowerShell represents the directories that the system searches for modules and resources.
- The `$PSHOME\Modules` directory generally houses system-wide PowerShell modules. It also includes **Desired State Configuration** (**DSC**) resources, usually in `$PSHOME\Modules\PSDesiredStateConfiguration\DSCResources`.
- User-specific modules are those installed by users and might use different locations based on the operating system. On Windows 10 and higher, the location is `$HOME\Documents\PowerShell\Modules`, On Linux or Mac, it is usually `$HOME/.local/share/powershell/Modules`.
- The `AllUsers` location usually stores modules accessible to all users. This location is `$env:PROGRAMFILES\PowerShell\Modules` on Windows and `/usr/local/share/powershell/Modules` on Linux or Mac.

These paths can vary based on factors such as the Windows version and folder redirection settings.

The Windows operating system contains many different local PowerShell modules depending on the installed version of Windows, PowerShell, and other applications containing available modules. To view the available PowerShell modules within Windows, you can execute the following command:

```
Get-Module -ListAvailable
```

To retrieve only the core modules included with PowerShell, use the **PS** prefix, which is common to all:

```
Get-Module -ListAvailable | Where-Object { $_.Name -like "PS*" }
```

If you want to find modules that are for PowerShell 7, you can look in the **"$PSHOME/ Modules"** directory or filter on the version of the module:

```
Get-Module -ListAvailable | Where-Object {
    $_.Path -like "C:\Program Files\PowerShell\7\Modules\*"
}


Get-Module -ListAvailable | Where -Object {
    $_.Version -like "*7*"
}
```

You can also search for a specific module by name. For example, to find the **Microsoft.PowerShell.Utility** module you would use:

```
Get-Module Microsoft.PowerShell.Utility
```

If you are looking for a particular type of module, like security-related ones, you can filter them using the **Where-Object** cmdlet based on their description:

```
Get-Module -ListAvailable | Where-Object { $_.Name -like "*Security*" }
```

PowerShell modules vary between different versions and the software installed on your system. However, here are five standard modules that you are likely to find on systems running either PowerShell 7 or PowerShell 5.1:

- **Microsoft.PowerShell.Management**.
- **Microsoft.PowerShell.Utility**.
- **PSReadLine**.
- **PackageManagement**.
- **PowerShellGet**.

While these modules are generally available in both PowerShell 7 and PowerShell 5.1, some cmdlets or functionalities may differ between versions due to changes and improvements in the PowerShell platform. For example, within a Windows Server 2022 Domain Controller, you might find the following PowerShell modules available:

- **Microsoft.PowerShell.Utility:** This module provides various utility functions, such as those for working with files, folders, and objects.

- **Microsoft.PowerShell.Management:** This module provides various management functions, such as those for working with Active Directory, Windows PowerShell, and other Windows features.
- **Microsoft.PowerShell.Core:** This module provides the core functionality of PowerShell, such as the ability to run scripts, import modules, and manage objects.
- **Microsoft.WSMan.Management:** This module offers functions for managing the Windows Server Manager, including creating, modifying, and deleting sessions and listeners.
- **ActiveDirectory:** This module provides commands for managing Active Directory domains, **Active Directory Lightweight Directory Services (AD LDS)** configuration sets, and Active Directory Database Mounting Tool instances.
- **DnsServer:** This module contains commands for managing **Domain Name System (DNS)** servers, facilitating the configuration of server settings, zones, and records.
- **PSDiagnostics:** This module offers diagnostic capabilities in PowerShell, providing functions for analyzing and troubleshooting PowerShell sessions, remoting, and workflows.
- **CimCmdlets:** This module delivers cmdlets that interact with **Common Information Model (CIM)** classes, enabling the retrieval, management, and manipulation of CIM instances on local and remote computers.

When listing the currently loaded or available modules, one of the fields displays a list of the cmdlets available for use. The list of commands truncates by default. You can format the output for specified modules as shown below:

```
(Get-Module -Name Microsoft.WSMan.Management `
-ListAvailable).ExportedCommands.Values | Select-Object -Property Name


(Get-Module -Name ActiveDirectory `
-ListAvailable).ExportedCommands.Values | Select-Object -Property Name
```

You use the **Import-Module** command to import a local PowerShell module. The cmdlets make use of various parameters outlined below:

- **Name**: Specifies the name of the module to import.
- **Alias, Function, Cmdlet**: These parameters allow you to import only specific aliases, functions, or cmdlets from the module.
- **DisableNameChecking**: Suppresses the warnings generated when a cmdlet in the module does not follow the standard cmdlet verb-noun naming.
- **Force**: Forces the command to run without asking for user confirmation.

- **Global**: Imports the module into the global session state.
- **NoClobber**: Prevents the command from overwriting existing commands with the same names as those in the imported module.
- **PassThru**: Returns a module object for each module imported.
- **Prefix**: Adds a prefix to the names of imported commands to avoid name conflicts.
- **Scope**: This parameter determines if the module loads into the global or local scope.
- **Verbose**: Provides detailed information about the operation performed by the command.

The standard syntax for importing a module is:

`Import-Module "Module Name"`

You can, however, utilize the parameters to change the import process as required. Here are some examples of how to use the different available parameters:

- Import a module by its name:

  `Import-Module -Name PowerShellGet`

- Import a module with a version number within the specified range:

  `Import-Module -Name PowerShellGet -MinimumVersion 2.0.0 -MaximumVersion 2.9.9`

- Import a module into the global session state:

  `Import-Module -Name PowerShellGet -Global`

- Imports a module and returns a PSModuleInfo for the imported module:

  `Import-Module -Name PowerShellGet -PassThru`

- Import a module and override ("clobber") cmdlets with the same names:

  `Import-Module -Name PowerShellGet -AllowClobber`

- Add a prefix to the nouns in the cmdlet names for the imported module:

  `Import-Module -Name PowerShellGet -Prefix "PG"`

The following three examples for Windows, Linux, and macOS show importing modules and using a command:

- Windows:
  - Import the module:

    `Import-Module ActiveDirectory`

  - Use a cmdlet from the module

    `Get-ADUser -Filter * | Select-Object -First 10`

- Linux
  - Import the module:
    ```
    Import-Module Microsoft.PowerShell.Management
    ```
  - Use a cmdlet from the module:
    ```
    Get-ChildItem -Path / -File | Select-Object -First 10
    ```
- macOS
  - Import the module:
    ```
    Import-Module PowerShellGet
    ```
  - Use a cmdlet from the module:
    ```
    Find-Module -Tag 'Azure'
    ```

Many other modules are available depending on the version of the Windows operating system, installed applications, and the PowerShell version. Always refer to the official PowerShell documentation or use the `Get-Help` cmdlet for accurate, version-specific information.

Import external PowerShell modules

External PowerShell modules significantly improve the built-in capabilities of PowerShell, making it a highly flexible scripting environment. Many third-party developers and organizations create and maintain modules for PowerShell. These modules expand the capabilities of PowerShell beyond what Microsoft offers. They allow users to interact with various systems, applications, and services such as databases, web APIs, cloud platforms, and DevOps tools.

One of the primary reasons for importing external modules is to incorporate their specific features into your PowerShell scripts or sessions. For instance, if you need to interact with a cloud service like **Amazon Web Services (AWS)**, **Google Compute (GC)**, or Microsoft's Azure, you can import their respective PowerShell modules and gain access to a vast array of cmdlets designed explicitly for that platform.

These modules are typically available from several sources. The PowerShell Gallery, maintained by Microsoft, is the most comprehensive and trusted source. Other software vendors might host their PowerShell modules on their websites or public code repositories like GitHub.

To import an external module, you use the `Install-Module` cmdlet. It downloads and installs the module from the specified source, most commonly the PowerShell Gallery. The command `Install-Module` will download and install a module, making it available for import in your PowerShell sessions. For example, the following command will install the PowerShell module **PSWindowsUpdate**, used to manage the Windows Update Client:

`Install-Module -Name PSWindowsUpdate`

The `Install-Module` cmdlet also uses multiple parameters, allowing you to adjust the import process depending on your needs. The available parameters are:

- **Name**: Specifies the name of the module to install.
- **RequiredVersion**: Specifies the exact version of the module to install.
- **MinimumVersion and MaximumVersion**: You can use these parameters to set a range of module versions suitable for installation.
- **Repository**: This parameter defines the repository for installing the module.
- **AllowClobber**: Allows cmdlets in the installed module to override commands in other modules with the same names.
- **Scope**: This parameter specifies if the installation applies to the module for the current user only or all users.
- **Force**: Forces the command to run without asking for user confirmation.
- **Credential**: Specifies a user account with the rights to install the module.
- **Proxy and ProxyCredential**: These parameters specify a proxy server for the command.
- **SkipPublisherCheck**: Bypasses the publisher check.
- **AllowPrerelease**: If specified, PowerShell installs a pre-release version of the module if one is available.
- **AcceptLicense**: When specified, PowerShell automatically accepts the software license agreement terms for the module to install.

You can utilize the parameters to change the import process as required. Here are some examples of how to use the different available parameters:

- Install a module by its name:

    `Import-Module -Name PSWindowsUpdate`

- Install the module regardless of its current installation status:

    `Import-Module -Name PSWindowsUpdate -Force`

- Install a module from the specified repository:

    `Install-Module -Name PSWindowsUpdate -Repository PSGallery`

- Install a module for all users:

    `Install-Module -Name PSWindowsUpdate -Scope AllUsers`

- Install a specific version of a module:

  `Install-Module -Name PSWindowsUpdate -RequiredVersion 2.2.4.1`

- Install a pre-release version and automatically accept the license agreement:

  `Install-Module -Name PSWindowsUpdate -AllowPrerelease -AcceptLicense`

After installing, you use the **Import-Module** cmdlet to load the module into your current session. For example, the following command will load the installed module, making its cmdlets and functions available:

`Install-Module PSWindowsUpdate`

`Import-Module PSWindowsUpdate`

Accepting the untrusted repository prompt may be necessary to install external modules successfully. Refer to the following figure:

```
PS C:\> Install-Module -Name PSWindowsUpdate

Untrusted repository
You are installing the modules from an untrusted repository. If you trust this repository,
change its InstallationPolicy value by running the Set-PSRepository cmdlet. Are you sure you
want to install the modules from 'PSGallery'?
[Y] Yes  [A] Yes to All  [N] No  [L] No to All  [S] Suspend  [?] Help (default is "N"):
```

Figure 3.2: Untrusted repository confirmation

After importing the external module, you can use its functionalities, such as built-in cmdlets. You can use the **Get-Command** cmdlet to find the available cmdlets within the module. Refer to the following figure:

```
PS C:\> Get-Command -Module PSWindowsUpdate

CommandType     Name                             Version
-----------     ----                             -------
Alias           Clear-WUJob                      2.2.0.3
Alias           Download-WindowsUpdate           2.2.0.3
Alias           Get-WUInstall                    2.2.0.3
Alias           Get-WUList                       2.2.0.3
Alias           Hide-WindowsUpdate               2.2.0.3
Alias           Install-WindowsUpdate            2.2.0.3
Alias           Show-WindowsUpdate               2.2.0.3
Alias           UnHide-WindowsUpdate             2.2.0.3
Alias           Uninstall-WindowsUpdate          2.2.0.3
Cmdlet          Add-WUServiceManager             2.2.0.3
Cmdlet          Enable-WURemoting                2.2.0.3
Cmdlet          Get-WindowsUpdate                2.2.0.3
Cmdlet          Get-WUApiVersion                 2.2.0.3
Cmdlet          Get-WUHistory                    2.2.0.3
Cmdlet          Get-WUInstallerStatus            2.2.0.3
Cmdlet          Get-WUJob                        2.2.0.3
Cmdlet          Get-WULastResults                2.2.0.3
```

Figure 3.3: Using Get-Command to view available cmdlets for imported module

The following three examples for Windows, Linux, and macOS show installing, importing modules, and using a command:
- Windows
    - Utilize Pester is a unit-testing framework for PowerShell:

        ```
        Install-Module -Name Pester -Repository PSGallery -Force
        Import-Module -Name Pester
        Invoke-Pester -Script @{
        Path = '.\tests\';Parameters = @{ TestValue = 'SomeValue' }
        }
        ```
- Linux
    - Install PowerShellGet and find modules:

        ```
        Install-Module -Name PowerShellGet -Repository PSGallery -Force
        Import-Module -Name PowerShellGet
        Find-Module -Name *Get*
        ```
- macOS
    - Update the PowerShell command line editing experience:

        ```
        Install-Module -Name PSReadLine -Repository PSGallery -Force
        Import-Module -Name PSReadLine
        ```

Once you install a PowerShell module, you may need to update or remove the module. You can achieve this by using the **Update-Module** or **Remove-Module** commands. For example:
- Updates the specified module to the latest version:

    `Update-Module -Name PSWindowsUpdate`
- Removes the specified module from the current session:

    `Remove-Module -Name PSWindowsUpdate.`

Mastering the import process opens a world of opportunities in PowerShell. By utilizing external PowerShell modules, you can significantly enhance the capability of scripting and automation tasks. Windows, macOS, and Linux environments can easily leverage these modules, underlining PowerShell's cross-platform robustness. You can bring these resources from sources such as the PowerShell Gallery using the Install-Module cmdlet. Import-Module brings these modules into the current session, making the cmdlets readily available.

How to use the help system

PowerShell's help system is an essential tool that provides important information about cmdlets, functions, scripts, and modules. To use the help system, you need to use the **Get-Help** cmdlet followed by the name of the cmdlet or topic you need help with. The following example will display information about the **Get-Process** cmdlet:

`Get-Help Get-Process`

The help content usually includes a brief description of the cmdlet or function, the syntax, a list of parameters, examples of usage, and sometimes even links to additional online resources. Refer to the following figure:

```
PS C:\> Get-Help Get-Process

NAME
    Get-Process

SYNTAX
    Get-Process [[-Name] <string[]>] [-Module] [-FileVersionInfo] [<CommonParameters>]

    Get-Process [[-Name] <string[]>] -IncludeUserName [<CommonParameters>]

    Get-Process -Id <int[]> [-Module] [-FileVersionInfo] [<CommonParameters>]

    Get-Process -Id <int[]> -IncludeUserName [<CommonParameters>]

    Get-Process -InputObject <Process[]> [-Module] [-FileVersionInfo] [<CommonParameters>]

    Get-Process -InputObject <Process[]> -IncludeUserName [<CommonParameters>]


ALIASES
    gps
    ps


REMARKS
    Get-Help cannot find the Help files for this cmdlet on this computer. It is displaying only partial help.
        -- To download and install Help files for the module that includes this cmdlet, use Update-Help.
        -- To view the Help topic for this cmdlet online, type: "Get-Help Get-Process -Online" or
           go to https://go.microsoft.com/fwlink/?LinkID=2096814.
```

Figure 3.4.: Results from executing Get-Help Get-Process

A vital feature of the PowerShell help system is that it is interactive. You can control how much detail you want to see by adding parameters such as **Detailed**, **Examples**, or **Full** to the **Get-Help** command. The following are examples of using the supported parameters:

- View basic help information:

    `Get-Help Get-Process`

- View detailed help information:

    `Get-Help Get-Process -Detailed`

- View all the help information:

  `Get-Help Get-Process -Full`

- View examples from the help information:

  `Get-Help Get-Process -Examples`

- View parameter-specific help information for the specified command:

  `Get-Help Get-Process -Parameter Name`

You can also use the **ShowWindow** parameter to open a new window that presents help content in a well-structured manner, which is extremely useful when dealing with complex cmdlets with many parameters. Refer to the following figure:

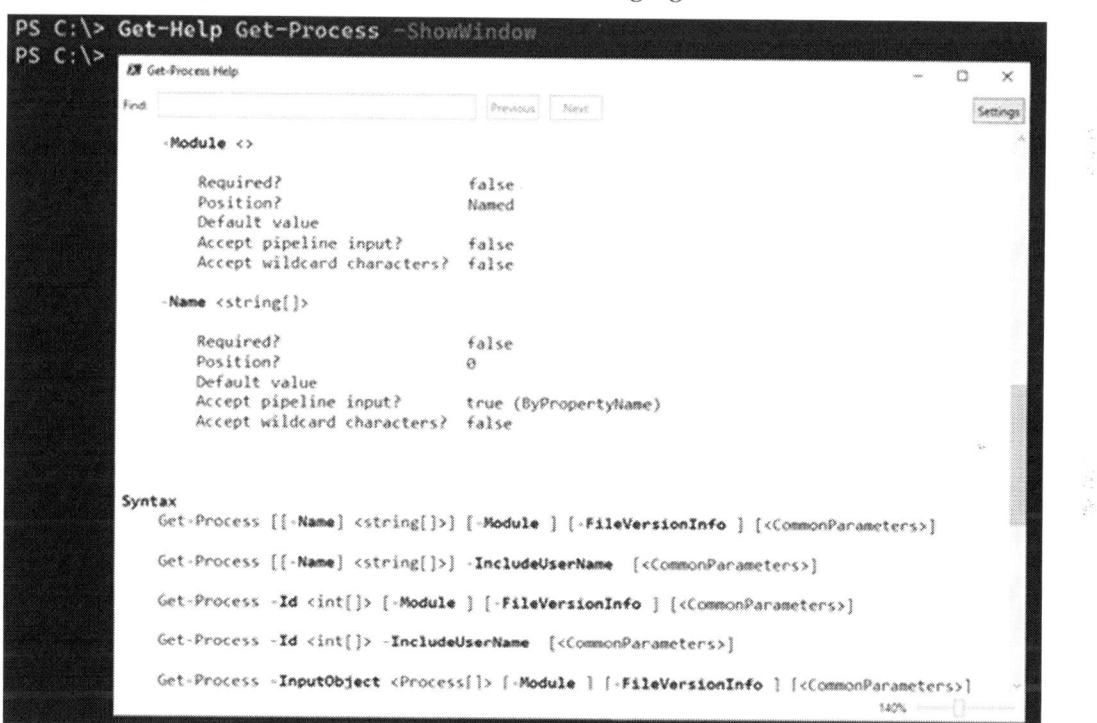

Figure 3.5: Open a new window with help information

You can also use wildcard characters with **Get-Help** if you need clarification on the exact cmdlet name. For instance, passing ***process** within the command will return all help topics that include **process** in their name. Refer to the following figure:

```
PS C:\> Get-Help *process

Name                         Category    Module
----                         --------    ------
Enter-PSHostProcess          Cmdlet      Microsoft.PowerShell.Core
Exit-PSHostProcess           Cmdlet      Microsoft.PowerShell.Core
Debug-Process                Cmdlet      Microsoft.PowerShell.Man…
Get-Process                  Cmdlet      Microsoft.PowerShell.Man…
Start-Process                Cmdlet      Microsoft.PowerShell.Man…
Stop-Process                 Cmdlet      Microsoft.PowerShell.Man…
Wait-Process                 Cmdlet      Microsoft.PowerShell.Man…
Start-AppvVirtualProcess     Function    AppvClient
Get-AppvVirtualProcess       Function    AppvClient
```

Figure 3.6: Retrieving details for commands containing *process in the name

It is vital to keep the help system up to date, which you can do by executing the **Update-Help** command. It will download the newest help files from Microsoft servers, ensuring your local help content is current:

```
PS C:\> Update-Help
Updating Help for module PowerShellGet [Downloading Help Content...  ]
```

Figure 3.7: Executing Update-Help within Windows

The help system breaks down each help topic into the following sections:

- **Synopsis**: This section provides a summary of what the cmdlet does. It gives you a quick understanding of the purpose of the cmdlet.
- **Syntax**: This section shows the cmdlet's structure and acceptable parameters. This section provides the different ways to use the cmdlet.
- **Description**: This section contains a more detailed explanation of what the cmdlet does. It may also include important context or background information.
- **Examples**: This section provides examples of using the cmdlet in different situations or with other parameters.
- **Parameters**: This section provides detailed explanations of each parameter the cmdlet can accept. For each parameter, it will provide its data type, whether it is mandatory or optional, and what it does.
- **Inputs**: This section describes the types of information the cmdlet can accept.
- **Outputs**: This section describes the type of output the cmdlet produces.
- **Notes**: This section contains essential information that did not fit the other sections. It often includes tips, tricks, pitfalls, or further crucial details.
- **Related links**: This section provides hyperlinks to associated cmdlets or further resources for learning about the cmdlet.

Getting Started with Modules and Providers | 35

The PowerShell help system also supports categories. Using the **Category** parameter with **Get-Help**, you can narrow your search to a particular category, such as cmdlets, functions, providers, or scripts. For example, if you execute the **Get-Help** command searching for the word **remoting** in the name, the following returns:

```
PS C:\> Get-Help -Name Remoting

Name                                            Category
----                                            --------
Install-PowerShellRemoting.ps1                  External…
Disable-PSRemoting                              Cmdlet
Enable-PSRemoting                               Cmdlet
Enable-WURemoting                               Cmdlet
Enable-ServerManagerStandardUser…               Function
Disable-ServerManagerStandardUse…               Function
```

Figure 3.8: View basic information using Get-Help and searching for "Remoting"

Adding the **Category** parameter and setting that to **Cmdlet** removes items you do not want to see:

```
PS C:\> Get-Help -Name Remoting -Category Cmdlet

Name                    Category    Module
----                    --------    ------
Disable-PSRemoting      Cmdlet      Microsoft.PowerShell.Core
Enable-PSRemoting       Cmdlet      Microsoft.PowerShell.Core
Enable-WURemoting       Cmdlet      PSWindowsUpdate
```

Figure 3.9: Filter the returned information by category

To help you when working with PowerShell and remove the need to type the **Get-Help** command, you can now get help while typing. If you press the *F1* key, a **PSReadLine** function pulls up the full help for the cmdlet to the left of the cursor. If the cursor is just to the left of a parameter, it explicitly shows its description. When you press Q, it exits the help view and returns to your command exactly where you left off. Using *Alt+H* triggers another function showing help information for the parameter immediately left of the cursor, right below the command line. You can read the parameter description while continuing to type your command with this feature. Refer to the following figure:

```
PS C:\> Get-Process -Name

-Name <System.String[]>

DESC: Specifies one or more processes by process name. You can type multiple proces
s names (separated by commas) and use wildcard characters. The parameter name ('Nam
e') is optional.
Required: false, Position: 0, Default Value: None, Pipeline Input: True (ByProperty
Name), WildCard: true
```

Figure 3.10: Viewing the name parameter details after pressing Alt+H

The help system in PowerShell is a robust learning tool that assists you in mastering the use of PowerShell. It is always available, offering guidance and information about the PowerShell language and its features.

Review WMI within PowerShell

Windows Management Instrumentation (WMI) is an essential component of Windows that helps administrators and developers interact with system resources. WMI cmdlets offer ways to manage system components, including operating systems, disk drives, services, and processes. In the context of PowerShell, WMI is instrumental in scripting administrative tasks.

The WMI cmdlets are unavailable within PowerShell 7 as they are deprecated and replaced with the **Common Information Model (CIM)** commands. PowerShell 5.1 still provides the WMI cmdlets, allowing you to use them alongside the CIM commands within the Windows operating system. Executing the following command in both PowerShell 5.1 and 7 will display the count of WMI cmdlets available:

`(Get-Command -Noun *WMI*).Count`

PowerShell 5.1 and PowerShell 7+ can run side-by-side, allowing you to take advantage of either option. To view the available WMI cmdlets within PowerShell 5.1, you can execute the following command:

`Get-Command -Noun *WMI*`

A total of five commands will return; refer to the following figure:

```
PS C:\> Get-Command -Noun *WMI* | Select-Object Name

Name
----
Get-WmiObject
Invoke-WmiMethod
Register-WmiEvent
Remove-WmiObject
Set-WmiInstance
```

Figure 3.11: View cmdlets with nouns containing "WMI"

The `Get-WmiObject` cmdlet in PowerShell retrieves information from the WMI infrastructure. It is one of the most used cmdlets for interacting with WMI. It allows you to retrieve information from WMI classes, which could include data on software, hardware, or system settings. Here is the basic syntax:

```
Get-WmiObject `

-Class <Class> `

-Namespace <Namespace> `

-ComputerName ComputerName>
```

The three parameters allow you to configure the system information to retrieve by class and type and the machine to execute the command on:

- **Class:** This parameter specifies the name of the WMI class you want to access. The WMI class determines what kind of data you will be working with.
- **Namespace:** This parameter specifies the WMI namespace containing the class you want to access. It uses the default namespace defined in the Windows registry if you do not specify a namespace.
- **ComputerName:** This parameter specifies the name of the computer you want to access. It will access the local computer if you do not specify a computer name. You can enter a single computer name or an array of computer names.

The WMI service, which **Get-WmiObject** utilizes, is only available on Windows. Only the Windows operating system supports the WMI cmdlets. You cannot use them on macOS and Linux systems.

WMI namespaces and classes represent different aspects of the WMI structure, and understanding their differences can help you better utilize WMI in PowerShell. A namespace in WMI is a category or container used to organize classes representing similar types of items or from similar domains. For instance, classes that relate to networking might be in one namespace, while classes that represent hardware components might be in another. This structure helps ensure that the class names are unique within each namespace and makes it easier to locate the appropriate class for a particular management task.

Within these namespaces are classes, which are essentially templates that define a particular kind of object. Each class represents a type of item that you might want to manage or inspect, such as a disk drive, a piece of software, or a service running on a computer. A class defines the properties an instance of the class can have and the supported methods (actions). For example, the **Win32_Process** class represents a process on a Windows system and includes methods to create, terminate, and get information about a process. So, while namespaces organize the classes into logical and functional groups, classes define the objects within those groups with their properties and methods.

There are various classes and namespaces available for WMI; a few are:

Classes:
- **Win32_Process:** Represents a process on an operating system. You can use it to list all running processes, like the task manager.
- **Win32_Service:** Represents a service on an operating system. It can start, stop, or retrieve the status of services on a system.
- **Win32_ComputerSystem:** Provides information about a computer system, such as total physical memory, domain roles, manufacturer, model, and so on.
- **Win32_OperatingSystem:** Represents an operating system. You can get information like the last boot-up time, free physical memory, and operating system version.
- **Win32_BIOS:** Represents the attributes of the computer system's essential **input/output services** (**BIOS**). You can retrieve information like the BIOS version, manufacturer, and release date.

Namespaces:
- **Root\CIMv2:** This is the primary namespace for Windows Management Instrumentation. It includes classes for the operating system, processes, services, and hardware.
- **Root\Subscription:** This namespace stores permanent event consumer classes and instances. Event consumers are components that perform an action when a specified event occurs, such as sending an email or writing to a log file.
- **Root\StandardCimv2:** This namespace provides improved performance and additional classes over Root\CIMv2.
- **Root\directory\LDAP:** When accessing Active Directory objects, you engage this namespace with the WMI **Active Directory Service Interfaces** (**ADSI**) Provider.
- **Root\WMI:** This is a special namespace that includes several system classes.

To retrieve system information, you can execute the following commands:
- Retrieve operating system architecture information:

    `Get-WmiObject -Class Win32_OperatingSystem`
- Retrieve computer information:

    `Get-WmiObject -Class Win32_ComputerSystem`
- Retrieve computer BIOS information:

    `Get-WmiObject -Class Win32_BIOS`
- Retrieve processor information:

    `Get-WmiObject -Class Win32_Processor`

- Retrieve information about the Active Directory domain:

  `Get-WmiObject -Class Win32_NTDomain`

The `Get-WmiObject` command supports providing a namespace along with the class to retrieve further information. A few examples are:

- List all the services on the system:

  `Get-WmiObject -Namespace "root\CIMv2" -Class Win32_Service`

- List all installed software on the system:

  `Get-WmiObject -Namespace "root\CIMv2" -Class Win32_Product`

- List all user accounts in Active Directory:

  `Get-WmiObject -Namespace "root\directory\LDAP" -Class ds_user`

There are other WMI cmdlets available to assist in retrieving system information.

Another cmdlet, `Invoke-WmiMethod`, can call methods of WMI objects, effectively allowing you to modify system settings. The following is an example of the `Invoke-WmiMethod` cmdlet to shut down a computer:

```
$computerName = "localhost"

$className = "Win32_OperatingSystem"

$methodName = "Win32Shutdown"

$shutdownCode = 1

$methodParameters = @{ Flags = $shutdownCode; Reserved = 0 }


Invoke-WmiMethod `

-ComputerName $computerName `

-Class $className `

-Name $methodName `

-ArgumentList $methodParameters
```

In addition, the `Set-WmiInstance` and `Remove-WmiObject` cmdlets can change or delete instances of WMI objects, allowing you to manage system resources more dynamically. For example, let us say you have a Windows Service, such as **wuauserv** (Windows Update), and you want to change its startup type to Automatic. Define the service name and desired startup type:

`$serviceName = "wuauserv"`

```
$startMode = "Automatic"
```
- Get the instance of the service:
```
$service = Get-WmiObject -Query "SELECT * FROM Win32_Service WHERE Name = '$serviceName'"
```
- Change the start mode:
```
$service.ChangeStartMode($startMode)
```

The **Remove-WmiObject** cmdlet deletes an instance of an existing WMI class. For example, to remove static IP address configuration from a network adapter, you first retrieve the WMI object representing that IP address entry, and then you can remove it.

- Get the WMI object for the static IP address entry:
```
$staticIP = Get-WmiObject `
-Class Win32_NetworkAdapterConfiguration `
-Filter "IPEnabled = TRUE"
```
- Remove the static IP address entry:
```
$staticIP | Remove-WmiObject
```

Lastly, the **Register-WmiEvent** cmdlet allows you to react to WMI events, providing a mechanism to automate tasks based on system events. The WMI cmdlets provide a comprehensive toolset for interacting with and managing Windows systems using PowerShell.

Review CIM within PowerShell

The open standard, **Common Information Model (CIM)**, represents how IT environments manage elements. Windows operating systems now integrate CIM cmdlets, which you can access through PowerShell. The CIM cmdlets replace the WMI cmdlets providing performance improvements and compatibility with standards-based management tools.

WMI and CIM are integral parts of Windows PowerShell but operate differently. The CIM cmdlets offer comparable functionalities to the WMI cmdlets but have better standard compliance, performance, and ease of use, especially when dealing with remote systems.

Although both WMI and CIM build upon the same underlying CIM standard, leading to a substantial overlap in classes and namespaces, they are different. The root/cimv2 namespace is common to both WMI and CIM, and many of the classes in this namespace, such as **Win32_Processor** or **Win32_OperatingSystem**, are the same or very similar in both WMI and CIM. Newer versions of Windows have introduced namespaces and classes that follow the CIM standard. You access these through CIM cmdlets, but they may need to be fully functional with WMI cmdlets. Although there are similarities and overlapping classes and namespaces between WMI and CIM, they are not identical.

You can execute the **Get-**command to view the available CIM cmdlets. Refer to the following figure:

```
PS C:\> Get-Command -Noun *CIM*

CommandType     Name                          Version    Source
-----------     ----                          -------    ------
Cmdlet          Get-CimAssociatedInstance     7.0.0.0    CimCmdlets
Cmdlet          Get-CimClass                  7.0.0.0    CimCmdlets
Cmdlet          Get-CimInstance               7.0.0.0    CimCmdlets
Cmdlet          Get-CimSession                7.0.0.0    CimCmdlets
Cmdlet          Invoke-CimMethod              7.0.0.0    CimCmdlets
Cmdlet          New-CimInstance               7.0.0.0    CimCmdlets
Cmdlet          New-CimSession                7.0.0.0    CimCmdlets
Cmdlet          New-CimSessionOption          7.0.0.0    CimCmdlets
Cmdlet          Register-CimIndicationEvent   7.0.0.0    CimCmdlets
Cmdlet          Remove-CimInstance            7.0.0.0    CimCmdlets
Cmdlet          Remove-CimSession             7.0.0.0    CimCmdlets
Cmdlet          Set-CimInstance               7.0.0.0    CimCmdlets
```

Figure 3.12: View cmdlets with nouns containing "WMI"

The **Get-CimInstance** cmdlet, like **Get-WmiObject**, allows you to retrieve instances of a specific CIM class, giving you access to system information. It is one of the most used cmdlets for interacting with CIM. Here is the basic syntax:

```
Get-CimInstance `

-ClassName <ClassName> `

-Namespace <Namespace> `

-ComputerName <ComputerName>
```

The three parameters allow you to configure the system information to retrieve by class and type and the machine to execute the command:

- **ClassName**: Select the name of the CIM class you want to retrieve instances from. It is a mandatory parameter.
- **Namespace**: Sets the namespace where the CIM class resides. This parameter is optional and defaults to the root namespace.
- **ComputerName**: Specify the remote computer name from which you want to retrieve CIM instances. This parameter is optional; if not specified, the command runs on the local computer.

The following examples show retrieving system information using the command **Get-CimInstance**:

- Retrieve operating system information:

  `Get-CimInstance -ClassName Win32_OperatingSystem`

- Retrieve processor information:

  `Get-CimInstance -ClassName Win32_Processor`

- Retrieve disk drive information:

  `Get-CimInstance -ClassName Win32_LogicalDisk`

- Retrieve network adapter information:

  `Get-CimInstance -ClassName Win32_NetworkAdapter`

With the **Invoke-CimMethod** command, you can execute actions on managed objects by calling methods defined in CIM classes. Suppose you have a requirement to shut down a remote computer. The Shutdown method, available in the **Win32_OperatingSystem** class, allows for shutting down a computer:

- Get the CIM instance for the operating system:

  `$os = Get-CimInstance -ClassName Win32_OperatingSystem`

- Use Invoke-CimMethod to shut down the computer:

  ```
  Invoke-CimMethod `
  -InputObject $os `
  -MethodName "Shutdown"
  ```

The **New-CimInstance**, **Set-CimInstance**, and **Remove-CimInstance** commands allow you to create, modify, and remove instances of CIM objects, giving you control over managed resources.

The CIM cmdlets enable remote management for Windows, Linux, and macOS systems through the WS-Management protocol.

Conclusion

PowerShell modules and providers form the backbone of a PowerShell environment, serving as the primary mechanism for extending functionality and managing resources. Built-in PowerShell providers enable interactions with data stores, treating them like file systems. These include providers for the file system, registry, certificate store, environment variables, and more. You can install external PowerShell modules from sources such as the PowerShell Gallery. These modules also extend the capabilities of PowerShell, providing specialized functionalities tailored to a wide range of tasks and environments.

The WMI and CIM commands within PowerShell. WMI is a core component of Windows, providing a standardized structure for querying and managing system resources. At the same time, CIM cmdlets offer a more modern, performant, and cross-platform solution for system management.

The help system provides comprehensive details about cmdlets, their parameters, and their usage through illustrative examples.

In conclusion, thoroughly understanding these components and how to use them effectively improves your PowerShell knowledge and makes script writing more efficient and flexible. The next chapter will review how to execute various PowerShell commands.

Join our book's Discord space

Join the book's Discord Workspace for Latest updates, Offers, Tech happenings around the world, New Release and Sessions with the Authors:

https://discord.bpbonline.com

Chapter 4
Executing PowerShell Commands

Introduction

This chapter will review the fundamentals of executing commands using PowerShell. It will include understanding the different types of cmdlets and executing pre-existing commands in a Windows environment. We will also focus on specific modules. We will then review the command response or return object, which is essential to efficiently interacting with PowerShell. We will explain how PowerShell and Visual Studio Code work together effortlessly, allowing you to accomplish more with PowerShell scripts. Lastly, we will cover writing and debugging scripts, giving you a complete understanding of how to use PowerShell in Visual Studio Code.

Structure

In this chapter, we will cover the following topics:
- Discovering commands to execute
- Understanding the different types of commands.
- Executing existing commands within a Windows computer.

- Executing commands from specific modules.
- Understanding the command return or response object.
- Using PowerShell in Visual Studio Code.

Objectives

By the end of this chapter, you will understand the fundamentals of executing commands using PowerShell. You will know the various types of cmdlets and be able to execute pre-existing commands in a Windows environment, including those from specific modules. You will also develop an understanding of the command response or return object, a critical aspect for efficient interaction with PowerShell. Additionally, you will see how PowerShell and Visual Studio Code merge, enabling you to achieve more with your PowerShell scripts. You will also learn to write and debug scripts using Visual Studio Code, improving your PowerShell proficiency and scripting skills in various settings.

Discovering commands to execute

Discovering the various commands you can execute is critical to mastering PowerShell. PowerShell provides several built-in cmdlets to help you with this task, notably `Get-Command`, `Get-Help`, and `Get-Module`. These cmdlets allow you to explore commands, learn about them, and find the commands you need for any task.

As the name suggests, the `Get-Command` cmdlet lets you get basic information about all the commands that PowerShell knows, including cmdlets, functions, aliases, and scripts. By default, `Get-Command` displays the name, command type, and module (if any) a command is part of. To display a list of all available commands, type `Get-Command` into the PowerShell prompt and hit *Enter*:

```
Get-Command
```

You will get the following output:

CommandType	Name	Version	Source
Alias	Add-AppPackage	2.0.1.0	Appx
Alias	Add-AppPackageVolume	2.0.1.0	Appx
Alias	Add-AppProvisionedPackage	3.0	Dism
Alias	Add-PnPAdaptiveScopeProperty	1.12.0	PnP.PowerShell
Alias	Add-PnPPropertyBagValue	1.12.0	PnP.PowerShell
Alias	Add-PnPSiteClassification	1.12.0	PnP.PowerShell
Alias	Add-ProvisionedAppPackage	3.0	Dism
Alias	Add-ProvisionedAppSharedPackageContainer	3.0	Dism
Alias	Add-ProvisionedAppxPackage	3.0	Dism
Alias	Add-ProvisioningPackage	3.0	Provisioning
Alias	Add-TrustedProvisioningCertificate	3.0	Provisioning
Alias	Apply-WindowsUnattend	3.0	Dism
Alias	Attach-DbaDatabase	1.1.145	dbatools
Alias	Copy-PnPFolder	1.12.0	PnP.PowerShell
Alias	Decode-SqlName	21.1.18256	SqlServer
Alias	Detach-DbaDatabase	1.1.145	dbatools
Alias	Disable-PhysicalDiskIndication	2.0.0.0	Storage
Alias	Disable-PhysicalDiskIndication	1.0.0.0	VMDirectStorage
Alias	Disable-StorageDiagnosticLog	2.0.0.0	Storage
Alias	Disable-StorageDiagnosticLog	1.0.0.0	VMDirectStorage
Alias	Dismount-AppPackageVolume	2.0.1.0	Appx
Alias	Enable-PhysicalDiskIndication	2.0.0.0	Storage
Alias	Enable-PhysicalDiskIndication	1.0.0.0	VMDirectStorage
Alias	Enable-StorageDiagnosticLog	2.0.0.0	Storage
Alias	Enable-StorageDiagnosticLog	1.0.0.0	VMDirectStorage

Figure 4.1: List all available PowerShell commands

You will see a list of all commands, and you might notice quite a lot of them. But do not worry; you can narrow down this list. If you are interested in a specific command or want to search for commands that include a particular term, you can use the **Name** parameter:

`Get-Command -Name Get-Process`

It will return information about the command named **Get-Process**. You can use wildcard characters to find all commands containing a specific word. For instance, to find all commands that have the word **Process**, you could use:

`Get-Command *Process*`

It will return any command with the word **Process** anywhere in its name. While **Get-Command** is excellent for discovering what commands exist, the **Get-Help** cmdlet discussed previously is your primary tool for learning how to use these commands. **Get-Help** displays information about the function and syntax of a command, its parameters, examples of its use, and links to more detailed help.

To use **Get-Help**, type **Get-Help** followed by the name of the command you are interested in. For example, if you wanted to learn more about the **Get-Process** command, you could type:

`Get-Help Get-Process`

Modules in PowerShell are packages that contain cmdlets, providers, functions, variables, and aliases. Use the **Get-Module** function to discover the currently imported modules in your PowerShell session and the commands they provide. To obtain a list of modules currently loaded in your session, run the **Get-Module** command without any parameters.

`Get-Module`

If you want to explore all the available modules, not just those loaded into your session, you can use the **ListAvailable** parameter:

`Get-Module -ListAvailable`

Once you have found a module of interest, you can use **Get-Command** to list all its commands. For example, to see all the commands in the **PSReadLine** module, you can use the following:

`Get-Command -Module PSReadLine`

You will get the following output:

```
CommandType     Name                            Version     Source
-----------     ----                            -------     ------
Function        PSConsoleHostReadLine           2.2.6       PSReadLine
Cmdlet          Get-PSReadLineKeyHandler        2.2.6       PSReadLine
Cmdlet          Get-PSReadLineOption            2.2.6       PSReadLine
Cmdlet          Remove-PSReadLineKeyHandler     2.2.6       PSReadLine
Cmdlet          Set-PSReadLineKeyHandler        2.2.6       PSReadLine
Cmdlet          Set-PSReadLineOption            2.2.6       PSReadLine
```

Figure 4.2: All PowerShell Commands within the Specified Module

Additionally, you can use the **CommandType** parameter to filter the type of commands you want to view, such as cmdlets, scripts, functions, and so on. The following examples show using the **Get-Command** cmdlet in various ways.

The following examples filter the results using the **CommandType** property:

> **Note:** Some example commands will not return any values due to requiring other PowerShell Modules, Files, or Folders. An example is the Get-Command -CommandType Configuration, which only returns values if you are using PowerShell Desired State Configuration (DSC).

```
# Get All Aliases (Returns Values)
Get-Command -CommandType Alias

# Get All Applications (Returns Values)
Get-Command -CommandType Application

# Get All Options (Returns Values)
Get-Command -CommandType All

# Get All Cmdlets (Returns Values)
Get-Command -CommandType Cmdlet

# Get All Configuration (May Not Return Values)
Get-Command -CommandType Configuration

# Get All External Scripts (Returns Values)
Get-Command -CommandType ExternalScript

# Get All Functions (Returns Values)
Get-Command -CommandType Function

# Get All Filters (May Not Return Values)
Get-Command -CommandType Filter

# Get All Scripts (May Not Return Values)
Get-Command -CommandType Script
```

The **ParameterName** property for the **Get-Command** in PowerShell is a convenient way to find specific commands with a specified parameter. It allows you to filter out commands based on the parameters they accept.

- For instance, if you are looking for commands that accept a **Path** parameter, you would use:

```
Get-Command -ParameterName Path
```

- If you want to find cmdlets that accept **ComputerName** as a parameter, use:

```
Get-Command -ParameterName ComputerName
```

- You can search for commands with a **Credential** parameter by executing:

```
Get-Command -ParameterName Credential
```

- Suppose you want to find cmdlets that accept an **Encoding** parameter. You can find them with:

```
Get-Command -ParameterName Encoding
```

- If you are working with services and need cmdlets that use the **Name** parameter, use:

```
Get-Command -ParameterName Name
```

- To find commands that utilize a **Filter** parameter, the command would be:

```
Get-Command -ParameterName Filter
```

- You can find cmdlets that accept a **Force** parameter when working with files by running:

```
Get-Command -ParameterName Force
```

- To discover cmdlets that use a **Verbose** parameter, use:

```
Get-Command -ParameterName Verbose
```

- When looking for commands that can take a **WarningAction** parameter, use:

```
Get-Command -ParameterName WarningAction
```

- If you need cmdlets that use the **ErrorAction** parameter, use the following:

```
Get-Command -ParameterName ErrorAction
```

Using the **ParameterName** property is a powerful way to discover the functionality available in PowerShell and locate the correct command for your needs. This approach can significantly reduce the time you spend hunting for the valid cmdlet when scripting in PowerShell. And once you have the command you need, **Get-Help** can assist you further in understanding how to utilize it effectively.

The following three examples for Windows, Linux, and macOS show finding commands to execute:

- Windows:
    - Find all cmdlets related to users in the **Microsoft.PowerShell.LocalAccounts** module.

    ```
    Get-Command -Module Microsoft.PowerShell.LocalAccounts -Noun *User*
    ```

- Linux:
    - Retrieve all available cmdlets that handle text objects.

      `Get-Command -Noun *Text*`
- macOS:
    - Return a list of all cmdlets available within the **PowerShellGet** module.

      `Get-Command -Module PowerShellGet -Noun Module`

The **Get-Command** cmdlet in PowerShell is excellent for discovering and investigating the commands available to you. However, the sheer volume of available commands can sometimes be overwhelming. To help, you can use other commands such as **Format-List**, **Where-Object**, and **Sort-Object**. They can help you filter, sort, and display command information in an easier way to analyze and understand.

For example, if you wanted to find all commands with a specific noun, you might use **Where-Object** to filter the results, returning all commands with **Process** as a noun:

`Get-Command | Where-Object {$_.Noun -eq 'Process'}`

Once you have a list of commands, you can display the information in a more readable format. The **Format-List** cmdlet can help you by showing each command's name and definition in a list format:

`Get-Command | Where-Object {$_.Noun -eq 'Process'} | Format-List Name, Definition`

If you want to sort these commands based on their names, you will use the **Sort-Object** cmdlet to display the commands alphabetically:

`Get-Command | Where-Object {$_.Noun -eq 'Process'} | Sort-Object Name | Format-List Name, Definition`

If you are searching for a specific parameter within a range of commands, you can utilize **Where-Object** to list all commands that contain the **Path** parameter:

`Get-Command | Where-Object {$_.Parameters.Keys -contains 'Path'} | Format-List Name`

Finally, if you want to sort the commands based on the count of parameters, you could use the **Sort-Object** cmdlet as follows:

`Get-Command | Where-Object {$_.Parameters.Keys -contains 'Path'} | Sort-Object -Property {$_.Parameters.Count} | Format-List Name, Parameters`

Using **Format-List**, **Where-Object**, and **Sort-Object** together with **Get-Command**, you can filter through the vast array of PowerShell commands, finding what you need precisely and efficiently. You can combine all the available properties and commands to refine your search for commands. The following example uses multiple property filters combined with the previously used commands:

```
$commands = Get-Command

$filteredCommands = $commands | Where-Object {

    $_.CommandType -eq 'Cmdlet' -and

    $_.Source -like 'Microsoft.*' -and

    $_.Noun -like '*Service*' -and

    ($_.Parameters.Keys.Count -gt 2)

}

$sortedFilteredCommands = $filteredCommands | `

    Sort-Object Source, Noun | `

        Format-Table -Property Name, Source, `

            @{Name='ParameterCount';Expression={$_.Parameters.Keys.Count}}

$sortedFilteredCommands
```

The PowerShell filters commands provided by Microsoft that contain **Service** in the name and more than two parameters will be displayed, as shown:

Name	Source	ParameterCount
Get-Service	Microsoft.PowerShell.Management	18
New-Service	Microsoft.PowerShell.Management	21
Remove-Service	Microsoft.PowerShell.Management	15
Restart-Service	Microsoft.PowerShell.Management	20
Resume-Service	Microsoft.PowerShell.Management	19
Set-Service	Microsoft.PowerShell.Management	23
Start-Service	Microsoft.PowerShell.Management	19
Stop-Service	Microsoft.PowerShell.Management	21
Suspend-Service	Microsoft.PowerShell.Management	19

Figure 4.3: Microsoft PowerShell commands containing service in the name and multiple parameters

You can also use advanced techniques such as using **Get-Command** with wildcard characters, exploring modules, and tapping into .NET assemblies. To explore commands within .NET assemblies, you need to complete specific steps. The following example will investigate available commands within the **System.Text.RegularExpressions** DLL within Windows:

1. To load the `System.Text.RegularExpressions` assembly, you can use the following:

   `Add-Type -AssemblyName "System.Text.RegularExpressions"`

2. Once the assembly is loaded, you can use the .NET methods available within this assembly. For instance, if you want to use a static method from the Regex class, you will use the following format:

   `[System.Text.RegularExpressions.Regex]::Method()`

3. To use the Escape static method to escape a string, use the following command:

   `[System.Text.RegularExpressions.Regex]::Escape('Text')`

4. To create a Regex object to check if a string contains any digit, use the `IsMatch` instance method. First, create the Regex object:

   `$regexObj = New-Object System.Text.RegularExpressions.Regex("\d")`

5. Now you can use the `IsMatch` method on the Regex object to check if a string contains a digit:

   `$regexObj.IsMatch('Text')`

The entire PowerShell should look like this:

```
Add-Type -AssemblyName "System.Text.RegularExpressions"

$escapedString=[System.Text.RegularExpressions.Regex]::Escape("PowerShell")

Write-Output "Escaped String: $escapedString"

$regexObj = New-Object System.Text.RegularExpressions.Regex("\d")

$containsDigit = $regexObj.IsMatch("PowerShell")

Write-Output "Does the string contain a digit? $containsDigit"
```

The command will return **True** if there is a digit in the string and **False** otherwise. The result can be stored in a variable for further processing if necessary.

> **Note:** In newer versions of PowerShell, the Add-Type cmdlet is available and functions similarly to previous versions. However, there might be differences in available .NET assemblies between .NET Framework and .NET Core.

One thing to note is that while PowerShell provides cmdlets for almost everything, certain advanced tasks might require direct use of .NET classes and their methods. While .NET assemblies provide extensive capabilities, it is essential to understand the classes, methods, and properties they expose before attempting to use them in PowerShell.

Another tool for discovering PowerShell commands is the command prediction feature, available in PowerShell 7 and above. Predictive IntelliSense improves command-line efficiency by suggesting possible completions as you type. The feature uses machine learning to predict the rest of a command based on your command history, giving you intelligent suggestions in real time. Predictive IntelliSense can save you time by reducing the keystrokes needed to complete a command, especially for long cmdlets or paths. It looks something like this:

```
Get-ChildItem -Recurse "C:\Windows\System32\drivers\etc"
```

Figure 4.4: Command prediction within PowerShell 7

Using **Integrated Development Environments (IDEs)** like Visual Studio Code or PowerShell ISE can provide IntelliSense features to help discover and complete PowerShell commands, making finding and executing PowerShell commands more efficient and intuitive. The Visual Studio Code IntelliSense for command is shown in the following figure:

```
Start-Pro
    Start-Proce...    Start-Process [-FilePath] <string> [[-Arg...
    Start-MpRollback
    Start-AppvVirtualProcess
    Start-AppBackgroundTask
    Start-DbaDbEncryption
    Start-MpRollback
```

Figure 4.5: Visual Studio Code IntelliSense for Command

The properties windows looks like the following figure:

```
Start-Process -
    FilePath                                               [string]
    ArgumentList
    Credential
    WorkingDirectory
    LoadUserProfile
    NoNewWindow
    PassThru
    RedirectStandardError
    RedirectStandardInput
    RedirectStandardOutput
    Verb
    WindowStyle
```

Figure 4.6: Visual Studio Code IntelliSense for Command Properties

Understanding how to utilize the `Get-Command` cmdlet is critical to becoming proficient with PowerShell. It is a powerful tool, enabling you to explore, understand, and use the vast array of commands and functionalities within PowerShell. You can filter, sort, and dissect the commands based on their properties, module source, and parameters. This ability to explore .NET assemblies significantly extends the range of functionalities you can leverage. Remember, the `Get-Command` cmdlet is **not** just for discovering commands; it **is** a door to understanding PowerShell's expansive capabilities. Knowing `Get-Command` will make you a more effective and efficient PowerShell user, whether working in a Windows, Linux, or macOS environment.

Understanding the different types of commands

PowerShell commands, commonly called cmdlets, are the core of the PowerShell scripting language. They provide the functionality to manage and automate tasks in your Windows environment. This section will guide you through the commands in PowerShell: cmdlets, functions, scripts, and aliases. By understanding the distinctions between these, you can effectively leverage PowerShell's power to accomplish various tasks.

Cmdlets

Command-lets (**cmdlets**) form the backbone of PowerShell. They are lightweight commands that perform a specific function. PowerShell cmdlets use the .NET Framework to manipulate objects directly in the pipeline. Cmdlets use a **Verb-Noun** naming system. The verb describes the command's action, and the noun describes the object that the command acts upon. For example, in the cmdlet, `Get-Process`, `Get` is the verb indicating an action of retrieving, and `Process` is the noun specifying the retrieved. PowerShell supports a diverse set of verbs designed to work with different actions within a command. Examples of these verbs include:

- **Get** for retrieving data.
- **Set** for defining data.
- **Add** for adding data or values.
- **Remove** for deleting specific elements.
- **New** for creating new instances or objects.

Other important verbs are **Start** and **Stop**, used for initiating or terminating processes. You use the **Invoke** verb to run commands or actions and **Test** to check conditions or verify. Using these standard verbs helps maintain consistency and clarity across different PowerShell commands.

Functions

Functions in PowerShell are named blocks of script used as independent units, providing flexibility in script design. They can take input parameters, perform operations, and return results. Whether straightforward or complex, functions serve a variety of purposes. You can use them to modularize code, making it more readable and maintainable. A function, once defined, can be reused across multiple scripts, saving time and effort. An example could be a function designed to log events, which you can use across different scripts in a project. Here is an example of a simple PowerShell function that multiplies two numbers:

```
function Multiply-Numbers {

    param (

        [Parameter(Mandatory=$true)]

        [int]$number1,

        [Parameter(Mandatory=$true)]

        [int]$number2

    )

    return $number1 * $number2

}
```

To use this function, you would call it by its name and supply the parameters like so, which would return an answer of 50:

```
Multiply-Numbers -number1 5 -number2 10
```

Scripts

Scripts in PowerShell are files containing a series of commands to perform specific tasks, often used for automating repetitive or complex operations. PowerShell scripts use the .ps1 extension and can contain any valid PowerShell commands. To run a script, you type the path of the script file at the PowerShell command prompt, or you can execute them from within the script editor. For example, you could write a script to list all the processes on your computer and export the list to a CSV file. This script might look something like this:

```
$processes = Get-Process

$processes | Export-Csv -Path "C:\Temp\Processes.csv" -NoTypeInformation
```

Aliases

Aliases in PowerShell are shorthand ways to refer to cmdlets or functions. They help make your scripts more concise and easier to type at the command line. For example, the **Get-ChildItem** cmdlet, which lists items in a directory, has the alias **ls**, a shorter and more familiar command for many users coming from Unix-like systems. You can view the list of defined aliases using the **Get-Alias** cmdlet:

`Get-Alias`

The following output will be displayed:

```
CommandType     Name
-----------     ----
Alias           ? -> Where-Object
Alias           % -> ForEach-Object
Alias           ac -> Add-Content
Alias           cat -> Get-Content
Alias           cd -> Set-Location
Alias           chdir -> Set-Location
Alias           clc -> Clear-Content
Alias           clear -> Clear-Host
Alias           clhy -> Clear-History
Alias           cli -> Clear-Item
Alias           clp -> Clear-ItemProperty
Alias           cls -> Clear-Host
Alias           clv -> Clear-Variable
Alias           cnsn -> Connect-PSSession
Alias           compare -> Compare-Object
Alias           copy -> Copy-Item
Alias           cp -> Copy-Item
Alias           cpi -> Copy-Item
Alias           cpp -> Copy-ItemProperty
Alias           cvpa -> Convert-Path
Alias           dbp -> Disable-PSBreakpoint
Alias           del -> Remove-Item
Alias           diff -> Compare-Object
Alias           dir -> Get-ChildItem
```

Figure 4.7: List of Current Aliases

Using the **Set-Alias** command, you can create aliases for basic commands and functions, scripts, files, and executables. For example, to create an alias **np** for the Notepad application, you could use:

`Set-Alias -Name "np" -Value Notepad`

The following example defines a **Get-LargestFiles** function that retrieves the largest files in the specified path. It then creates an alias **glf** for this function. After setting the alias, you can use **glf** to call the **Get-LargestFiles** function:

```
function Get-LargestFiles {
    param(
        [Parameter(Position=0, Mandatory=$true)]
        [string]$path,
        [Parameter(Position=1)]
        [int]$top = 10
    )

    Get-ChildItem -Path $path -Recurse -File |
    Sort-Object Length -Descending |
    Select-Object -First $top
}

Set-Alias -Name glf -Value Get-LargestFiles
glf -path "C:\Temp" -top 10
```

Developing a deep understanding of the various types of commands forms the cornerstone of practical scripting in PowerShell. These command types include:

- Cmdlets
- Functions
- Scripts
- Aliases

Each serves distinct roles and has specific use cases that can significantly enhance the effectiveness of your programming. Understanding when and how to use each command type effectively enables you to craft more efficient, readable, and powerful scripts. It can elevate your scripting skills and empower you to tackle more complex tasks with confidence and proficiency.

Executing existing commands within a Windows computer

In Windows, PowerShell comes with numerous built-in modules to manage various aspects of the operating system. Some of the core modules include:

- **Microsoft.PowerShell.Management:** This is the main module for managing Windows. It provides cmdlets to manipulate services, processes, and the registry.
- **Microsoft.PowerShell.Utility:** It offers various utility cmdlets that handle format conversion, text manipulation, and more.
- **Microsoft.PowerShell.Security:** It helps manage the security aspects of PowerShell, including cmdlets for managing **Access Control Lists (ACLs)** and the PowerShell execution policy.
- **Microsoft.PowerShell.Host:** It is mainly for interaction with the PowerShell host. Scripts do not typically use cmdlets from this module.
- **Microsoft.PowerShell.Diagnostics:** This module provides cmdlets to work with Event Logs and performance counters.
- **Microsoft.WSMan.Management:** It offers cmdlets to manage and configure WS-Management, a protocol used for remote systems management.
- **CimCmdlets:** This module provides cmdlets to manage resources using the **Common Information Model (CIM)**, a standard for representing systems, applications, networks, devices, and other managed components.

Remember that the availability of certain modules can depend on the specific roles and features installed on your Windows machine and the version of PowerShell you are using. As discussed previously, you can use the **Get-Module** cmdlet without any parameters to get a list of all loaded modules in your PowerShell session.

With Windows already loading various modules, you do not need to worry about ensuring the module loads and the commands are available. It helps when working with multiple Windows machines to execute the same command or write PowerShell scripts you wish to distribute and execute on various Windows machines. For instance, suppose you need to retrieve system information from Windows clients running different versions of the Windows operating system. Use the default-loaded **Windows Management Instrumentation (WMI)** and **Common Information Model (CIM)** commands. The following code retrieves the operating system information using the **Win32_OperatingSystem** class and outputs the OS Name, Version, and Manufacturer:

```
$info = Get-CimInstance -ClassName Win32_OperatingSystem

Write-Output "OS Name: $($info.Caption)"

Write-Output "OS Version: $($info.Version)"

Write-Output "OS Manufacturer: $($info.Manufacturer)"
```

It is important to note that you can use all verb types when executing commands. It is common to manage the entire Windows operating system using PowerShell. The following are three examples of managing different components or features within Windows:

- **Managing Scheduled Tasks**
  - Retrieve all the scheduled tasks enabled on the system:

    `Get-ScheduledTask | Where-Object {$_.State -eq 'Ready'}`
  - Create a new scheduled task to launch Notepad at a specific time:

    `$action = New-ScheduledTaskAction -Execute 'Notepad.exe'`

    `$trigger = New-ScheduledTaskTrigger -At 12:00 -Once`

    `Register-ScheduledTask Task -Action $action -Trigger $trigger`
  - Remove a scheduled task named Task:

    `Unregister-ScheduledTask -TaskName "Task01" -Confirm:$false`
- **Querying Windows Event Logs**
  - Retrieve the 10 most recent system events:

    `Get-EventLog -LogName System -Newest 10`
  - Create a new event log:

    `New-EventLog -LogName "MyNewLog" -Source "NewLog"`
  - Remove an event log named **NewLog**:

    `Remove-EventLog -LogName "NewLog"`
- **Working with Files and Folders**
  - Find all .log files in the C:\Logs directory and its subdirectories modified in the last 7 days:

    `Get-ChildItem -Path C:\Logs -Filter *.log -Recurse | Where-Object {$_.LastWriteTime -gt (Get-Date).AddDays(-7)}`
  - Create a new directory and a new text file:

    `New-Item -Path C:\NewDirectory -ItemType Directory`

    `New-Item -Path C:\NewDirectory\NewFile.txt -ItemType File`
  - Remove a directory and its contents:

    `Remove-Item -Path C:\NewDirectory -Recurse -Force`

Executing commands from specific modules

PowerShell's extensive library is one of its most outstanding features, offering a wealth of pre-packaged scripts called cmdlets. These cmdlets are grouped into modules, each providing a specific set of functionalities. You can leverage their cmdlets to perform various tasks by importing these modules. One such module is the `NetTCPIP` module, which is included in Windows and provides functionality for managing TCP/IP settings.

For example, you can use the **Get-NetIPAddress** cmdlet from the **NetTCPIP** module to retrieve IP address configuration data from your system. While some Windows systems load this module by default, using the **Import-Module** cmdlet to confirm its availability before execution remains a good practice:

`Import-Module NetTCPIP`

`Get-NetIPAddress`

The **ActiveDirectory** module provides cmdlets for managing Active Directory. For instance, the **Get-ADUser** cmdlet can fand so onh information about a specific user. Like before, we will use **Import-Module** to ensure the module is loaded:

`Import-Module ActiveDirectory`

`Get-ADUser -Filter 'Name -like "Liam Cleary"'`

PowerShell also includes a built-in module for managing the system's event logs, called **Microsoft.PowerShell.Management**. This module offers the **Get-EventLog** cmdlet to retrieve entries from the event logs. To use this cmdlet, you first need to import the module:

`Import-Module Microsoft.PowerShell.Management`

`Get-EventLog -LogName System -Newest 5`

Managing network connections is an essential task on any system, and the **NetAdapter** module makes this easy. This module provides the **Get-NetAdapter** cmdlet, which retrieves the status of all network adapters on the system:

`Import-Module NetAdapter`

`Get-NetAdapter`

For disk management, PowerShell offers the **Storage** module. The **Get-Volume** retrieves all volume information:

`Import-Module Storage`

`Get-Volume`

While PowerShell is a Windows-native framework, it is also available on Linux through PowerShell Core. While PowerShell Core does not support all the modules available on Windows, several useful modules are still available. One is **PackageManagement**, which provides a unified interface for software discovery, installation, and inventory. It is important to note that the syntax for importing a module in Linux is the same as in Windows:

```
Import-Module PackageManagement

Find-Package nano
```

Importing external modules in PowerShell extends its native capabilities by providing cmdlets that perform specialized tasks. External modules can offer anything from additional ways to interact with the operating system to interacting with cloud services and even handling tasks in third-party software. PowerShell's modular nature makes it an incredibly versatile tool adaptable to many scenarios.

External modules ensure that the scripts are clean, efficient, and reusable. Since modules encapsulate related functions and cmdlets, you can import only the necessary modules, keeping the scripting environment lean and optimized.

For example, the **SqlServer** module provides cmdlets to manage SQL Server. After installing and importing the module with:

```
Install-Module -Name SqlServer

Import-Module SqlServer
```

Using the following command, you can retrieve a list of databases on a SQL Server instance:

```
Get-SqlDatabase -ServerInstance 'localhost'
```

The PowerShell Gallery is the primary repository for PowerShell content. It provides a central hub where developers can share and acquire scripts, **Desired State Configuration** (**DSC**) resources, modules, and other useful tools. By using the **PowerShellGet** cmdlets such as `Install-Module`, `Find-Module`, and `Update-Module`, you can manage your modules directly from the PowerShell Gallery.

Apart from the PowerShell Gallery, you can also import modules manually from local or network paths. If you have a module saved in a directory, you can import it into your PowerShell session using the `Import-Module` cmdlet followed by the path to the module. When you install a module from an external source, ensure that you trust the module's source, considering security risks. The community contributes many modules to the PowerShell Gallery, so reviewing the code and ensuring it is from a trusted source before installation is essential.

Enterprise environments often utilize an internal repository for PowerShell modules. This internal repository affords better control over installable modules and guarantees access to only trusted and approved modules for the team. The following example creates a function within a file that needs saving as a module using the `.psm1` extension. Notice the use of `Export-ModuleMember` ensuring that PowerShell understands the purpose of the file. You can then import the newly created module using the path to the `.psm1` file:

```
function Say-Hello {
    param(
        [Parameter(Mandatory=$true)]
        [string]$Name
    )
    Write-Host ("Hello, " + $Name)
}
Export-ModuleMember -Function Say-Hello
```

```
Import-Module .\MyModule.psm1
```

If you are creating and using your own PowerShell module, place the **.psm1** file in one of the directories specified in **$Env:PSModulePath**, or set the full path when importing the module. Like any other created PowerShell module, you can view and execute the available functions as needed:

Get-Module -Name MyModule

You will get the following output:

ModuleType	Version	PreRelease	Name	ExportedCommands
Script	0.0		MyModule	Say-Hello

Figure 4.8: The Loaded Module and the Available Function

To execute the function from within the module, you execute the following within the PowerShell console:

Say-Hello -Name "Liam Cleary"

The PowerShell Gallery and these other options for importing modules expand the functionality of PowerShell, making it a powerful tool for managing and automating tasks in a wide variety of environments.

Understanding the command return or response object

In PowerShell, every command or cmdlet you execute typically returns an object or a set of objects. These objects are instances of .NET classes that carry data and behavior.

The information contained in these objects can then be manipulated, transformed, or even passed on to other cmdlets as input.

The terms **return object** and **response object** often refer to the same thing – the output or result of a **cmdlet**, **function**, or **script**. However, there are specific contexts where these terms can have distinct meanings.

A **return object** usually refers to the output a user-defined function or script sends back. The **return** keyword in PowerShell functions specifies the output and immediately halts the function execution. For example, this function accepts a number and returns its double:

```
function Get-Double {

    param($number)

    return $number * 2

}
```

A **response object**, on the other hand, is a term generally used to refer to the result of a cmdlet or script, irrespective of whether it is executed from a function or directly in the console. It represents the output object (or objects) you can interact with once a command executes.

In the case of the `Get-Process` cmdlet, the response objects are the process objects that the cmdlet outputs, providing information about the processes running on your system. It is crucial to understand that PowerShell functions automatically output any value or object not captured or stored (for example, in a variable) — you do not necessarily need the return keyword to produce output. For example, this function will output the same result as the previous one, even without the **return** keyword:

```
function Get-Double {

    param($number)

    $number * 2

}
```

These objects come in various types, often mirroring the data types you interact with. Here are some of the most common response object types in PowerShell:

- **String objects**: These are textual data. PowerShell often returns it as a string object when manipulating or retrieving text-based data. For example, the `Get-Content` cmdlet used on a text file returns a string object for each line of the text:

    ```
    $myText = Get-Content -Path .\MyFile.txt

    $myText.GetType()
    ```

- **Integer objects**: These are numerical data without decimals. For instance, when you perform a mathematical operation, PowerShell returns an integer object:

  `$myNum = 5 - 2`

  `$myNum.GetType()`

- **Boolean objects**: These represent true or false values. Many cmdlets return boolean objects to indicate the success or failure of an operation:

  `$myBool = Test-Path -Path .\MyFile.txt`

  `$myBool.GetType()`

- **Array objects**: These are collections of other objects. When you gather multiple objects into a list, PowerShell treats it as an array object:

  `$myArray = 1,2,3,4`

  `$myArray.GetType()`

- **Custom objects**: You can create custom objects with the **New-Object** cmdlet or the **[PSCustomObject]** accelerator. These objects can contain properties that are string, integer, boolean, array, or even other custom objects.

  `$myObject = New-Object -TypeName PSObject`

  `$myObject | Add-Member `` `

  ``  -Type NoteProperty ` ``

  ``  -Name "Name" ` ``

  `  -Value "Liam Cleary"`

  `$myObject.GetType()`

Understanding PowerShell response object types is critical for several reasons:

- **Data manipulation**: Knowing the data type you are dealing with allows you to manipulate it more effectively. Different data types have different methods and properties that can be accessed and used. For instance, string objects have methods like **.ToUpper()** or **.Split()**, whereas arrays have methods like **.Sort()** or **.Count**.

- **Troubleshooting**: When a script does not behave as expected, it is often due to data being in an unexpected format. Knowing the response object type helps identify such issues.

- **Efficient coding**: Different data types have different performances for various operations. For example, if you need to frequently access items by a key, using a hashtable (a specific type of object) instead of an array can significantly speed up your code.

- **Integration**: When integrating with other systems (like databases, web APIs, or other software), you often need to provide data in a specific type. Understanding the response object type helps ensure you supply data in the correct format.
- **Script flexibility**: Knowledge of object types allows you to write more flexible scripts. For example, by understanding that a cmdlet returns an array of objects, you can code your script to handle multiple items simultaneously, making it more robust.

Understanding these concepts will allow you to write more effective and flexible scripts.

To further understand the structure and properties of returned objects, the `Get-Member` cmdlet is invaluable. It allows you to examine the object type and the properties and methods it contains. For example, `Get-Disk | Get-Member` will show you all the properties and methods available on the disk objects `Get-Disk` returns. The following examples show how to use `Get-Member` to retrieve properties and methods:

- **Working with Files**
  - If you are working with file system objects, you can use `Get-Member` to discover properties like the file's size, creation time, or last access time:

    ```
    Get-ChildItem C:\temp\somefile.txt | Get-Member
    ```

  - You can see all the available properties and methods for the file object using `Get-Member`, helping you write scripts that interact with the file system.

- **Processing CSV Data**
  - Suppose you are processing CSV data and need to figure out the column names in the file. `Get-Member` can help:

    ```
    Import-Csv "C:\Temp\File.csv" | `
    Get-Member -MemberType NoteProperty
    ```

  - It will output a list of the properties on the CSV object corresponding to the CSV file's column names. Knowing these property names allows you to write scripts to manipulate the data.

- **Exploring Custom Objects**
  - If you are working with custom objects or unfamiliar objects returned by cmdlets or functions, you can use `Get-Member` to understand what you are dealing with:

    ```
    Get-Process | Get-Member
    ```

  - It will display all properties and methods related to the process objects retrieved by the `Get-Process` cmdlet. You can find out what actions you can perform on the process object (like kill) and what properties are available (like CPU or ID) from the output.

Using PowerShell in Visual Studio Code

Visual Studio Code (VSCode) offers a compelling PowerShell scripting and development environment. It is a free, open-source, and cross-platform code editor developed by Microsoft, enabling scripting in PowerShell across Windows, macOS, and Linux. By leveraging VSCode, you are getting a scripting editor and a full-fledged IDE for PowerShell.

VSCode supports PowerShell language features through the PowerShell extension. This extension provides features like syntax highlighting, code snippets, and IntelliSense (code completions), greatly enhancing your scripting experience. Moreover, it offers powerful debugging tools that can set breakpoints, step through code, and inspect variables, enhancing your ability to write and debug complex scripts. In VSCode, you can leverage the integrated terminal that supports PowerShell. This terminal allows you to execute scripts, run individual commands, and see the output inside the VSCode interface without switching to a separate PowerShell console. It also has a feature to run a code selection, which is handy when developing and testing a part of your script.

One key benefit of VSCode is its robust extension marketplace. Apart from the PowerShell extension, you can find and install various other extensions to augment your PowerShell scripting capabilities. For example, the Git extension can be used for version control, allowing you to keep track of your script modifications and collaborate with others more effectively. These extensions are displayed in the following figure:

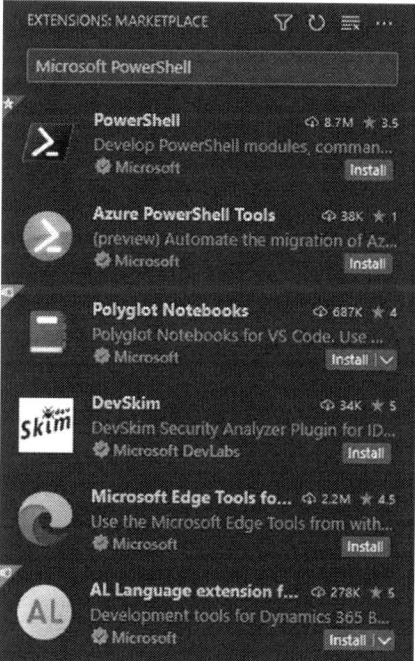

Figure 4.9: Visual Studio Code PowerShell Extensions

However, like any tool, VSCode has a few cons. The learning curve may be steep for those used to simple text editors or the **Integrated Scripting Environment (ISE)**, given the vast array of features and configurations VSCode offers.

To use VSCode for PowerShell scripting, you will need to install both VSCode and the PowerShell extension, as shown:

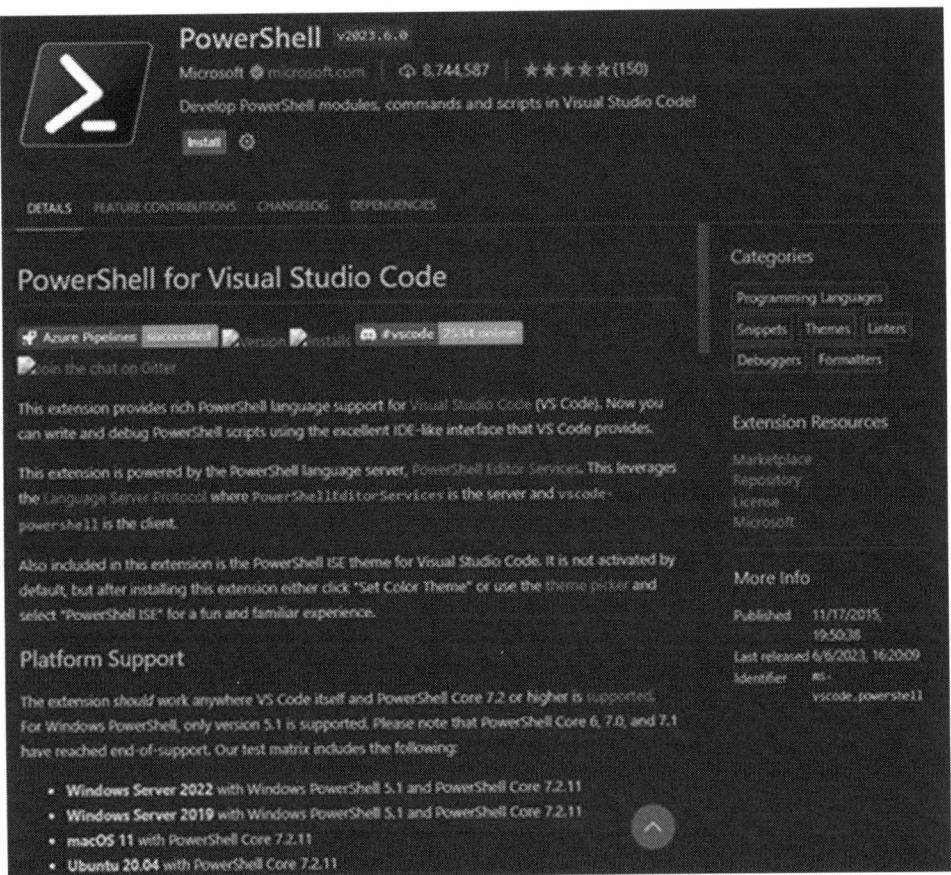

Figure 4.10: Visual Studio Code PowerShell Extension

You also need to install PowerShell on your machine, with PowerShell 5.1 or higher recommended for the best compatibility and features.

VSCode and PowerShell complement each other well. You could write a script, leveraging IntelliSense for quicker development and the integrated terminal to test individual calls. The VSCode PowerShell Intellisense looks like the following figure:

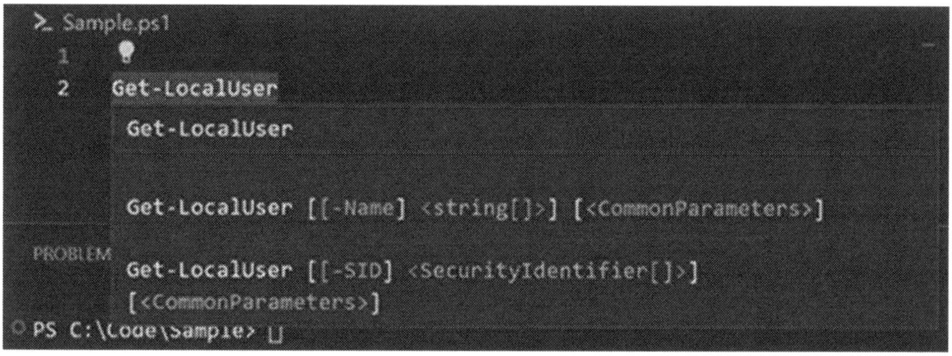

Figure 4.11: Visual Studio Code PowerShell Intellisense

The VSCode Integrated PowerShell Terminal is displayed below:

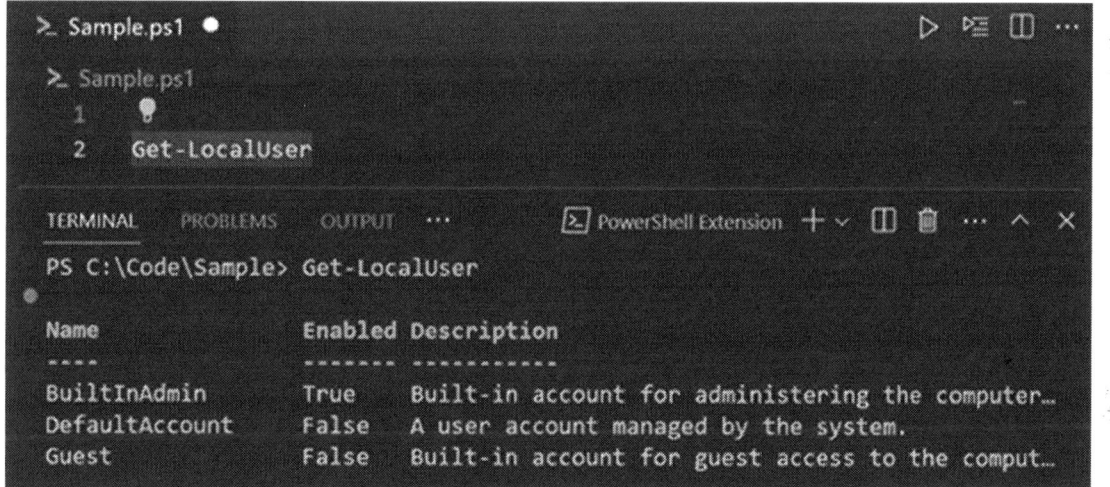

Figure 4.12: Visual Studio Code Integrated PowerShell Terminal

As your script grows, the debugging features become invaluable, and when your script is ready, you can even use Git for version control right within VSCode.

Using PowerShell in Visual Studio Code combines the flexibility and power of PowerShell with the robust features of a modern IDE, making it a powerful combination for any PowerShell developer.

Conclusion

To effectively use PowerShell, it is crucial to grasp the command structure, execution, and practical application of command return or response objects. When combined with knowledge of using modules and specific commands from them, your PowerShell toolkit becomes even more powerful. Visual Studio Code is an excellent tool to enhance the benefits of using PowerShell. By understanding these components, you can use PowerShell's versatility and robustness, improving your scripting and automation skills, whether on a Windows machine or using Visual Studio Code. This knowledge lays the foundation for advanced script development, opening numerous opportunities for automating tasks, managing systems, and simplifying IT processes.

Join our book's Discord space

Join the book's Discord Workspace for Latest updates, Offers, Tech happenings around the world, New Release and Sessions with the Authors:

https://discord.bpbonline.com

CHAPTER 5
Working with Variables and Pipelines

Introduction

In this chapter, we will look at using variables and pipelines in PowerShell. We will begin by understanding the pipeline operator, which lets you use the output of one command as input for another. We will then explore variables in PowerShell, learning how to create and manage them, from simple string variables to more complex objects. We will discuss how to declare and cast variable types, which helps you control the data type a variable can hold. We will also show you how to pass variables between commands, a helpful technique for saving and reusing data throughout your PowerShell scripts. Lastly, we will cover various pipeline filtering techniques, which help you to extract and work with the specific data you need.

Structure

In this chapter, we will cover the following topics:
- Understanding the pipeline operator
- Executing commands that flow into single and multiple pipelines
- Using variables in PowerShell
- Creating and managing variables in PowerShell

- Declaring and casting variable types
- Passing variables between commands
- Techniques for filtering data in the pipeline

Objectives

After reading this chapter, you will have a solid grasp of how to work with variables and pipelines in PowerShell. Specifically, you can use the pipeline operator to execute commands flowing into single and multiple pipelines. You will also become familiar with variables in PowerShell, their function in storing values, and how to create and manage them effectively. Additionally, you will learn how to create and manage variables and pass them between commands, a helpful technique for storing and reusing data across commands and scripts. Finally, you will learn different pipeline filtering techniques that enable you to extract and work with specific data you need.

Understanding the pipeline operator

The pipeline operator in PowerShell, represented by the | symbol, is a powerful feature that enables the chaining of commands, creating workflows that pass objects from one command to another. This chaining effect uses the output from one command as the input for the next. Below, you will find the syntax format for the pipeline operator:

Command 1 | Command 2

In this syntax, you run **Command 1**, and its output then pipes to **Command 2**. **Command 2** will then process this output. The pipeline operator provides for more efficient code, enabling the performance of complex tasks with fewer lines of code and in a more readable format. Understanding the pipeline operator is fundamental to mastering PowerShell. It operates differently from other shell environments, passing objects, not just text, through the pipeline. This object-oriented nature provides greater flexibility and depth when working with commands, as each command in the pipeline can manipulate the objects in diverse ways, such as by filtering, transforming, or exporting. You can chain multiple commands using the pipeline operator, each building upon the previous command's output. It allows you to perform a series of operations in a single line of code, saving you time and effort. Below, you will find the syntax format for the pipeline operator with multiple commands:

Command 1 | Command 2 | Command 3 | ...

For this to work effectively, **Command 2**, **Command 3**, and so forth should be able to accept the output of the preceding command as their input. As a real-world example, you might need to retrieve a running process list and filter them based on specific criteria. With the pipeline operator, you can accomplish this in one line of code:

```
Get-Process | Where-Object { $_.CPU -gt 50 }
```

You will get the following **output:**

```
Handles  NPM(K)    PM(K)     WS(K)    CPU(s)      Id SI ProcessName
-------  ------    -----     -----    ------      -- -- -----------
   2622     670   193780    174168    231.00     820  0 lsass
    827     110   259600    193900    233.45    3784  0 MsMpEng
    310      18     3980     10772     75.13    1364  0 svchost
    452      18    12324     22924    260.13    3132  0 svchost
    309      17    16888     20364    147.97    6136  0 svchost
   2225       0       44        64     91.08       4  0 System
    463      25    18288     34792    149.81    4304  0 WmiPrvSE
```

Figure 5.1: List processes with 50% CPU Usage

In this example, the **Get-Process** command retrieves a list of all running processes, and the **Where-Object** command filters the processes based on the CPU usage being greater than 50. The pipeline operator allows the **Get-Process** command to pass its output actively as input to the **Where-Object** command.

When you pass objects through a pipeline, PowerShell attempts to bind the output objects to the next command's input parameters. If a command in the pipeline accepts pipeline input, it has parameters designated to receive input values from the pipeline. There are two types of pipeline parameter binding: **ByValue** and **ByPropertyName:**

- **ByValue** occurs when the cmdlet accepts pipeline input of a particular **.NET** type. PowerShell binds the entire output object to the parameter if the output object matches the expected input type. For example, if you pipe a string to **Get-Content**, it binds to the Path parameter because **Get-Content** can accept string values as the Path parameter.
- **ByPropertyName** occurs when the cmdlet accepts pipeline input where a parameter can accept input from a property on the incoming object with the same name. If an output object has a property that matches the name of a parameter, PowerShell binds that property value to the parameter. For example, if you pipe an object with Path to **Get-Content**, it binds the Path property to the Path parameter.

PowerShell will first try to bind **ByValue**. If it cannot, it will then try to bind **ByPropertyName**. If neither binding methods are successful, the object will not be bound, and it could lead to errors or unexpected results. Understanding how pipeline parameter binding works is essential to designing and troubleshooting pipelines in PowerShell.

The pipeline operator is not limited to just two commands. You can chain together as many commands as you need, allowing you to perform complex operations efficiently. The output of each command in the pipeline becomes the input for the next command, creating a seamless flow of data. For example, you could use the same pattern as before, but this time use **Get-Process** to retrieve a list of processes, pass this to **Sort-Object** to sort by CPU usage, and then pass the sorted list to **Select-Object** to select the top five processes:

`Get-Process | Sort-Object CPU -Descending | Select-Object -First 5`

The following figure is the result:

```
Handles  NPM(K)    PM(K)     WS(K)     CPU(s)      Id  SI ProcessName
-------  ------    -----     -----     ------      --  -- -----------
    421      17    12128     22884     260.14    3132   0 svchost
    798     109   258280    192748     233.45    3784   0 MsMpEng
   2628     670   193796    174200     231.06     820   0 lsass
    462      25    18304     34836     149.88    4304   0 WmiPrvSE
    309      17    17012     20456     148.00    6136   0 svchost
```

Figure 5.2: Display the top 5 processes in descending order using the CPU Property

The pipeline operator is more than just a convenient way to chain commands together. It provides a range of advantages that can significantly enhance your PowerShell experience. One of the main benefits of using the pipeline operator is increased efficiency. By chaining commands together, you can perform multiple operations in a single line of code, reducing the need for repetitive tasks. The following example retrieves all processes, sorts them by CPU usage, selects the top 5, and displays the name and CPU usage:

`Get-Process | Sort-Object CPU -Descending | Select-Object -First 5 | Format-Table Name, CPU`

It not only saves you time but also improves your productivity. Instead of writing separate scripts for each task, you can simultaneously accomplish them using the pipeline operator. The pipeline operator also promotes code reusability. Once you have a set of commands that perform a specific task, you can easily reuse them by piping them into different inputs. It eliminates the need to rewrite the same code repeatedly, making your scripts more modular and maintainable. Using the pipeline operator allows you to filter and sort data easily. PowerShell provides a wide range of cmdlets (commands) that enable you to manipulate and process data. Combining these cmdlets with the pipeline operator allows you to filter and sort data based on specific criteria, making extracting the information easier. This flexibility is beneficial when working with large datasets or searching for particular information within a data set.

The pipeline operator offers more than just efficiency, code reusability, and data manipulation. By understanding how to use this operator effectively, you can perform complex tasks in a simplified manner, improving your productivity and the readability of your scripts. It is, without a doubt, an essential tool in PowerShell.

Executing commands that flow into single and multiple pipelines

PowerShell is proficient at processing large amounts of data efficiently. This operator directs the output of one command, the upstream command, into another, the downstream command, transforming the data step by step. In the previous section, we looked at some basic examples of using the pipeline operator. The pipeline operator makes it easy to handle command execution that flows into single or multiple pipelines.

Let us recap with a basic example. Say you want to retrieve a list of running processes on your system and sort them by CPU usage; you would use the following:

```
Get-Process | Sort-Object -Property CPU -Descending
```

In the example, **Get-Process** retrieves all running processes, and **Sort-Object -Property CPU -Descending** sorts them in decreasing order of CPU usage. The pipeline operator connects these commands, enabling the smooth data flow from **Get-Process** to **Sort-Object**.

PowerShell pipelines are not limited to just one pipe; you can create a series of pipes for more complex data manipulation. Let us show this by adding a **Select-Object** command to the previous pipeline to limit the output to the top five processes:

```
Get-Process | Sort-Object -Property CPU -Descending | Select-Object -First 5
```

Here, **Select-Object -First 5** receives the sorted process list and trims it down to the top five processes in terms of CPU usage. This example shows how easily you can chain commands to refine and format your output.

For an advanced example, let us construct a pipeline that retrieves event logs. We will then filter these logs for specific entries and output the final data to a CSV file using the following code:

```
Get-EventLog -LogName System | Where-Object { $_.EntryType -eq "Error" } | Export-Csv -Path C:\Temp\Errors.csv
```

> **Note:** You will need to update the "Path" property to your desired path

This pipeline first uses **Get-EventLog -LogName System** to retrieve system event logs. Then **Where-Object { $_.EntryType -eq "Error" }** filters out all entries except those marked as **Error**. Finally, **Export-Csv -Path C:\Temp\Errors.csv** exports the filtered list of error entries to a CSV file.

You can use pipeline operators with all supported PowerShell commands. It is not just limited to basic commands for sorting or filtering. For example, let us say you want to get a list of all users in your Active Directory, sort them by their last name, filter those enabled, and select specific properties for each user object, such as their security group memberships, then output the results to a GridView. Here is how you could achieve this:

```
Import-Module ActiveDirectory


Get-ADUser -Filter * -Property GivenName, Surname, Enabled, MemberOf |

Sort-Object -Property Surname |

Where-Object {$_.Enabled -eq $True} |

ForEach-Object {

    $groups = $_.MemberOf | ForEach-Object { (Get-ADGroup $_).Name }

    $properties = @{

        'First Name' = $_.GivenName

        'Last Name' = $_.Surname

        'Username' = $_.SamAccountName

        'Enabled' = $_.Enabled

        'Groups' = $groups -join ', '

    }

    New-Object PSObject -Property $properties

} | Select-Object 'First Name', 'Last Name', 'Username', 'Enabled', 'Groups' | Out-GridView
```

The Grid View is shown in the following screenshot:

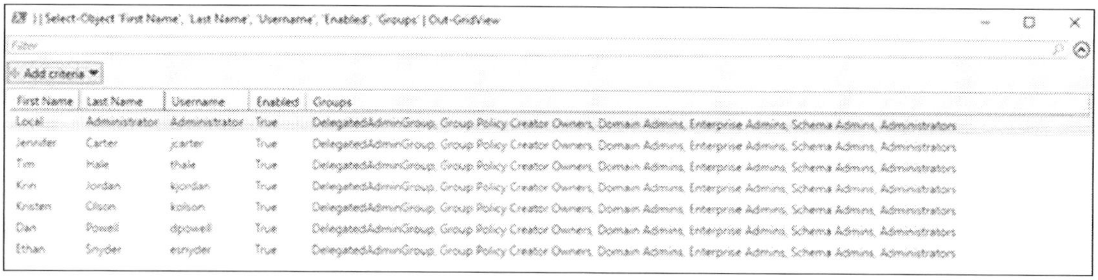

Figure 5.3: Grid View of active directory users and group details

Let us walk through each line of the PowerShell:

- **Import-Module ActiveDirectory:** This line loads the Active Directory module into the current PowerShell session. This module contains the cmdlets required to interact with Active Directory, such as **Get-ADUser** and **Get-ADGroup**.

- **Get-ADUser -Filter * -Property GivenName, Surname, Enabled, MemberOf |:** This line fetches all Active Directory users (-Filter *) and retrieves specified properties for each user: **GivenName**, **Surname**, **Enabled**, and **MemberOf**. The **MemberOf** property contains a list of distinguished names for the security groups the user is a member of. The output is piped (|) to the next command.

- **Sort-Object -Property Surname |:** This line sorts the users by the Surname property. Then, the script pipes the sorted output to the next command.

- **Where-Object {$_.Enabled -eq $True} |:** This line filters the sorted list to include only the Enabled users set to True, meaning the users whose accounts are active. We then pipe the filtered output to the next command:

    ```
    ForEach-Object {
    $groups = $_.MemberOf | ForEach-Object { (Get-ADGroup $_).Name }
    $properties = @{
    'First Name' = $_.GivenName
    'Last Name' = $_.Surname
    'Username' = $_.SamAccountName
    'Enabled' = $_.Enabled
    'Groups' = $groups -join ', '
    }
    New-Object PSObject -Property $properties
    } |
    ```

In this code, for each user object coming from the **pipeline ($_)**, we first retrieve the names of the groups the user is a member of **($groups)**. Then, we create an ordered hashtable ($properties) representing a new custom object with properties **First Name**, **Last Name**, **Username**, **Enabled**, and **Groups**. We then create a new PSObject using **New-Object PSObject -Property $properties**. This new object has the properties defined in the $properties hashtable. We then send this object down the pipeline:

```
Select-Object 'First Name', 'Last Name', 'Username', 'Enabled', 'Groups' | Out-GridView
```

Lastly, **Select-Object** chooses which properties we want to display and in what order. The script pipes the output into **Out-GridView**, presenting the results in a sortable and filterable table.

Using variables in PowerShell

Variables in PowerShell serve as foundational building blocks that hold various data values, spanning from basic data types like strings, integers, and date-time objects to more intricate structures, such as arrays, hash tables, and custom objects. They are labeled containers storing information, streamlining data retention, retrieval, and manipulation, particularly in extensive scripts or when passing data between functions or modules.

Setting or declaring a variable in PowerShell is designed to be intuitive. To initiate a variable, you employ the dollar sign **$** directly, followed by the desired name of the variable. For example, the following code assigns **Hello, World!** to **$MyVariable**.

```
$MyVariable = "Hello, World!"
```

This unique identification using the dollar sign is a distinct trait of PowerShell, distinguishing variable names from other elements or commands within the script. For instance, **$UserName** might store a user's name, and **$DateOfBirth** could hold a specific date.

Similarly, variables enhance the readability of scripts by providing descriptive names to data. Instead of constantly reevaluating expressions or re-fetching data, you can refer to a variable that holds the result. This abstraction makes the script more efficient and easier to maintain and debug. As scripts become more complex, the ability to segment and manage data using variables becomes indispensable, underscoring their pivotal role in practical PowerShell scripting.

Variable names are not case-sensitive. This behavior aligns with PowerShell's overall design philosophy, prioritizing user-friendliness and accessibility. For example, suppose you create a variable named **$MyVariable**. In that case, you can reference it using **$myvariable**, **$MYVARIABLE**, or any other combination of cases, and PowerShell will treat it as the same variable. However, while PowerShell itself does not differentiate based on the case, it is essential to remember that if your scripts interact with other case-sensitive systems or platforms, you must use the correct case.

Additionally, even though PowerShell is case-insensitive for variable names, it is a good practice to maintain consistent casing throughout your scripts. Doing so can help improve readability and reduce potential confusion for anyone reviewing or maintaining the code in the future.

You can access variables and manipulate existing values easily. For example, you can append further string values to the existing variable:

`$MyVariable += ", how are you?"`

You can create a variety of variables to store different types of data, such as:

- **Scalar variables:** These variables hold a single value and can store different data types, such as integers, strings, Boolean, or dates:

    `$Name = "John Doe"`

    `$Age = 30`

    `$IsActive = $true`

- **Array variables:** These variables hold multiple values. An array variable can be created by enclosing a comma-separated list of values in parentheses:

    `$MyArray = 1,2,3,4,5`

- **HashTable variables (Associative Arrays):** Hash tables allow storing of key-value pairs. The key-value pairs hold either single or multiple values:

    `$hashTable = @{Name="John"; Age=25}`

- **Script variables:** A script or function defines these. They are private to the script or function and are not available outside the scope of that script or function:

    `$script:MyScriptVariable = "This is a script variable"`

- **Global variables:** These variables are available to all scripts and functions running in the current session:

    `$global:MyGlobalVariable = "This is a global variable"`

- **Environment variables:** These variables can influence software behavior on the system:

    `$env:USERNAME`

- **Object variables:** PowerShell is an object-oriented scripting language allowing you to store complex objects with their properties and methods in variables:

    `$ProcessObj = Get-Process | Select-Object -First 1`

- **PSDrive Variables:** You can work with different data stores, such as the registry and certificate stores, as though they were file system drives by using these:

  `New-PSDrive -Name HKCUSoftware -PSProvider Registry -Root HKEY_CURRENT_USER\Software`

Each type serves different needs, offering flexibility and efficiency when scripting. Variables play a significant role in PowerShell scripts and are indispensable for tasks that require data storage, retrieval, and manipulation. By understanding and using variables, you can write more efficient and flexible scripts in PowerShell.

Creating and managing variables in PowerShell

Creating and managing variables in PowerShell is a straightforward and essential process for writing effective scripts and managing data within your scripting environment. Variables support strong typing, where you can specify a particular data type for a variable, and casting, where you can convert a variable from one type to another. Managing the content and scope of variables ensures your scripts are robust and maintainable.

There are multiple ways of creating variables within PowerShell, such as:

- **Using direct assignment:** You can create a variable by prefixing the variable name with a dollar sign **$** and assigning it a value using the = operator. For example:

  `$MyVariable = "Hello, World!"`

- **Strong typing:** To ensure that a variable only holds a specific data type, you can specify the type during the creation. For example, to create an integer variable:

  `[int]$MyNumber = 42`

- **Using cmdlets:** You can also use the `New-Variable` cmdlet to create variables, providing options to specify the name, value, description, and other properties.

  `New-Variable -Name "MyVariable" -Value "This is a variable."`

Maintaining PowerShell variables involves updating, clearing, removing, setting the scope, inspecting the variable, and choosing if the variable is writable. They are described as follows:

- **Changing values:** You can easily change the value of a variable by simply reassigning it with the = operator:

  `$MyVariable = "New value."`

- **Clearing values:** If you need to clear the value of a variable, you can use the `Clear-Variable` cmdlet or set the variable to **$null**:

```
Clear-Variable -Name "MyVariable"
$MyVariable = $null
```

- **Removing variables:** You can remove a variable entirely from the session using the Remove-Variable cmdlet:

```
Remove-Variable -Name "MyVariable"
```

- **Read-only variables:** You can create a read-only variable using the **New-Variable** or **Set-Variable** cmdlets with the **-Option ReadOnly** flag to prevent accidental modifications:

```
Set-Variable -Name "MyVariable" -Option ReadOnly
```

- **Variable scope:** PowerShell supports different scopes (global, local, script, private) for variables. You can define the scope during the creation or using the **Set-Variable** cmdlet:

```
$global:MyVariable = 10
Set-Variable -Name "MyVariable" -Scope Global
```

- **Inspecting variables:** You can use the **Get-Variable** cmdlet to list existing variables or filter them by name or scope:

```
Get-Variable -Name "MyVariable"
```

PowerShell provides ***-Variable** cmdlets to interact with and manipulate variables within your PowerShell session. You typically use them when you want to perform operations on variables beyond just assigning and retrieving values, and they prove particularly useful in scripts and functions. The available cmdlets are:

- **Get-variable:** This command retrieves the value of a variable. It can be helpful if you want to retrieve the value of a variable in a way that is consistent with the other **Get** cmdlets:

```
$MyVariable = 10
Get-Variable -Name MyVariable
```

- **Set-Variable:** This command sets the value of a variable. It can be helpful if you want to set the value of a variable in a way that is consistent with the other **Set** cmdlets.

```
Set-Variable -Name MyVariable -Value 20
Write-Host $MyVariable
```

- **New-Variable:** This command creates a new variable. It can be helpful to explicitly create a variable before you use it rather than just assigning a value to a new variable name.

```
New-Variable -Name MyVariable -Value 30
```

`Write-Host $MyVariable`

- **Remove-Variable**: This command deletes a variable. It can be helpful to explicitly delete a variable to free up memory or prevent it from being used later in the script.

  `Remove-Variable -Name MyVariable`

  `Write-Host $MyVariable`

- **Clear-Variable**: This command clears the value of a variable. It can be helpful if you want to reset a variable's value without deleting the variable itself.

  `Clear-Variable -Name MyVariable`

  `Write-Host $MyVariable`

By understanding these methods for creating and maintaining variables, you will be well-equipped to manage data within your PowerShell scripts and create more flexible, robust solutions.

Declaring and casting variable types

In PowerShell, you can declare variables with specific types and cast variables to convert one type to another. You might need to declare the variable type within PowerShell for many reasons:

- **Type safety:** Ensures that the variable can only hold values of a particular type, preventing unintended data types from being assigned:

  ```
  [int]$MyInt = 123
      try {
          $MyInt = "Hello"
      }
      catch {
          Write-Output "Error: $_"
      }
  ```

- **Code clarity:** Makes the code easier to understand and maintain by clearly indicating what type of data is expected in a variable.
- **Performance optimization:** In some scenarios, explicitly specifying a type can benefit performance by reducing the need for runtime type resolution.
- **Error prevention**: Helps catch errors early in the development cycle if a variable assigns a wrong type. The following example does not use an explicit type declaration:

```
$UserAge = "twenty-three"
if ($UserAge -lt 18) {
Write-Output "User is a minor."
}
```

The following example uses an explicit type declaration:

```
[int]$UserAge = "twenty-three"
if ($UserAge -lt 18) {
Write-Output "User is a minor."
}
```

The output is as follows:

```
PS C:\> [int]$UserAge = "twenty-three"
MetadataError: Cannot convert value "twenty-three" to type "System.Int32
". Error: "The input string 'twenty-three' was not in a correct format."
```

Figure 5.4: Using a variable type declaration for errors

- **Integration with .NET:** Facilitates interaction with .NET classes and methods that expect specific types.

When declaring a variable, you can specify its type using square brackets and the type name. For example, `[int]$MyInt = 5` explicitly declares a variable as an integer type. Similarly, `[string]$MyString = "Hello"` declares a string variable.

If you try to assign a value that does not match the declared type, PowerShell will attempt to convert it or throw an error if the conversion fails. Casting in PowerShell refers to converting a variable from one type to another. It is a way to tell PowerShell how to treat a variable in a specific context. PowerShell is generally type-agnostic, determining the best way to handle the variable types automatically. But sometimes, you need to define or convert the variable type explicitly. You might need to cast a variable type within PowerShell for many reasons:

- **Type conversion:** Enables conversion between different types, such as turning a string into an integer or a base64 string into a byte array.
- **Data parsing:** Converting raw data into a more usable or meaningful format, like transforming a date string into a DateTime object.
- **Compatibility with other systems:** Helps in preparing data for interaction with other systems, services, or APIs that expect specific types.

- **Enhancing functionality:** Allows leveraging the methods and properties of a specific type, for instance, casting a general object to a FileInfo object to access file-related methods.
- **Null handling:** Casting to nullable types can provide more elegant handling of null or missing values.
- **Enum handling:** Facilitates the usage of enumerations, enabling the conversion of string representations of enum values into actual enum types.

You perform explicit casting by using the desired type inside square brackets. The example below converts a string to an integer:

`$intValue = [int]"42"`

If a variable contains a string representing a date, you can cast it to a **DateTime** object using `$date = [datetime]"2022-01-01`. Casting is also beneficial when working with objects, like converting a Base64 string to bytes:

`$Base64String = "SSBsb3ZlIFBvd2VyU2hlbGw="`

`$Bytes = [System.Convert]::FromBase64String($Base64String )`

`$Bytes -join ' '`

`$DecodedString = [System.Text.Encoding]::UTF8.GetString($Bytes )`

`$DecodedString`

Take a look at the following figure for the output:

```
PS C:\> $Base64String = "SSBsb3ZlIFBvd2VyU2hlbGw="
PS C:\> $Bytes = [System.Convert]::FromBase64String($Base64String )
PS C:\> $Bytes -join ' '
73 32 108 111 118 101 32 80 111 119 101 114 83 104 101 108 108
PS C:\> $DecodedString = [System.Text.Encoding]::UTF8.GetString($Bytes )
PS C:\> $DecodedString
I love PowerShell
```

Figure 5.5: Decoding a Base64 string value

Sometimes you need to convert a value to a nullable type, such as `$NullableInt = [nullable[int]]$Value`. It allows the integer to have a null value, unlike regular integers.

PowerShell also allows for casting arrays, such as `$IntArray = [int[]]$values`, assuming `$values` contains an array that can be converted to integers. If you have a double value and want to cast it to an integer, you can do so like this:

`$doubleValue = 23.567`

Write-Output "Original Double Value: $doubleValue"

$integerValue = [int]$doubleValue

Write-Output "Casted Integer Value: $integerValue"

The following example starts with a custom object, **$Object,** with a **FilePath** property. Initially, this property is just a string, but then we cast it to **System.IO.FileInfo** and display the type before and after casting:

$Object = [PSCustomObject]@{

    Name = "MyFile";

    FilePath = "C:\Documents\File.txt"

}

$FileInfo = [System.IO.FileInfo]$Object.FilePath

Write-Output "Type before casting: $($obj.FilePath.GetType().FullName)"

Write-Output "Type after casting: $($FileInfo.GetType().FullName)"

While you often see casting with built-in types, such as Strings, Integers, and Booleans, you can also cast using custom classes and .NET types. The following example defines a custom class **Car** with properties **Brand** and **Year**. A separate object, **$MyObject**, with matching properties is created. Then, **$MyObject** is cast to type **Car**:

Class Car {

    [string]$Brand

    [int]$Year

}

$MyObject = [PSCustomObject]@{

    Brand = 'Ford'

    Year = '2020'

}

```
$Object = [Car]$MyObject

$Object
```

.NET provides a vast library of types and classes often used in PowerShell. You can cast between these types, especially if there is a meaningful way to convert from one type to another. Imagine you have a string representing an IPv4 or IPv6 address and want to validate its format or extract its bytes. The **System.Net.IPAddress** class can assist:

```
$IpString = "192.168.1.254"

$IpAddress = [System.Net.IPAddress]::Parse($IpString)


Write-Output "Address: $($IpAddress.ToString())"

Write-Output "Address Family (IPv4 or IPv6): $($IpAddress.AddressFamily)"

Write-Output "Bytes: $($IpAddress.GetAddressBytes())"
```

In PowerShell, as in many other programming and scripting languages, an enumeration (often abbreviated to enum) represents a distinct type that consists of a set of named constants. Each constant in an enumeration maps to a unique number, typically an integer.

Enumerations are useful for defining a set of allowed values that can be easily read and understood. They make code more readable and reduce the likelihood of invalid values. Casting can be a handy way to convert a string to an enumeration type when dealing with enums. This example casts the string **Red** to its corresponding value in the **System.ConsoleColor** enumeration:

```
$Color = [System.ConsoleColor]"Red"
```

In some cases, a direct casting may fail if the conversion is complex; then, you might need to use methods like **Parse** or **TryParse** provided by the type, such as:

```
$StringDate = "2023-05-27"

[System.DateTime]::Parse($StringDate)
```

The methods provide a more controlled way to convert from one type to another and offer some benefits over simple casting:

- **Error handling (TryParse):** Casting a variable using a simple typecast can cause an error if the conversion fails. It can lead to script termination if not appropriately handled. **TryParse** provides a way to attempt a conversion and get a Boolean result indicating whether the transformation was successful or not. It allows for graceful error handling.

  ```
  $result = 0
  ```

```
[int]::TryParse("42", [ref]$result)
[int]::TryParse("NotANumber", [ref]$result)
```

- **Explicit Parsing (Parse):** Sometimes, you want to enforce that a string must be of a specific format, particularly when converting to complex types like DateTime. Parse allows you to specify the exact format and culture information, giving you more control over the conversion process. Parse will throw an exception if the parsing fails, so you will need to use try-catch blocks if there is a risk of failure. The following example uses the specified date and converts it to a correctly formatted date time object:

  ```
  $Date = [DateTime]::Parse("2020-12-31")
  ```

- **Performance considerations:** In scenarios where you need to cast many variables, using **TryParse** can be more performance-friendly, as it avoids exceptions that can be expensive in terms of performance.

- **Code clarity**: Using **Parse** and **TryParse** makes the intention of your code more straightforward, especially to others who might read your code later. It shows that you are explicitly trying to convert a value from one type to another and have considered the possibility of conversion failure.

Understanding how to declare and cast variable types in PowerShell provides more control over your data. It can help prevent errors, especially when dealing with complex objects or interacting with .NET libraries.

Passing variables between commands

Passing variables between commands in PowerShell is a fundamental concept that allows for powerful scripting and automation. You create efficient and dynamic scripts by chaining together different commands and sharing data between them. You can pass variables between commands using various methods, such as the pipeline, functions, or parameters. For example, you can assign a list of process names to a variable **$Processes** and then pass that variable to the **Get-Process** cmdlet like this:

```
$Processes = "explorer", "winlogon"; Get-Process -Name $Processes
```

The pipeline operator | is a general method to pass data from one command to another. You create a seamless flow of information by taking the output of one command and feeding it into the next. The following example gets all the items in the **C:\Documents** folder and passes them to **ForEach-Object**, which extracts and outputs the names:

```
$Files = Get-ChildItem -Path C:\Documents; $Files| ForEach-Object { $_.Name }
```

You can also define functions with parameters that accept input and then call those functions within your scripts, passing variables as needed. For example, this function accepts two values and writes their values when executed:

```
function Show-Details ($Name, $Age) {
    Write-Host "Name: $Name, Age: $Age"
}


$Name = "Alice"

$Age = 30


Show-Details -Name $Name -Age $Age
```

The output is shown below:

Figure 5.6: Execute the custom function

When working with cmdlets that require specific input types, you may need to transform or filter the data before passing it along. Use commands like **Where-Object**, **Select-Object**, or **ForEach-Object** to achieve this. The following example will get all the enabled Active Directory users and print their names:

```
$Users = Get-ADUser -Filter *; $Users | Where-Object { $_.Enabled -eq $true } | ForEach-Object { $_.Name }
```

Splatted variables allow you to pass several parameters as a single unit. It is useful when you have a command requiring multiple parameters and want to organize them neatly. Here is an example of using splatting:

```
$Params = @{

Path = "C:\Documents"

Filter = "*.txt"

}

Get-ChildItem @Params
```

Use cmdlet binding and define parameters that accept pipeline input in your custom functions. It enables more complex pipeline usage and allows custom functions to accept input from other cmdlets. For example, adding cmdlet binding tells PowerShell to accept values for the specified parameter from the pipeline:

```
function Get-UserInformation {
    [CmdletBinding()]
    param (
        [Parameter(ValueFromPipeline=$true)]
        [string]$UserName
    )

    process {
        Write-Host "Processing user: $UserName"
    }
}
```

You can directly pass values as part of the pipeline to the function:

```
"Sue", "David", "Tom", "Lucy" | Get-UserInformation
```

Seamlessly passing information from one command to the next creates a coherent and efficient pipeline that optimizes processing and simplifies code readability. The flexibility in accepting pipeline input and utilizing cmdlet binding in custom functions allows for the creation robust and reusable components. Understanding and mastering this is an essential skill in PowerShell.

Techniques for filtering data in the pipeline

Filtering data in the pipeline is an essential aspect of PowerShell scripting. It allows for the narrowing down and manipulation of information according to specific criteria. The **Where-Object** cmdlet, for instance, is instrumental in filtering objects based on their properties. You can filter processes that use more than a certain amount of CPU:

```
Get-Process | Where-Object {$_.CPU -gt 10}
```

Comparison operators like **-eq**, **-gt**, **-lt** are also widely used for filtering. This example uses the **-eq** operator for retrieving stopped processes:

```
Get-Service | Where-Object { $_.Status -eq 'Stopped' } | ForEach-Object {
Write-Output $_.DisplayName }
```

We will get the following output:

```
PS C:\> Get-Service | Where-Object { $_.Status -eq 'Stopped' } | `
>> ForEach-Object { Write-Output $_.DisplayName }
Agent Activation Runtime_20004a0
AllJoyn Router Service
Application Layer Gateway Service
Application Identity
Application Management
App Readiness
Microsoft App-V Client
AppX Deployment Service (AppXSVC)
ASP.NET State Service
AssignedAccessManager Service
Cellular Time
ActiveX Installer (AxInstSV)
```

Figure 5.7: List stopped processes by display name

This example uses the **-gt** operator for retrieving processes where the CPU usage is above 10:

```
Get-Process | Where-Object { $_.CPU -gt 10 } | ForEach-Object { Write-Output
$_.ProcessName }
```

The following figure displays the output:

```
PS C:\> Get-Process | Where-Object { $_.CPU -gt 10 } | `
>> ForEach-Object { Write-Output $_.ProcessName }
Adobe Desktop Service
CefSharp.BrowserSubprocess
CefSharp.BrowserSubprocess
CHERRY-Utility-Software
chrome
Code
Creative Cloud
Creative Cloud UI Helper
Dropbox
explorer
firefox
ms-teams
```

Figure 5.8: List stopped processes by process name

This example uses **-eq** and **-lt** operators to retrieve stopped processes:

`Get-EventLog -LogName System | Where-Object { $_.EntryType -eq 'Error' -and $_.EventID -lt 1000 } | ForEach-Object { Write-Output $_.Message }`

Additionally, **Select-Object** provides a way to select specific properties, such as:

`Get-Service | Select-Object -Property DisplayName, Status`

Script blocks can provide more complex filtering, while **ForEach-Object** enables custom actions. You might use a script block to filter processes:

```
Get-Process | Where-Object { $_.CPU -gt 10 -and $_.Id -ne $PID } | ForEach-Object {
    Write-Host ("Process " + $_.ProcessName + " with ID " `
+ $_.Id + " is using more than 10 CPU.")
}


Get-Service | ForEach-Object {
    if ($_.Status -eq 'Running') {
        Write-Output $_.Name
    }
}
```

The following figure is the output:

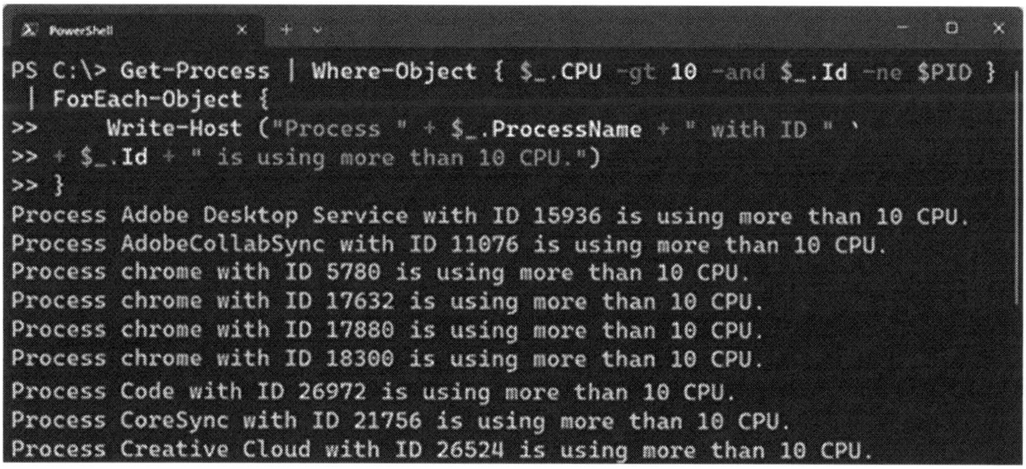

Figure 5.9: List processes using more than 10 seconds of CPU time and the ID does not match the PID

Regex matching is another powerful tool, enabling pattern matching such as `Get-Process | Where-Object { $_.Name -match '^w.*' }`. Many cmdlets have built-in filtering options, such as in the `Get-EventLog` cmdlet shown below:

`Get-EventLog -LogName Application -EntryType Error`

The versatility continues with combining multiple filters for complex queries, using the `-Filter` parameter with Active Directory cmdlets, and sorting as a form of filtering. Even wildcards can be employed, for example, `Get-Service -Name 'w*'`, and the if statement can be combined with `ForEach-Object`:

```
Get-Service -Name 'w*' | ForEach-Object {
    if ($_.Status -eq 'Running') {
        Write-Host ("Service " + $_.DisplayName + " is running.")
    } else {
        Write-Host ("Service " + $_.DisplayName + " is not running.")
    }
}
```

The following screenshot displays the output:

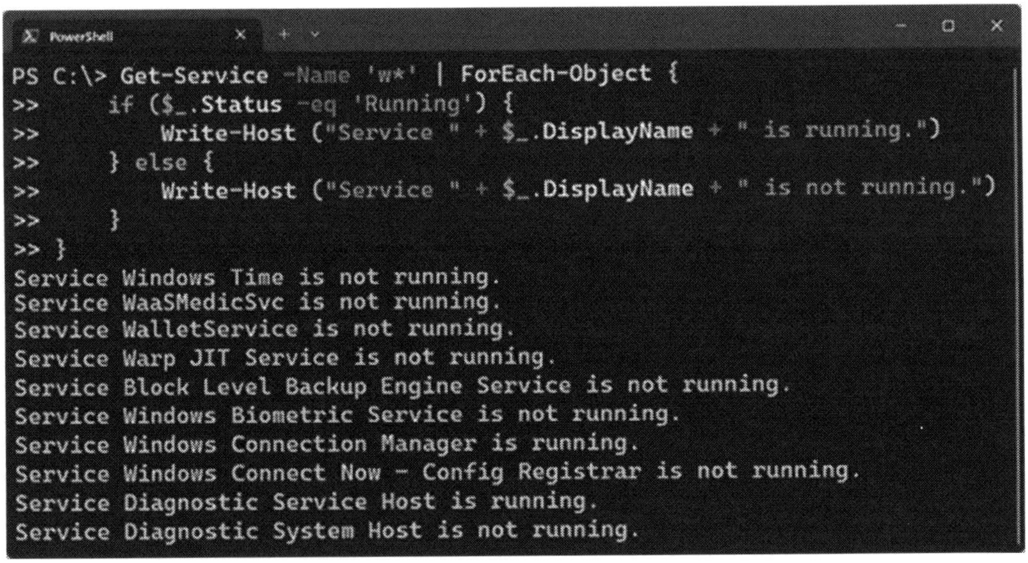

Figure 5.10: List services starting with 'W' and display their running status

Custom functions and filtering data with types add further depth to the possibilities. You might cast variables for precise filtering with **$numbers | Where-Object { $_ -is [int] }**, or utilize the **-Exclude** and **-Include** parameters to refine the results further.

The techniques for filtering data within PowerShell pipelines are rich and varied, allowing for highly customized and accurate data retrieval. From simple equality checks to complex scripting blocks, mastering these filtering techniques is vital to handling PowerShell data manipulation and automation tasks. Whether working with file system objects, processes or querying Active Directory, these techniques enable you to craft precise and efficient scripts.

Conclusion

It is essential to thoroughly understand variables and pipelines and how they can be applied practically. When you combine this knowledge with an understanding of commands and their specific parameters, you can harness the power of PowerShell to a greater extent. Using efficient variables allows for storing and retrieving data across commands and scripts. At the same time, knowledge of pipelines empowers you to execute a series of commands, enabling you to handle complex tasks easily. Mastering data filtering techniques in the pipeline will enhance your data manipulation skills, making your scripts more precise and effective. Additionally, passing variables between commands enables complex data exchanges and operations. With this knowledge, you can create advanced scripts for automation, system management, and simplifying IT processes. As you become more proficient in PowerShell, you can confidently and efficiently tackle more complex tasks and projects.

In the upcoming chapter, you will learn how PowerShell uses objects such as custom objects, string arrays, and various variable data types. You will also delve into the Export and Import cmdlets for data portability and the integration of .NET objects, which will aid you in utilizing the .NET framework in PowerShell.

Join our book's Discord space

Join the book's Discord Workspace for Latest updates, Offers, Tech happenings around the world, New Release and Sessions with the Authors:

https://discord.bpbonline.com

CHAPTER 6
Deep Diving PowerShell Objects

Introduction

This chapter will delve into the PowerShell objects. We will start by understanding the fundamentals of PowerShell objects, which are central to the flexibility and power of the scripting language. Next, we will examine the creation and management of string arrays, essential constructs for handling multiple pieces of data in an organized manner. We will then move to creating and managing custom objects, allowing you to define custom structures tailored to your needs. It will lead us to work with object properties and methods, improving how you can manipulate and leverage these objects. We will introduce the `[PSCustomObject]` data type, a versatile way to define and work with objects in PowerShell. We will discuss setting specific data types within PowerShell variables to ensure accuracy in your scripting tasks. We will also cover the Export and Import cmdlets, vital for data persistence and transfer. Finally, we will work with .NET objects within PowerShell, expanding your toolbox for automation and scripting.

Structure

In this chapter, we will cover the following topics:

- Understanding PowerShell objects
- Creating and managing string arrays

- Working with object properties and methods
- Creating and managing custom objects
- Using [PSCustomObject] data type
- Setting specific data types within Powershell variables
- Using the Export and Import cmdlets
- Understanding and working with .NET objects in PowerShell

Objectives

After reading this chapter, you will understand the object-oriented core of PowerShell. You will get introduced to PowerShell objects and dive into creating and managing string arrays, custom objects, and the `[PSCustomObject]` data type. The chapter will guide you in setting data types for your PowerShell variables, ensuring data consistency, and reducing potential errors. You will also learn about data portability by understanding the Export and Import cmdlets, ensuring you can seamlessly transfer and use data across different scripts and sessions. To finish, we will dive into integrating .NET objects within PowerShell, equipping you with the skills to harness the vast .NET framework directly within your scripts.

Understanding PowerShell objects

PowerShell objects are fundamental building blocks that drive its operations and scripting capabilities. Unlike traditional shells that primarily operate with text, PowerShell's power lies in its object-oriented nature. Every command or cmdlet you execute in PowerShell produces an object as its output, even if that object is simply a string of text. For instance, when you run the command **Get-Service**, it does not just return plain text; it retrieves a list of service objects, each with its own set of properties and methods. It allows for a more structured and intricate interaction with the data.

You can think of objects as containers holding related data and actions. Properties describe the object's attributes, such as name or size, while methods represent actions the object can perform or undergo. Take the following command to see this in action:

`$file = Get-Item C:\Files\Text-Document.txt`

This cmdlet fetches an object representing the file and stores it in the **$file** variable. If you explore **$file | Get-Member**, you will get a detailed list of its properties, like its length or last access time, and the methods it supports, as shown in *Figure 6.1* and *Figure 6.2*:

```
PS C:\> $file | Get-Member -MemberType Method

   TypeName: System.IO.FileInfo

Name                       MemberType Definition
----                       ---------- ----------
AppendText                 Method     System.IO.StreamWriter AppendText()
CopyTo                     Method     System.IO.FileInfo CopyTo(string destFileName), S…
Create                     Method     System.IO.FileStream Create()
CreateAsSymbolicLink       Method     void CreateAsSymbolicLink(string pathToTarget)
CreateText                 Method     System.IO.StreamWriter CreateText()
Decrypt                    Method     void Decrypt()
Delete                     Method     void Delete()
Encrypt                    Method     void Encrypt()
Equals                     Method     bool Equals(System.Object obj)
GetHashCode                Method     int GetHashCode()
GetLifetimeService         Method     System.Object GetLifetimeService()
GetObjectData              Method     void GetObjectData(System.Runtime.Serialization.S…
GetType                    Method     type GetType()
InitializeLifetimeService  Method     System.Object InitializeLifetimeService()
MoveTo                     Method     void MoveTo(string destFileName), void MoveTo(str…
Open                       Method     System.IO.FileStream Open(System.IO.FileStreamOpt…
OpenRead                   Method     System.IO.FileStream OpenRead()
OpenText                   Method     System.IO.StreamReader OpenText()
```

Figure 6.1: Execute Get-Member for a file object to view the available methods

```
PS C:\> $file | Get-Member -MemberType Property

   TypeName: System.IO.FileInfo

Name              MemberType Definition
----              ---------- ----------
Attributes        Property   System.IO.FileAttributes Attributes {get;set;}
CreationTime      Property   datetime CreationTime {get;set;}
CreationTimeUtc   Property   datetime CreationTimeUtc {get;set;}
Directory         Property   System.IO.DirectoryInfo Directory {get;}
DirectoryName     Property   string DirectoryName {get;}
Exists            Property   bool Exists {get;}
Extension         Property   string Extension {get;}
FullName          Property   string FullName {get;}
IsReadOnly        Property   bool IsReadOnly {get;set;}
LastAccessTime    Property   datetime LastAccessTime {get;set;}
LastAccessTimeUtc Property   datetime LastAccessTimeUtc {get;set;}
LastWriteTime     Property   datetime LastWriteTime {get;set;}
LastWriteTimeUtc  Property   datetime LastWriteTimeUtc {get;set;}
Length            Property   long Length {get;}
LinkTarget        Property   string LinkTarget {get;}
Name              Property   string Name {get;}
UnixFileMode      Property   System.IO.UnixFileMode UnixFileMode {get;set;}
```

Figure 6.2: Execute Get-Member for a file object to view the available properties

Another instance is the **Get-Process** cmdlet. When executed, it brings forward process objects that encapsulate details about running processes, which can be filtered, sorted, and manipulated because of their object nature.

A significant advantage of these objects is that they can be piped from one cmdlet to another, allowing for sequential operations without complex parsing. Imagine wanting to find all text files modified today. You could utilize something like:

```
Get-ChildItem C:\ -Recurse | `
    Where-Object { $_.Extension -eq ".txt"
        -and $_.LastWriteTime.Date -eq (Get-Date).Date }
```

In this code, each part of the pipeline returns objects that the following segment processes.

PowerShell objects provide:
- A robust framework.
- Facilitating complex data operations.
- Ensuring consistency.
- Allowing for complex manipulations with relative ease.

Creating and managing string arrays

A string array is a collection of string elements stored together sequentially. It makes it simpler to aggregate similar data types, especially textual information. To create a string array, you can initialize it with values like the following:

```
$MyArray = ("Apple", "Banana", "Cherry")
```

The elements within this array are ordered, with indexing starting at zero., which means **$myArray[0]** would return **Apple**.

However, you can manipulate pre-existing arrays and dynamically add items to an array. If you had to add **Pear** to **$MyArray**, you can use this command:

```
$MyArray += "Pear"
```

Yet, there is a caveat; arrays in PowerShell are immutable by nature. When you **add** an item, PowerShell creates a new array and copies all the elements, which can be performance-intensive for large arrays. Alternatively, array lists or generic lists offer a more efficient approach for dynamic lists.

For example, executing this initializes an **ArrayList**:

```
$MyList = [System.Collections.ArrayList]@(
```

"Apple",

"Banana",

"Cherry")

With this, adding an element becomes straightforward:

$MyList.Add("Pear")

$MyList

Unlike standard arrays, you can remove items using the **Remove** method:

$MyList.Remove("Banana")

$MyList

Sorting string arrays is another common task. With PowerShell, the **Sort-Object** cmdlet does this efficiently. Executing **$MyArray | Sort-Object** returns the array in alphabetical order. Conversely, filtering items in a string array involves the **Where-Object** cmdlet. If you wish to find all strings in **$MyArray** containing the letter **A**, you can execute this code:

$MyArray | Where-Object { $_ -like '*A*' }

PowerShell's ability to seamlessly transition between singular strings and string arrays is compelling. For instance, if you apply a method or operation suitable for a string on a string array, PowerShell intuitively applies that operation to each string. When you execute **$MyArray.ToUpper()**, PowerShell will convert every string in **$MyArray** to uppercase, showcasing its inherent skill for object handling.

You can also join multiple string arrays and then perform various actions, such as filtering on shared values. In the following example, we join our existing **$MyList** string array with another string named **$MyExtraList**:

$MyExtraList = ("Grape", "Kiwi", "Mango")

$MyFruitsList = $MyList + $MyExtraList

With both the string arrays joined, we can now look for common values from another string array:

$MyCheckList = ("Apple", "Passionfruit", "Cherry", "Guava")

$MyCommonList = $MyFruitsList | Where-Object { $_ -in $MyCheckList }

This figure shows the executed command and the two common values found within the main **$MyFruitsList** and within **$MyCheckList**:

```
PS C:\> $MyFruitsList | Where-Object { $_ -in $MyCheckList }
Apple
Cherry
```

Figure 6.3: Retrieve the common fruits between two string arrays

If you have a larger data set within a string array, you can use **Slicing** to retrieve a specific segment of the values. For example, using our string array **$MyFruitsList**, we can retrieve the fruits by their integer ID. For example, the following code selects the elements from the array at indices 1, 2, and 3. The first number, **1**, is the starting index. The **..** is the range operator in PowerShell, and **3** is the ending index:

$MySlicedList = $MyFruitsList[1..3]

The figure below shows the items in the original **$MyFruitsList** array, then what is available after slicing using indices:

```
PS C:\> $MyFruitsList
Apple
Banana
Cherry
Grape
Kiwi
Mango

PS C:\> $MyFruitsList[1..3]
Banana
Cherry
Grape
```

Figure 6.4: Retrieve the sliced fruits for indices 1, 2 and 3

As you delve deeper into PowerShell scripting, learning the creation and management of string arrays proves invaluable. These arrays act as versatile tools, streamlining data manipulation and enhancing the efficiency and readability of your scripts.

Working with object properties and methods

Objects are key to PowerShell. Each object is a structured package of information comprising properties and methods. Properties describe the object's attributes or characteristics. If you imagine an object as a person, properties are akin to their age, name, or occupation — details that describe who they are. On the other hand, methods represent actions the object can perform, like a person being able to walk, talk, or read.

For instance, PowerShell returns an object when you use the **Get-Item** cmdlet on a file:

$File = Get-Item -Path "C:\Files\Word-Document.docx"

This object has properties like **LastAccessTime**, describing when the file was last accessed, or **Length**, indicating its size. You can extract a specific property using the variable name plus the required property like this:

$File.Length

Beyond properties, this object may also have methods. Consider the delete method, which allows for the file's removal. For example, invoking the delete method would execute the action:

$File.Delete()

PowerShell offers cmdlets like **Select-Object**, allowing users to extract specific properties from an object, and **Where-Object**, enabling the filtering of objects based on property values. For example, to filter files older than a year, you can use the following code:

$Files = Get-ChildItem "C:\Files" | `

Where-Object {$_.LastWriteTime -lt (Get-Date).AddYears(-1)}

It is essential to recognize that not all objects will have methods associated with them. The existence of methods depends on the type of object and its design. PowerShell provides commands like **Get-Member** to further explore an object's properties and methods. When piping an object **Get-Member**, it returns a list of its members, providing a list of its capabilities. The same applies to many other object types, such as hard disk drives, running processes, and regular string objects.

The following figure displays the local disk (C Drive) and the available methods provided by the object type:

```
PS C:\> $drive = Get-PSDrive -LiteralName C
PS C:\> $drive | Get-Member

   TypeName: System.Management.Automation.PSDriveInfo

Name                    MemberType     Definition
----                    ----------     ----------
CompareTo               Method         int CompareTo(System.Management.Automation.PSDri...
Equals                  Method         bool Equals(System.Object obj), bool Equals(Syst...
GetHashCode             Method         int GetHashCode()
GetType                 Method         type GetType()
ToString                Method         string ToString()
Credential              Property       pscredential Credential {get;}
CurrentLocation         Property       string CurrentLocation {get;set;}
Description             Property       string Description {get;set;}
DisplayRoot             Property       string DisplayRoot {get;}
MaximumSize             Property       System.Nullable[long] MaximumSize {get;}
Name                    Property       string Name {get;}
Provider                Property       System.Management.Automation.ProviderInfo Provid...
Root                    Property       string Root {get;}
VolumeSeparatedByColon  Property       bool VolumeSeparatedByColon {get;}
Free                    ScriptProperty System.Object Free {get=## Ensure that this is a...
Used                    ScriptProperty System.Object Used {get=## Ensure that this is a...
```

Figure 6.5: Retrieve the C drive and display available actions

The following retrieves a single process. and the available methods provided by the object type:

```
PS C:\> $process = Get-Process | Select-Object -First 1
PS C:\> $process | Get-Member

   TypeName: System.Diagnostics.Process

Name                    MemberType      Definition
----                    ----------      ----------
Handles                 AliasProperty   Handles = Handlecount
Name                    AliasProperty   Name = ProcessName
NPM                     AliasProperty   NPM = NonpagedSystemMemorySize64
PM                      AliasProperty   PM = PagedMemorySize64
SI                      AliasProperty   SI = SessionId
VM                      AliasProperty   VM = VirtualMemorySize64
WS                      AliasProperty   WS = WorkingSet64
Parent                  CodeProperty    System.Object Parent{get=GetParentProcess;}
Disposed                Event           System.EventHandler Disposed(System.Object, …
ErrorDataReceived       Event           System.Diagnostics.DataReceivedEventHandler …
Exited                  Event           System.EventHandler Exited(System.Object, Sy…
OutputDataReceived      Event           System.Diagnostics.DataReceivedEventHandler …
BeginErrorReadLine      Method          void BeginErrorReadLine()
BeginOutputReadLine     Method          void BeginOutputReadLine()
CancelErrorRead         Method          void CancelErrorRead()
CancelOutputRead        Method          void CancelOutputRead()
Close                   Method          void Close()
```

Figure 6.6: Retrieve a single running process and display available actions

The following displays the available methods provided by the string object type:

```
PS C:\> $string = "PowerShell is Great!"
PS C:\> $string | Get-Member

   TypeName: System.String

Name                    MemberType   Definition
----                    ----------   ----------
Clone                   Method       System.Object Clone(), System.Object IClone…
CompareTo               Method       int CompareTo(System.Object value), int Com…
Contains                Method       bool Contains(string value), bool Contains(…
CopyTo                  Method       void CopyTo(int sourceIndex, char[] destina…
EndsWith                Method       bool EndsWith(string value), bool EndsWith(…
EnumerateRunes          Method       System.Text.StringRuneEnumerator EnumerateR…
Equals                  Method       bool Equals(System.Object obj), bool Equals…
GetEnumerator           Method       System.CharEnumerator GetEnumerator(), Syst…
GetHashCode             Method       int GetHashCode(), int GetHashCode(System.S…
GetPinnableReference    Method       System.Char&, System.Private.CoreLib, Versi…
GetType                 Method       type GetType()
GetTypeCode             Method       System.TypeCode GetTypeCode(), System.TypeC…
IndexOf                 Method       int IndexOf(char value), int IndexOf(char v…
IndexOfAny              Method       int IndexOfAny(char[] anyOf), int IndexOfAn…
Insert                  Method       string Insert(int startIndex, string value)
IsNormalized            Method       bool IsNormalized(), bool IsNormalized(Syst…
LastIndexOf             Method       int LastIndexOf(char value), int LastIndexO…
```

Figure 6.7: Retrieve a string value and display available actions

You can view the available properties and methods for standard objects, existing cmdlets, and custom objects you create within PowerShell scripts.

Creating and managing custom objects

PowerShell's object-centric nature provides a robust platform for creating and working with custom objects. These custom objects allow you to structure data in a way that is tailored to your specific needs, offering an adaptable data management approach. For instance, you can craft an object representing a user with properties like name, age, and department. You can create a custom object in PowerShell using the **New-Object** cmdlet paired with the **PSCustomObject** type. For example, this code creates a new empty object stored in the **$user** variable:

```
$user = New-Object PSCustomObject
```

You can add properties to this object using the **Add-Member** cmdlet. However, a more streamlined approach involves using the **[PSCustomObject]** type accelerator. A simple way to instantiate a custom object with predefined properties is:

```
$user = [PSCustomObject]@{Name="John"; Age=25; Department="HR"}
```

This structure offers the flexibility to access and modify properties like any standard object—for example, **$user.Name** retrieves the name of the user and **$user.Age = 30** updates the age. Collections of these custom objects pave the way for more intricate data structures.

Consider managing a list of users: **$usersList = @()** initializes an empty array. To append a new user object, you would use the following:

```
$usersList += [PSCustomObject]@{Name="Jane"; Age=28; Department="Finance"}
```

When paired with **ForEach-Object**, **Where-Object**, and other cmdlets, such collections enable powerful data manipulations. For instance, you can filter users older than **27** using the following code:

```
$usersList | Where-Object {$_.Age -gt 27}
```

One significant advantage of custom objects is their extensibility. As requirements evolve, we can seamlessly integrate new properties or methods. If there is a need to track the user's job title, you can use the following:

```
$user | Add-Member -Type NoteProperty -Name Title -Value "Manager"
```

Custom objects are not just passive data structures; they can encompass methods (actions). For example, to add a method that prints the user's full details, you utilize:

```
$user | Add-Member -Type ScriptMethod -Name DisplayDetails -Value {$this.
Name + ", " + $this.Age + ", " + $this.Department}
```

The following shows the newly added custom script method for the `$user` `[PSCustomObject]`:

```
PS C:\> $user | Get-Member

    TypeName: System.Management.Automation.PSCustomObject

Name           MemberType   Definition
----           ----------   ----------
Equals         Method       bool Equals(System.Object obj)
GetHashCode    Method       int GetHashCode()
GetType        Method       type GetType()
ToString       Method       string ToString()
Age            NoteProperty int Age=25
Department     NoteProperty string Department=HR
Name           NoteProperty string Name=John
Title          NoteProperty string Title=Manager
DisplayDetails ScriptMethod System.Object DisplayDetails();
```

Figure 6.8: Executing Get-Member to view the added Script Method

You can then execute the following code to call the new script method associated with the object:

`$user.DisplayDetails()`

PowerShell's flexibility shines when converting custom objects to other formats, enhancing interoperability. It is noticeable when transforming a user object into a JSON string:

`$user | ConvertTo-Json`

This adaptability highlights why understanding and leveraging custom objects is pivotal. They encapsulate data and behaviors, enabling organized, modular, and efficient scripting.

Using [PSCustomObject] data type

The `[PSCustomObject]` is excellent for creating structured data on the fly. At its core, a `[PSCustomObject]` is a flexible and extensible object type, letting you define and access properties dynamically. Unlike other data structures like arrays or hashtables, `[PSCustomObject]` allows for creating structured, property-based objects without requiring a formal class definition. While like hashtables, `[PSCustomObject]` is unique in its display behavior and property-based access mechanism, making it more readable and intuitive. Though the `[PSCustomObject]` in PowerShell offers several advantages, like any tool, it also has limitations.

Pros of using [PSCustomObject]:

- **Structured data representation**: Allows for creating objects with named properties, making data easier to understand and reference.
- **Dynamic nature**: You can dynamically add, remove, or modify properties on the fly.
- **Intuitive display**: When outputted to the console, `[PSCustomObject]` presents data in a neat table-like format, enhancing readability.
- **Easy conversion**: It can easily convert to other formats like JSON or XML using cmdlets like ConvertTo-Json.
- **Flexible initialization**: You can create a `[PSCustomObject]` from hashtables and other objects or combine them for nested structures.
- **Performance**: Creation of `[PSCustomObject]` can be faster than other methods or types like the older `PSObject` object creation method.
- **Compatibility**: Modern versions of PowerShell include it, so you don't need additional modules or libraries.

Cons of using [PSCustomObject]:

- **Immutability**: Once created, a `[PSCustomObject]` properties order is immutable. It means you cannot easily change the order of properties after creation.
- **Memory overhead**: Custom objects consume more memory than simpler data structures for large datasets.
- **Lack of methods**: Unlike formal .NET class objects, `[PSCustomObject]s` do not have methods by default. While you can attach custom methods, this is more complex than it would be with a defined class.
- **Potential complexity**: While creating simple custom objects is straightforward, more complex operations (like adding methods or managing nested objects) can introduce complexity, especially for beginners.
- **Type limitations**: `[PSCustomObject]` is a generic object type. If you need specialized behavior or strict typing, you must delve into complete .NET class creation.
- **Overuse**: Due to its flexibility, there might be a temptation to use `[PSCustomObject]` everywhere, even when simpler data structures or other object types might be more appropriate.

To get started with a `[PSCustomObject]` type, you can cast an existing hashtable like this:

```
$fruit = [PSCustomObject]@{
    Name = 'Apple'
```

```
    Color = 'Red'
}
$fruit
```

After creating a **[PSCustomObject]**, you can add extra properties, as shown:

```
$fruit | Add-Member -MemberType NoteProperty `
    -Name 'Taste' `
    -Value 'Sweet'
$fruit
```

Like most objects within PowerShell, you can also nest them to create complex data structures. For example, to create a custom object representing a bag of fruit and then populate it with fruit, you would change the existing PowerShell to this:

```
$fruitBag = [PSCustomObject]@{
BagColor = 'Blue'
    Fruits = [PSCustomObject]@{
        Apple = 'Red'
        Banana = 'Yellow'
    }
}
$fruitBag
```

You can also populate other object types with **[PSCustomObject]** data types. In this example, you create a standard list array but populate the list with the **[PSCustomObject]** items:

```
$fruitsList = @(
    [PSCustomObject]@{Name = 'Apple';Color = 'Red'},
    [PSCustomObject]@{Name = 'Banana';Color = 'Yellow'}
)
$fruitsList
```

You can also use the **[PSCustomObject]** when retrieving values from other object types and need to extract specific values or reformat the output. For example, we could take the output of executing **Get-Process** and create a new custom object from various properties:

```
$process = Get-Process | Select-Object -First 1
$customProcess = [PSCustomObject]@{
    Name = $process.ProcessName
    MemoryMB = $process.WorkingSet / 1MB -as [int]
}
$customProcess
```

The following selects the required values from the **Get-Process** command, which returns a **System.Diagnostics.Process** object, then creates a new custom object for rendering. For any created object, you can also execute the **GetType()** method to see the final object type, as shown:

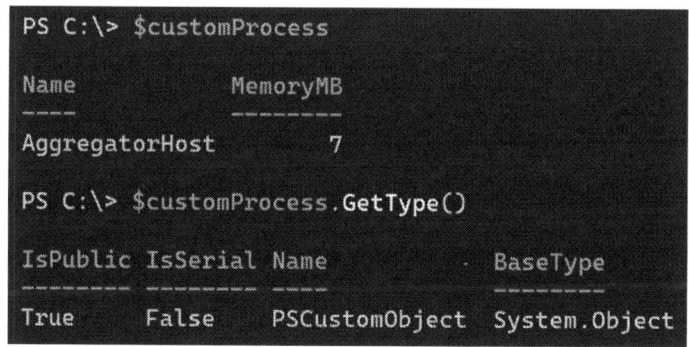

Figure 6.9: Creating a [PSCustomObject] from the results of executing Get-Process

While **[PSCustomObject]** effectively creates and manages structured data in PowerShell, understanding its strengths and limitations is crucial. Choosing when to use it — and when to opt for other data structures or objects can significantly influence the efficiency and clarity of your scripts.

Setting specific data types within PowerShell variables

You can specify the type for a variable, ensuring that only values of that type are stored, reducing the chances of unexpected errors during script execution. This deliberate type of definition is especially valuable in complex scripts or functions where the variable's intent needs to be precise.

When you do not specify a type for a variable in PowerShell, it defaults to the type [object]. This generic type allows the variable to hold any data type. However, while this offers flexibility, it does not provide the safety and clarity of a defined type. For instance, if you are expecting a variable only to hold strings and an integer gets assigned by mistake, you might encounter unforeseen consequences or errors.

When you assign a value to a variable without explicitly setting its type, PowerShell will automatically determine the most appropriate type based on the value. For example, if you assign a numeric value without decimals, PowerShell assumes it is an integer or a string if it is a series of characters enclosed in quotes.

Let us start with a basic example of setting a data type for a variable:

```
[string]$Name = "James Smith"

[int]$Age = 40

[bool]$IsMarried = $true
```

Now, let us look into more complex variable-type assignments, such as string arrays, hashtables, and **[PSCustomObject]**:

```
[string[]]$fruits = "Apple", "Banana", "Cherry"


[hashtable]$person = @{
    Name = "James Smith"
    Age = 40
    City = "New York"
}


[PSCustomObject]$employee = @{
    FirstName = "Lucy"
    LastName = "Smith"
    Department = "Human Resources"
}
```

The ability to set variable data types provides fantastic capabilities, especially when working with multiple data types. For example, let us say you are working on a project that requires tracking details of various organizational departments, including their associated projects and the employees working on them. You can store rows of values with their own data types using PowerShell, as shown:

```
[hashtable]$organizationDetails = @{
IT = @{
            Manager = "James Smith"
            Projects = @{
                Project1 = @{
                    Name = "Infrastructure Upgrade"
                    StartDate = [datetime]"2023-01-01"
                    EndDate = [datetime]"2023-12-31"
                    Employees = [string[]]@("Alice", "Bob", "Charlie")
                }
            Project2 = @{
                Name = "App Development"
                StartDate = [datetime]"2023-02-01"
                EndDate = [datetime]"2023-10-31"
                Employees = [string[]]@("David", "Eva")
            }
}
}
HR = @{
            Manager = "Lucy Smart"
            Projects = @{
                Project1 = @{
                    Name = "Recruitment Drive"
                    StartDate = [datetime]"2023-03-01"
                    EndDate = [datetime]"2023-06-30"
```

```
                Employees = [string[]]@("Frank", "Grace")
            }
        }
    }
}
```

The same applies when combining various data types with the **[PSCustomObject]** data type:

```
[PSCustomObject]$book = @{
    Title = "Advanced PowerShell Techniques"
    PublishedDate = [datetime]"2022-01-15"
    ISBN = "123-4567890"
    Authors = @(
        [PSCustomObject]@{
            FirstName = "Anna"
            LastName = "Bell"
            BirthDate = [datetime]"1990-05-20"
            Nationality = "American"
            OtherBooks = [string[]]@("PowerShell Basics", "PowerShell for Sysadmins")
        },
        [PSCustomObject]@{
            FirstName = "Chris"
            LastName = "Brown"
            BirthDate = [datetime]"1985-11-12"
            Nationality = "Canadian"
            OtherBooks = [string[]]@("Windows Administration", "Azure 101")
```

            }
)
    }

Setting specific data types for PowerShell variables helps control the behavior and expected outcomes. It reduces errors and clarifies the intended function of each variable, ensuring that other developers or administrators can read and understand the script with greater clarity. As with many aspects of PowerShell, the choice of when to strictly type variables and when to rely on PowerShell's dynamic typing depends on the specific task and the developer's intent.

Using the Export and Import cmdlets

PowerShell offers various cmdlets tailored to support multiple tasks, from system management to data processing. Among these cmdlets, the **Export-*** and **Import-*** stand out as useful for serialization and deserialization of data. These cmdlets allow you to save data into files and later retrieve it, making them pivotal in many use cases, from backup operations to data migration.

The **Export-*** cmdlets enable you to save PowerShell data structures, such as objects, hashtables, and arrays, to files in different formats (like **CSV**, **XML**, and **CLIXML**). The **Import-*** cmdlets facilitate the reading of these files, reviving the original data structures for further manipulation or analysis in the PowerShell environment. For example, **Export-Csv** saves an object or collection of objects in a comma-separated values (**CSV**) format. **Import-Csv** reads a **CSV** file and reconstructs the objects for use in the PowerShell session.

So why use these cmdlets? There are a few important reasons to utilize these types of commands. They are:

- **Data persistence:** With these cmdlets, you can make data persistent across sessions. Instead of retrieving data from sources repeatedly, you can extract it once, save it, and use the stored data in future sessions, reducing redundant operations.
- **Data sharing:** You can share data extracted in PowerShell among different systems or users. You can ensure interoperability with other platforms or software by exporting data into universally accepted formats like CSV or XML.
- **Backup:** Before making substantial changes to system configurations or data sets, it's prudent to have a backup. The **Export-*** cmdlets let you store a snapshot of your data for recovery purposes.

Exporting data, including the results from other commands, is achieved by calling the required **Export-*** command with the output path. The following examples export the results of **Get-Process**, **Get-Service**, and **Get-ChildItem** to CSV or XML flat files:

```
Get-Process | Export-Csv -Path "C:\Files\Processes.csv"

Get-Service | Export-Clixml -Path "C:\Files\Services.xml"

Get-ChildItem -Path "C:\Files" | Export-Csv -Path "C:\Files\Files.csv"

Get-ChildItem -Recurse | Export-Csv -Path "C:\Files\Files.xml"
```

The **Export-*** command supports the use of the pipeline operator. You can send objects and data to the commands, including any processing of the data or values, before the export begins. For example, you could retrieve all the currently running processes that use more than ten percent CPU time. Once identified, loop all the values, and create a custom PowerShell object ready for exporting:

```
$CustomProcesses = Get-Process |
    Where-Object {$_.CPU -gt 10} |
        ForEach-Object { [PSCustomObject]@{
            Name = $_.Name
            CPU = $_.CPU
            Id = $_.Id
        }
    } $CustomProcesses |
Export-Csv -Path "C:\Files\ProcessQuery.csv" -NoTypeInformation
```

The **Import-*** command supports importing data from CSV, XML, and JSON. There are two core commands: **Import-CSV** and **Import-CliXml**. **Import-CSV** reads a delimited file and returns the file's contents as objects with properties determined by the file's header row.

Let us say you have a CSV file named **Users.csv** with the following content:

```
Name,Age,Department

Susan,28,Engineering
```

Robert,32,Marketing

Jimmy,24,Human Resources

Alisha,36,IT

You can use **Import-CSV** to read this file:

$users = Import-CSV -Path "C:\Files\Users.csv"

After executing the above command, **$users** will be an array of objects. For example, to get the name of the second user, you would run the following:

$users[1].Name

Import-CliXml reads data from a previously saved file using **Export-CliXml** and recreates the saved object in memory. This method of storing and retrieving data preserves object types, allowing you to store complex objects and later import them while maintaining their structure and type. To start using this command, first, create an exported XML file using the following command:

```
$person = @{
    Name = "Braxton"
    Age = 28
    Address = @{
    Street = "123 North St"
    City = "Winchester"
    Zip = "22699"
    }
}
$person | Export-CliXml -Path "C:\Files\Person.xml"
```

The following figure displays the created XML file and structure:

```
C: > Files >  Person.xml
 7      <DCT>
 8        <En>
 9          <S N="Key">Name</S>
10          <S N="Value">Braxton</S>
11        </En>
12        <En>
13          <S N="Key">Address</S>
14          <Obj N="Value" RefId="1">
15            <TNRef RefId="0" />
16            <DCT>
17              <En>
18                <S N="Key">City</S>
19                <S N="Value">Winchester</S>
20              </En>
21              <En>
22                <S N="Key">Zip</S>
23                <S N="Value">22699</S>
24              </En>
```

Figure 6.10: XML Structure of the exported $Person variable

Let us say you close the PowerShell session and return later. To retrieve the **$person** object with all its properties and nested objects intact, use the following:

$person = Import-CliXml -Path "C:\Files\Person.xml"

You can now access properties like before, albeit they are imported ones, by using:

$person.Address.City

These cmdlets are instrumental for many PowerShell data storage, retrieval, and sharing tasks. By leveraging their capabilities, you get script flexibility, optimize processes, and ensure smooth data transfers across various platforms and sessions. While **Import-CSV** is excellent for more straightforward tabular data, **Import-CliXml** (in conjunction with **Export-CliXml**) offers a way to serialize and deserialize more complex data structures with full-type fidelity.

Understanding and working with .NET objects in PowerShell

PowerShell, while a robust scripting language, is built upon the .NET framework. This foundational connection allows PowerShell to interact seamlessly with .NET objects, expanding its capabilities beyond scripting. It grants you access to classes and functions provided by .NET, which can significantly enhance the power and functionality of your scripts. So why should you use .NET objects in PowerShell? Let us take a look at the following reasons:

- **Library:** .NET provides a vast library of prebuilt classes and methods.
- **Performance:** Certain operations, especially string manipulations or complex calculations, can be faster with .NET methods than native PowerShell commands.
- **Interoperability:** If you are working in environments where .NET applications are prevalent, using .NET objects in PowerShell ensures consistency and integration between your scripts and these applications.
- **Familiarity:** For those familiar with .NET or C#, leveraging .NET objects in PowerShell can make the transition to scripting smoother.

While using .NET objects can be powerful, there are a few considerations:

- **Complexity:** Introducing .NET objects can make scripts harder to read for those not familiar with .NET.
- **Portability:** Not all .NET classes are available across all versions of PowerShell or operating systems, especially if you're considering PowerShell Core on non-Windows platforms.
- **Overhead:** While .NET can enhance performance in some cases, it can also significantly introduce overhead if misused.

The following examples illustrate how to use .NET classes and functions within PowerShell:

```
# Basic String Manipulation - Join String Values Together
$MyString = [System.String]::Concat("Hello", " ", "World!")


# Working with Dates - Add 6 Days to Today's Date
$Today = [System.DateTime]::Now
$SixDaysFromNow = $Today.AddDays(6)


# Using a .NET Array List
$ArrayList = New-Object System.Collections.ArrayList
$null = $ArrayList.Add("Item1")
$null = $ArrayList.AddRange(@("Item2", "Item3"))
```

```
# Manipulating Files - Retrieve the File Size in Bytes

$FileBytes = [System.IO.File]::ReadAllBytes("C:\Files\File.txt")


# Working with Regular Expressions - Search Using a Specific Pattern

$Pattern = "[a-z]+"

$Regex = New-Object System.Text.RegularExpressions.Regex($Pattern)

$Matches = $regex.Matches("Hello World")
```

Previously we explored loading .NET DLLs and modules when working with PowerShell. Using this approach, you can use already loaded .NET libraries and prebuilt or custom .NET classes and functions. For example, let us say we have a folder with some files, and we need to compress them into a single .zip file using PowerShell and .NET. We can use the following PowerShell code:

```
Add-Type -AssemblyName "System.IO.Compression.FileSystem"

$sourceDirectory = "C:\Files"

$destinationZipFile = "C:\ZippedFiles\Files.zip"
```

You will get the following output.

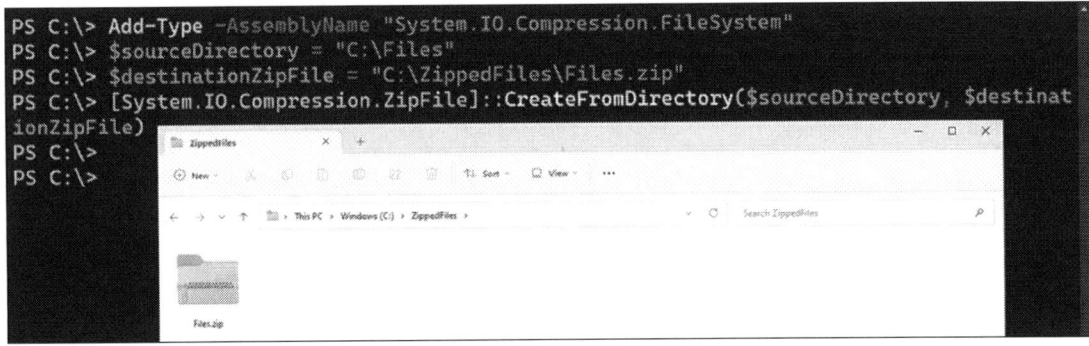

Figure 6.11: Zipped folder of files created using .NET classes and function

```
[System.IO.Compression.ZipFile]::CreateFromDirectory($sourceDirectory, $destinationZipFile)
```

You noticed that instead of **Import-Module**, we use **Add-Type** to bring in the required .NET classes and functions. **Add-Type** adds a Microsoft .NET class to the current PowerShell session. The primary purpose of **Add-Type** is to dynamically compile and generate types from source code. You can write **C#**, **VB**, or even **JScript** code directly in the PowerShell script, compile it on the fly, and then utilize the defined types and methods.

One of the most powerful features of Add-Type is the ability to embed C# code directly in your PowerShell script. It is useful when you need specific functionality that is easier or only possible to accomplish with .NET code. For example, we can create a .NET Class with a basic function, then use **Add-Type** to load it into the PowerShell session and use it:

```
Add-Type @"
public class MathUtilities {
    public static int Add(int a, int b) {
    return a + b;
    }
}
"@
[MathUtilities]::Add(11, 3)
```

The following calls the custom .NET function and displays the results:

```
PS C:\> [MathUtilities]::Add(11, 3)
14
```

Figure 6.12: Custom .NET addition function added to PowerShell session

Add-Type is a bridge between PowerShell and .NET, allowing you to tap into the vast .NET ecosystem, enhance script performance, and achieve tasks that might not work with just PowerShell.

With the files all zipped up, we can unzip them into a different location using the same loaded .NET library, classes, and functions, as shown:

```
$destinationExtractFolder = "C:\UnzippedFiles
[System.IO.Compression.ZipFile]::ExtractToDirectory($destinationZipFile, $destinationExtractFolder)
```

Using the capabilities of .NET within PowerShell opens doors to advanced operations and functionalities. At the same time, there is a learning curve, especially for those new to .NET. Understanding its strengths and weaknesses ensures that you use it efficiently and effectively.

Conclusion

Understanding the complexities of PowerShell objects is fundamental to achieving proficiency in scripting and automation tasks. When you delve deeper into creating and managing string arrays, you lay the foundation for effective data manipulation and storage. You also gain proficiency in creating and managing custom objects, enhancing your ability to structure data uniquely tailored to specific tasks. Familiarity with object properties and methods further refines the precision with which you can interact with and manipulate data.

Adopting the [PSCustomObject] data type provides a robust framework for custom data structures, adding flexibility to your scripts. Setting specific data types within PowerShell variables ensures data integrity and reduces the likelihood of errors due to incompatible data types. The Export and Import cmdlets' power lies in efficiently transferring data between scripts and sessions, ensuring data consistency and availability.

Finally, understanding and working with .NET objects in PowerShell lets you tap into various functionalities and connect PowerShell with the broader .NET framework. This knowledge equips you to design scripts, streamline complex tasks, and enhance your automation capabilities throughout your PowerShell journey.

In the upcoming chapter, you will delve into using functions and parameters in PowerShell. You will understand the foundational aspects of creating PowerShell functions to make informed decisions on their outputs. You will explore the dynamic nature of parameters, discovering how to create, use, and enhance them with default values and specific data types.

Join our book's Discord space

Join the book's Discord Workspace for Latest updates, Offers, Tech happenings around the world, New Release and Sessions with the Authors:

https://discord.bpbonline.com

CHAPTER 7
Using Functions and Parameters

Introduction

This chapter explains functions and parameters in PowerShell. We will start by learning the fundamentals of creating PowerShell functions, a vital skill that allows you to modularize and reuse code. Moving forward, we will dissect the anatomy of functions by addressing the crucial decision of determining the output of these functions. We will then transition into the parameters, diving into their addition to PowerShell functions to enhance flexibility. As we progress, we will focus on defining and invoking PowerShell functions, ensuring that you grasp the lifecycle of function execution. We will also explore setting default values and specifying data types for parameters and advanced parameter attributes, which include validation and input masks. Understanding the dynamics of passing and returning values in PowerShell functions is central to this chapter. Lastly, we will combine all we have learned and discuss designing complex scripts using functions.

Structure

In this chapter, we will cover the following topics:
- Creating PowerShell functions
- Choosing the output of functions

- Creating and using parameters in PowerShell functions
- Using default values and data types in parameters
- Advanced parameter features
- Passing and returning values in PowerShell functions
- Defining and calling PowerShell functions
- Combining functions into complex scripts

Objectives

After reading this chapter, you will understand the pivotal role of functions and parameters in PowerShell. You will be introduced to architecting PowerShell functions, allowing you to modularize and repeat code effortlessly. This chapter will guide you in determining the precise output of your functions, ensuring clarity and purpose in each function's return. You will also understand how to extend functions with parameters, refining their versatility and adaptability. You will learn to utilize parameters, ensuring your scripts remain dynamic and adaptable, and how to set default values and assign specific data types to parameters, ensuring precision in function execution. You will also review advanced parameter attributes enhancing functions and explain the dynamics of passing and returning values.

Creating PowerShell functions

Functions in PowerShell scripting are integral to any advanced script development. They act as standalone units or containers, each meticulously crafted to execute a distinct operation or a cluster of interrelated operations. Think of them as individual cogs in the machinery of a script, each designed with a specific purpose in mind. At the heart of this structure, the role of a function is primarily about encapsulation and reusability.

When you design a function, you segment your code, creating clear boundaries around a particular operation. It ensures that each piece of your script has a clear, well-defined responsibility. Moreover, because of their reusable nature, functions significantly reduce redundancy. For instance, if there is a need to repeat a certain logic in different parts of the script, you do not have to code it every single time manually. Instead, scripters can call the pre-defined function, making the code cleaner and more efficient. This approach streamlines the script development process and simplifies troubleshooting and maintenance. The ability to isolate issues within a specific function or to modify just one function without affecting the entirety of the script showcases the sophistication and modular approach that functions bring to PowerShell scripting.

Knowing the advantages and disadvantages of using functions within PowerShell is essential. The most common advantages are:

- **Enhanced script modularity:** Functions allow for the breakdown of complex scripts into individual units. Each unit or function addresses a particular sub-task, thus improving the overall organization and structure of scripts.
- **Improved readability:** The script becomes more readable by categorizing tasks into specific functions, allowing developers to better understand each code segment's flow and purpose.
- **Increased maintainability and debuggability:** Dividing scripts into functions makes it easier to maintain and debug. When issues arise, they can often isolate themselves into specific functions, speeding up the troubleshooting process.
- **Reusability of code:** Functions encapsulate tasks that may exist across multiple scripts. Instead of duplicating the code, you can call the function, ensure consistency, and reduce redundancy. It also means that changes to a function automatically reflect wherever you invoke it.

The most common disadvantages of functions are:

- **Over-compartmentalization:** There is a risk of fragmenting scripts excessively. Creating many small functions can convolute a script, making it challenging to follow its logic, especially if these functions disperse across various files.
- **Performance overhead:** Invoking functions, especially nested ones, can introduce slight overhead in terms of performance. It might not be noticeable in smaller scripts but can impact larger, more complex scripts.
- **Dependency management:** Managing these dependencies becomes intricate if functions rely on other functions or specific variables. It is especially true when functions source from multiple files or modules.
- **Increased complexity with global variables:** Functions, when used extensively, can complicate the management of global and scoped variables. It can lead to unintended side effects if not handled carefully.

Now, let us illustrate with some simple examples. Consider a task where you need to greet a user. Instead of writing the greeting logic everywhere, we can create it in a function, as shown below:

```
function Greet-User($UserName) {
    Write-Output "Hello, $UserName!"
}
```

With this function in place, greeting any user becomes easy:

`Greet-User -UserName "Liam"`

The following figure displays the returned message:

```
PS C:\> Greet-User -UserName "Liam"
Hello, Liam!
```

Figure 7.1: Display user greeting

Another practical application could be a function to retrieve disk space from a list of servers:

```
function Get-DiskSpace($ServerName) {
    Get-WmiObject Win32_LogicalDisk -ComputerName $ServerName |
    Where-Object { $_.DriveType -eq 3 } |
    Select-Object DeviceID, Freespace
}
```

When you invoke **Get-DiskSpace -ServerName "Server"**, you quickly fetch free disk space for a specific server. This task might repeat frequently in scripts. The great news is that you can review regular PowerShell commands and scripts and then convert them to use functions. For example, this script uses a variable population and writes the values to the console:

```
$HighCpuProcesses = Get-Process | Where-Object {$_.CPU -gt 50}
$HighCpuProcesses | Format-Table Name, Id, CPU
$NotRespondingProcesses = Get-Process | Where-Object {$_.Responding -eq $false}
$NotRespondingProcesses | Format-Table Name, Id
$TotalMemory = (Get-Process | Measure-Object -Property WS -Sum).Sum
Write-Output "Total memory usage by all processes: $TotalMemory bytes"
```

To make this more modular, we could convert this into functions instead:

```
function Get-HighCpuProcesses {
    Get-Process | Where-Object {$_.CPU -gt 50} | Format-Table Name, Id, CPU
}
```

```
function Get-NotRespondingProcesses {
    Get-Process | Where-Object {$_.Responding -eq $false} | Format-Table Name, Id
}

function Get-TotalMemoryUsage {
    (Get-Process | Measure-Object -Property WS -Sum).Sum
}

Get-HighCpuProcesses
Get-NotRespondingProcesses
$TotalMemory = Get-TotalMemoryUsage
Write-Output "Total memory usage by all processes: $TotalMemory bytes"
```

Creating functions for each task makes the code more readable and easier to maintain. Each function encapsulates a specific task, making it easier to understand, debug, or reuse in other scripts. Functions in PowerShell offer a powerful way to optimize, modularize, and enhance the efficiency of your scripts. As we delve more in-depth, we will explore advanced aspects of functions, building upon this foundational knowledge.

Choosing the output of functions

Like other programming languages, functions in PowerShell can produce output that you can capture, process further, or display. This output's type, structure, and amount can vastly impact how the function integrates with other PowerShell commands and scripts. Any value not captured or consumed within a function will be sent to the output stream by default. When you assign a variable but do not use it, the system treats its value as output. This behavior, while convenient, can lead to unintentional results if not managed deliberately.

To specifically produce output, PowerShell offers the return keyword. However, return is mainly a means to exit the function early. Any values specified after the return keyword go to the output stream, but the function sends any other unprocessed value. Consider this function:

```
function Get-Square {
```

```
    param($Number)

    $Results = $Number * $Number

    return $Results

    "This won't be displayed."

}
```

The following figure displays the execution of the "**Get-Square**" function, and its returned output:

```
PS C:\> Get-Square -Number 4
16
```

Figure 7.2: Execute 'Get-Square' and View Output

Here, the function will only output the squared value. Now, let us modify the function to return the squared value and the string:

```
function Get-Square {

    param($Number)

    $Results = $Number * $Number

    $Results

    "This will also be displayed."

}
```

The following figure displays the execution of the **Get-Square** function, and its returned output:

```
PS C:\> Get-Square -Number 4
16
This will also be displayed.
```

Figure 7.3: Execute Modified 'Get-Square' and View Output

Controlling function output is more than just limiting what is returned. It provides meaningful, structured data to pipe to other cmdlets or store for later use. Diving deeper into PowerShell functions, the decision on what a function outputs is essential, not just in terms of value but also in terms of format, type, and usability. You can think of a function's output as communicating with the rest of the script or other functions.

PowerShell operates with multiple streams: **Output**, **Error**, **Warning**, **Verbose**, and **Debug**. By default, when you are controlling the output of a function, you are interacting with the Output stream. However, knowing that these other streams exist can be helpful, especially for functions intended for broader use. The following example writes a value to three different output streams:

```
function Test-Streams {

    [CmdletBinding()]

    param($InputValue)


    Write-Output "This is the output: $InputValue"

    Write-Error "This is an error: $InputValue"

    Write-Verbose "This is verbose: $InputValue" -Verbose

}
```

The output, error, and verbose streams display content when calling this function. However, only the output stream's content can be piped or captured in a variable unless redirected. Any value not assigned to a variable or consumed inside a function will be sent to the output. It is implicit output. Explicit output uses cmdlets like **Write-Output** or the **return** keyword to indicate the output. Using cmdlets like **Write-Output** can make it explicit what the function is returning, whereas **Write-Host** directly displays information to the console without sending it down the pipeline. In this example, **"Hello, [name]!"** is sent to the output stream and can be piped or captured, while the second message is only displayed, as shown:

```
function Get-Message {

    param($Name)

    Write-Output "Hello, $Name!"

    Write-Host "This message is only for display."

}
```

Get-Message

The following figure displays the execution of the "**Get-Message**" function and its returned output:

```
PS C:\> Get-Message -Name Liam
Hello, Liam!
This message is only for display.
```

Figure 7.4: Execute 'Get-Message' and View Output

In PowerShell, everything is an object. Consider returning outputs as custom objects when designing a function, especially for reusable scripts or modules. It allows for more structured data, easier filtering, and better formatting. The following basic function returns the required properties to the console:

```
function Get-FileDetails {

    param($FilePath)

    $Size = (Get-Item $FilePath).length

    $CreationTime = (Get-Item $FilePath).creationTime

    Write-Output "File Size: $Size, Creation Time: $CreationTime"

}


Get-FileDetails
```

The following figure displays the execution of the "**Get-FileDetails**" function and its returned output:

```
PS C:\> Get-FileDetails -FilePath "C:\Files\Files.csv"
File Size: 1939, Creation Time: 08/22/2023 12:30:10
```

Figure 7.5: Execute 'Get-FileDetails' and view output

Let us modify this function to convert the string output to an object explicitly:

```
function Get-FileDetails {

    param($FilePath)

    $FileItem = Get-Item $FilePath


    $OutputObject = [PSCustomObject]@{

        Size = $FileItem.length

        CreationTime = $FileItem.creationTime
```

```
    }
    Write-Output $OutputObject
}
```

This version returns an object with properties **Size** and **CreationTime**, allowing for more advanced manipulations, like "**| Where-Object {$_.Size -gt 500}**".

Lastly, remember that you should not use **Write-Host** if you intend to capture or pipe the output. **Write-Host** speaks directly to the console, bypassing the usual streams, making it suitable for messages but not for returnable data.

Controlling and choosing the output of functions in PowerShell is a blend of understanding the pipeline, the various streams, and the difference between implicit and explicit outputs.

Creating and using parameters in PowerShell functions

Parameters allow your functions to be flexible and adaptable. Instead of hardcoding values, you can tailor the function's behavior based on variable input, making your scripts more dynamic and reusable. Think of them as the **settings** of your function; with different parameters, the same function can produce different results or perform different actions.

The most straightforward way to add a parameter to a function is by declaring it inside the **param** block at the beginning of the function. Let us say our function returns a simple message as shown below:

```
function Greet {
    Write-Output "Hello, World!"
}
```

To make the function more flexible, we can add a parameter to specify a name to write to the console, as shown:

```
function Greet {
    param($Name)
    Write-Output "Hello, $Name!"
}
```

When executing the function, we will need to provide the name value, which will display as part of the output message. For example, executing **Greet -Name Liam** would produce **Hello, Liam!**:

```
PS C:\> Greet -Name Liam
Hello, Liam!
```

Figure 7.6: Execute 'Greet -Name Liam' and View Output

By default, PowerShell treats parameters as positional. It means the order in which you provide arguments matters. However, it is often better to use named parameters for clarity, especially when a function has several parameters, as shown in the following example:

```
function Get-Name {

    param($FirstName, $LastName)

    Write-Output "My Name is: $LastName, $FirstName."

}
```

Executing **Get-Name 'Liam' 'Cleary'** and **Get-Name -FirstName 'Liam' -Lastname 'Cleary'** produces the same output, but the latter is more straightforward.

The distinction between positional and named parameters can significantly influence the usability and clarity of functions in PowerShell. There are three common approaches:

- Positional parameters
- Named parameters
- Combined positional and named parameters

When using positional parameters, they are in a specific order. The person executing the function must remember that order, which can be complicated when using multiple or complex functions. For example, this function requires an animal type and color in that order.

```
function Get-Animal{

    param($AnimalType, $AnimalColor)

    Write-Output "The $AnimalType is $AnimalColor in Color"

}


Get-Animal "Lion" "Golden"
```

The following figure displays the execution of the **Get-Animal** function and its returned output:

```
PS C:\> Get-Animal "Lion" "Golden"
The Lion is Golden in Color
```

Figure 7.7: Execute Get-Animal using positional parameters and view output

Modifying the function to use named parameters makes it clearer and easier. Each parameter has a name, and while calling the function, you specify the parameter's name followed by its value. The modified function looks like this:

```
function Get-Animal{

    param($AnimalType, $AnimalColor)

    Write-Output "The $AnimalType is $AnimalColor in Color"

}
```

```
Get-Animal -AnimalType "Lion" -AnimalColor "Golden"
```

The following figure displays the execution of the **Get-Animal** function with named parameters and its returned output:

```
PS C:\> Get-Animal -AnimalType "Lion" -AnimalColor "Golden"
The Lion is Golden in Color
```

Figure 7.8: Execute 'Get-Animal' Using Named Parameters and View Output

You can mix positional and named parameters. Positional parameters always come first, followed by named parameters. It is convenient when you use a few primary parameters in a set order and also have additional optional parameters, as shown in the following example:

```
function Get-Animal {

    param(

        $AnimalHabitat,

        [Parameter(Position=1)]$AnimalType,

        $AnimalColor

    )

        Write-Output "The $AnimalType from $AnimalHabitat is $AnimalColor
```

        in Color"

}

Get-Animal -AnimalHabitat "Savannah" "Lion" -AnimalColor "Golden"

The following figure displays the execution of the **Get-Animal** function with a mix of positional and named parameters and its returned output:

```
PS C:\> Get-Animal -AnimalHabitat "Savannah" "Lion" -AnimalColor "Golden"
The Lion from Savannah is Golden in Color
```

Figure 7.9: Execute 'Get-Animal' Using Mixed Parameters and View Output

While each approach has its advantages, the key is to ensure clarity and ease of use for the user. If a function has many parameters, named parameters can provide better clarity. For more straightforward functions, positional parameters often suffice.

Using default values and data types in parameters

Not all parameters need to be mandatory. Sometimes, you can provide a default value when you do not supply a parameter. Adjusting the **Get-Animal** function, we can make the animal habitat parameter optional:

```
function Get-Animal {

    param(

    $AnimalHabitat = "Savannah",

    $AnimalType,

    $AnimalColor

        )

    Write-Output "The $AnimalType from $AnimalHabitat is $AnimalColor in Color"

}
```

If we were to execute **Get-Animal -AnimalType 'Lion' -AnimalColor 'Golden'** it would display the same message as before, using the default value. The following shows the default value:

```
PS C:\> Get-Animal -AnimalType "Lion" -AnimalColor "Golden"
The Lion from Savannah is Golden in Color
```

Figure 7.10: Execute 'Get-Animal' and display the default value

If we called the same function, like the one below, it would show the value, not the default value added to the parameter:

Get-Animal -AnimalType 'Lion' -AnimalColor 'Golden' -AnimalHabitat 'Africa'

The following displays the value:

```
PS C:\> Get-Animal `
>> -AnimalType "Lion" `
>> -AnimalColor "Golden" `
>> -AnimalHabitat "Africa"
The Lion from Africa is Golden in Color
```

Figure 7.11: Execute 'Get-Animal' and display the passed value

We can define types of parameters for better error handling and input control. It ensures that the function receives data in the expected format. For example, if we need to ensure integer values for the parameter, then we can create a function using this syntax:

```
function Add-Numbers {
    param([int]$Number1, [int]$Number2)
    Write-Output ($Number1 + $Number2)
}
```

Sometimes, you may want the function to accept multiple values for a single parameter. Arrays and HashTables are perfect for these scenarios. For example, if we wanted to display names, we could create a function using a parameter type set to either an array or a hashtable:

```
function Get-Names {
    param([string[]]$Names)
    $Names | ForEach-Object { Write-Output "Name: $_" }
}
```

To execute this function, you use the following command:

Get-Names -Names "Susan", "David", "Maria", "Sophie", "Oliver", "Ananya"

The following figure shows the displayed values stored within the string array:

```
PS C:\> Get-Names -Names "Susan", "David", "Maria", "Sophie", "Oliver", "Ananya"
Name: Susan
Name: David
Name: Maria
Name: Sophie
Name: Oliver
Name: Ananya
```

Figure 7.12: Execute 'Get-Names' and display values

By setting default values for parameters, you can streamline function calls, providing a blend of simplicity for everyday use cases and adaptability for unique scenarios. Moreover, defining data types for parameters is not just a matter of formality—it reinforces type safety, minimizes runtime errors, and enhances code clarity.

Advanced parameter features

PowerShell extends its parameter capabilities with advanced features. Validation and input masks are powerful tools that enforce input constraints and formats, ensuring that input meets specific criteria before processing.

Parameter validation attributes are inherent to PowerShell and are employed to validate the input to a function. They offer an organized way to check parameter values against predefined criteria, preventing the execution of a function if the input does not comply. It enhances script robustness and reduces the chances of errors occurring due to improper or unexpected input. For instance:

```
function Get-Age {

    param (

    [ValidateRange(1,120)]

    [int]$Age

    )

    Write-Output "Your age is $Age years."

}
```

Here, the **ValidateRange** attribute ensures that the **$Age** parameter falls within the specified range. Any age outside the 1-120 scope will result in an error. You can also validate specific values or provide acceptable values as part of the parameter validation. In this case, you can use **ValidateSet** to wrap the parameter with the required list. For example, if we wanted to modify the `Get-Animal` function to provide the supported animals instead of allowing someone to type anything, we would change the function like this:

```
function Get-Animal {

    param(

        $AnimalHabitat = "Savannah",

        [ValidateSet("Lion", "Elephant", "Buffalo", "Leopard", "Rhinoceros",
        "Giraffe", "Cheetah", "Hippopotamus")]

        $AnimalType,

        $AnimalColor

    )

    Write-Output "The $AnimalType from $AnimalHabitat is $AnimalColor in Color"

}
```

When executing this function, you can only pass a valid animal, plus IntelliSense within PowerShell will let you loop through the values.

The following figure shows a correct and incorrect value passed to the function with its result:

```
PS C:\> Get-Animal -AnimalType "Cheetah" -AnimalColor "Golden with Black Spots"
The Cheetah from Savannah is Golden with Black Spots in Color

PS C:\> Get-Animal -AnimalType "Hyena" -AnimalColor "Golden with Black Spots"
Get-Animal: Cannot validate argument on parameter 'AnimalType'. The argument "Hyena" does not
 belong to the set "Lion,Elephant,Buffalo,Leopard,Rhinoceros,Giraffe,Cheetah,Hippopotamus" sp
ecified by the ValidateSet attribute. Supply an argument that is in the set and then try the
 command again.
```

Figure 7.13: Execute get-animals and test the validation set

Input masks represent another layer of input refinement. While PowerShell does not possess native **masking** like some other languages or platforms, you can simulate input masks using parameters combined with regex validation. It ensures that input adheres to a specific pattern. Consider this example where a user provides a phone number in a particular format:

```
function Get-PhoneNumber {

    param (

        [ValidatePattern('^\(\d{3}\)\s?\d{3}-\d{4}$')]
```

        [string]$PhoneNumber

)

    Write-Output "Your phone number is $PhoneNumber."
}

The **ValidatePattern** attribute above checks if the provided phone number matches the regex pattern, which expects a format like (123) 456-7890.

You could also modify the same function to validate many different data formats. For example, you could change it to check for valid email addresses using this pattern:

[ValidatePattern('^[\w.-]+@[\w.-]+\.\w+$')]

You could also change it to validate dates in a specific format using the following pattern:

[ValidatePattern('^\d{4}-\d{2}-\d{2}$')]

PowerShell's beauty is its ability to combine all these validation capabilities into the same function. Suppose you are building a function that receives a U.S. **Social Security Number (SSN)**. You want it to match the format ###-##-####, and also want to ensure it does not start with specific invalid numbers, for example, 000. The following function ensures the input adheres to the SSN pattern and checks the starting characters. Both validations must pass for the function to execute successfully:

function Get-SocialSecurityNumber {

    param (

        [ValidatePattern('^\d{3}-\d{2}-\d{4}$')]

        [ValidateScript({

            if ($_ -match '^000') {

                throw "SSN cannot start with '000'."

            }

            return $true

        })]

        [string]$SSN

)

    Write-Output "Your Social Security Number is $SSN."

}

The following figure shows the output from calling the "`Get-SocialSecurityNumber`" function:

```
PS C:\> Get-SocialSecurityNumber -SSN 000235678
Get-SocialSecurityNumber: Cannot validate argument on parameter 'SSN'. SSN cannot start with '000'.
PS C:\>
PS C:\>
PS C:\> Get-SocialSecurityNumber -SSN 123456789
Get-SocialSecurityNumber: Cannot validate argument on parameter 'SSN'. The argument "123456789" does not
 match the "^\d{3}-\d{2}-\d{4}$" pattern. Supply an argument that matches "^\d{3}-\d{2}-\d{4}$" and try
 the command again.
PS C:\>
PS C:\>
PS C:\> Get-SocialSecurityNumber -SSN 123-45-6789
Your Social Security Number is 123-45-6789.
```

Figure 7.14: Execute Get-SocialSecurityNumber and view the results

There are many different validation options available to use with parameters. Some standard options are:

- **ValidateRange:** Ensures that numeric values fall within a specified range.
- **ValidateNotNullOrEmpty**: Ensures that the parameter value is neither $null nor an empty string.
- **ValidateCount**: Validates that an array parameter value contains a minimum and maximum number of elements.
- **ValidateLength**: Validates the length of a string.
- **ValidatePattern**: As demonstrated in previous examples, use regex to validate the parameter value.
- **ValidateScript**: This is a powerful validation technique. It allows you to use a custom script block to validate the parameter value. Validation fails if the script block does not return $true or throws an exception.
- **ValidateSet**: Confirms that a parameter value is one of a predefined set of values, as shown earlier.
- **ValidateDrive**: Validates that the provided drive exists on the system.
- **ValidateUserDrive**: Ensures that a drive, represented by the parameter value, is either a user-mapped Windows drive or a Windows drive that the user can access.
- **ValidateNotNull**: Checks that the value is not $null.

When using the **ValidateScript** option, you can look up values from other systems and use that as the supported and provided options. For example, the following function uses a hashtable of animals mapped to their color. Within the function, the parameter queries for the animal type then returns both that and the color and writes it to the console:

```powershell
$AnimalColorLookup = @{
    'Lion' = 'Tawny';
    'Elephant' = 'Grey';
    'Buffalo' = 'Dark Brown';
    'Leopard' = 'Golden with Black Spots';
    'Rhinoceros' = 'Grey';
    'Giraffe' = 'Yellow with Brown Spots';
    'Cheetah' = 'Golden with Black Spots';
    'Hippopotamus' = 'Greyish Brown';
}

function Get-Animal{
    param(
        [ValidateScript({
            if ($animalColorLookup.ContainsKey($_)) {
                $true
            } else {
                throw "Animal $_ is not in the known list of animals."
            }
        })]
        [string]$AnimalType
    )
$Color = $AnimalColorLookup[$AnimalType]
Write-Output "The typical color of a/an $AnimalType is $Color."
}

Get-Animal -AnimalType 'Lion'
```

The following figure shows the output from calling the updated "**Get-Animal**" function:

```
PS C:\> Get-Animal -AnimalType "Lion"
The typical color of a/an Lion is Tawny.
PS C:\>
PS C:\>
PS C:\> Get-Animal -AnimalType "Giraffe"
The typical color of a/an Giraffe is Yellow with Brown Spots.
PS C:\>
PS C:\>
PS C:\> Get-Animal -AnimalType "Buffalo"
The typical color of a/an Buffalo is Dark Brown.
```

Figure 7.15: Execute 'Get-Animal', perform the lookup and view the results

Harnessing these parameter features provides several benefits:

- **User guidance**: Users get a clear cue about the expected format or range by constraining input, minimizing potential confusion.
- **Reduced error handling**: The need for extensive error handling mechanisms diminishes with proactive validation.
- **Enhanced security**: Submitting unsanctioned input makes scripts less vulnerable to malicious or unintended input.

It is essential to exercise control when utilizing script features to maintain efficiency and safety. Excessive restrictions can limit the ability to adapt, while overly complicated input formats can confuse users. Striking a balance is critical: ensure that constraints protect and guide without hindering usability.

PowerShell features, like validation attributes and simulated input masks, increase script reliability and user experience. You can craft user-friendly and resilient scripts against problems by setting clear input boundaries.

Passing and returning values in PowerShell functions

At its core, a PowerShell function accepts input through parameters, which can be positional or named. As previously reviewed, parameters represent various data types, from simple strings and integers to complex objects and arrays. This flexibility makes it easy to pass in just about any information you need a function to work with.

Returning values in PowerShell functions also differs from what some developers may typically use. In many programming languages, a return keyword designates a specific value or object the function sends back. While PowerShell does have a return keyword, it operates a bit differently. Any value or object that is not captured, assigned, or otherwise consumed in the function becomes part of the output. This behavior implies that a function can output multiple times, not just when the return keyword invokes.

For example, each **Write-Output** sends a value back in the following function, cumulatively building the function's output:

```
function Invoke-GenerateNumbers {

    param([int]$Count)

    for ($i = 0; $i -lt $Count; $i++) {

        Write-Output $i

    }

}
```

```
Invoke-GenerateNumbers -Count 6
```

The following figure displays the output:

```
PS C:\> Invoke-GenerateNumbers -Count 6
0
1
2
3
4
5
```

Figure 7.16: Populating the functions output by executing 'Invoke-GenerateNumbers'

PowerShell functions can accept input directly from the pipeline, making data processing streamlined and efficient.

For example, you can pass a range of numbers directly in the pipeline to a custom-created function to process each number within the range:

```
function Invoke-DoubleTheNumber {

    param([int]$Number)

    return $Number * 2

}
```

```
1..10 | ForEach-Object {Invoke-DoubleTheNumber -Number $_}
```

The following figure displays the output:

```
PS C:\> 1..10 | ForEach-Object {Invoke-DoubleTheNumber -Number $_}
2
4
6
8
10
12
14
16
18
20
```

Figure 7.17: Passing a pipeline number range to a custom function

You can also design functions to modify and return complex objects, making them powerful tools for data manipulation. For example, the following function takes a person object and an integer, adds the integer to the person's age, and returns the updated person object:

```
function Add-Age {

    param(

        [PSCustomObject]$Person,

        [int]$AgeToAdd

    )

    $Person.Age += $AgeToAdd

    return $Person

}


$kaylen = [PSCustomObject]@{ Name = "Kaylen"; Age = 40}

Write-Host $kaylen


Add-Age -Person $kaylen -AgeToAdd 5

Write-Host $kaylen
```

The following figure shows the function used to add five years to "**Kaylen**," who initially is 40 years old, making her 45 years old after the function call:

```
PS C:\> $kaylen = [PSCustomObject]@{ Name = "Kaylen"; Age = 40}
PS C:\> Write-Host $kaylen
@{Name=Kaylen; Age=40}
PS C:\>
PS C:\>
PS C:\> Add-Age -Person $kaylen -AgeToAdd 5
PS C:\> Write-Host $kaylen
@{Name=Kaylen; Age=45}
```

Figure 7.18: Results from executing the 'Add-Age' function

PowerShell functions offer flexibility and power through data input and output management, enabling the creation of efficient and versatile functions. PowerShell scripting relies heavily on functions, whether dealing with simple data types or complex objects.

Defining and calling PowerShell functions

PowerShell functions encapsulate a block of code that performs a specific task. These tasks can range from simple operations, such as adding two numbers, to more complex operations involving managing and manipulating entire systems. We have already delved into function parameters, outputs, and validation complexities. Now, let us refocus on the foundational aspect: how to define and subsequently call these functions.

As previously shown, you use the function keyword followed by the function's name and a block of code enclosed in curly braces {...}. The name should be verb-noun format, aligning with standard PowerShell cmdlet naming conventions. The following example is a simple function for returning a simple message:

```
function Get-Greeting {
    return "Hello, World!"
}
```

Once defined, calling a function is as straightforward as referencing its name:

```
Get-Greeting
```

Like any part of PowerShell, functions support variables, parameters, and complex logic. Adding parameters is as simple as adding **param** along with the type and name:

```
function Get-Greeting {
    param([string]$Name)
    return "Hello, $Name!"
```

}

Once defined, calling a function is as straightforward as referencing its name and parameters:

`Get-Greeting -Name "Liam"`

It is essential to understand the scope when working with functions. Variables defined inside a function are local to that function unless specified otherwise. However, you can use the global keyword to set global variables. The following update combines local and global variables within the **Get-Greeting** function:

```
$global:defaultLanguage = "English"


function Get-Greeting {
    param(
        [string]$Name,
        [string]$Language = $global:defaultLanguage
    )
    $Greetings = @{
        "English" = "Hello"
        "French" = "Bonjour"
        "Spanish" = "Hola"
        "German" = "Hallo"
    }

    if (-not $Greetings.ContainsKey($Language)) {
        Write-Warning "Language not supported. Using English as default."
        $Language = "English"
    }
    return "$($Greetings[$Language]), $Name!"
}
```

After updating, you can easily execute the function by calling its name and parameters, as shown below.:

```
Get-Greeting -Name "Alice"

Get-Greeting -Name "Mario" -Language "Spanish"

Get-Greeting -Name "Charlie" -Language "NonExistent"
```

The function will use the default language if the provided language does not match any of the languages stored within the **$Greetings** hashtable. The following three figures (*Figures 7.19, 7.20,* and *7.21*) show the output from executing the updated **Get-Greeting** function and the result based on using local and global variables and logic:

```
PS C:\> Get-Greeting -Name "Alice"
Hello, Alice!
```

Figure 7.19: *Results from executing the Add-Age function*

```
PS C:\> Get-Greeting -Name "Mario" -Language "Spanish"
Hola, Mario!
```

Figure 7.20: *Results from executing the Add-Age function*

```
PS C:\> Get-Greeting -Name "Charlie" -Language "NonExistent"
WARNING: Language not supported. Using English as default.
Hello, Charlie!
```

Figure 7.21: *Results from executing the Add-Age function*

Creating and using functions with additional capabilities will enhance existing scripts, make them reusable, and make them easier to manage and control.

Combining functions into complex scripts

Now that you can grasp the art of defining and calling functions, let us advance our understanding by integrating multiple functions into complex scripts. Combining functions allows you to create more structured, readable, and maintainable scripts.

Why combine functions? Think of individual functions as building blocks. While each block serves a purpose, combining them creates a more structured and meaningful entity. This modularity aids in troubleshooting and iterative development. For example, you needed PowerShell to calculate area and perimeter. Using functions, you can create the following:

```
function Get-Area {
```

```
    param(
        [double]$Length,
        [double]$Width
    )
    return $Length * $Width
}

function Get-Perimeter {
    param(
        [double]$Length,
        [double]$Width
    )
    return 2 * ($Length + $Width)
}

$length = 5.5
$width = 4.2
Write-Output "AREA: $(Get-Area -Length $length -Width $width)"
Write-Output "PERIMETER: $(Get-Perimeter -Length $length -Width $width)"
```

The following figure shows the output of the two separately executed functions:

```
PS C:\> Write-Output "AREA: $(Get-Area -Length $length -Width $width)"
AREA: 23.1
PS C:\>
PS C:\>
PS C:\> Write-Output "PERIMETER: $(Get-Perimeter -Length $length -Width $width)"
PERIMETER: 19.4
```

Figure 7.22: Results from executing both functions

Though creating two functions works and is easy to use, there is no reason for them being separate. The following is an example of two functions combined into one:

```
function Get-RectangleProperties {
```

```
    param (
        [double]$Length,
        [double]$Width
    )

    $Area = $Length * $Width
    $Perimeter = 2 * ($Length + $Width)

    return [PSCustomObject]@{
        Area = $Area
        Perimeter = $Perimeter
    }
}

$rectangleProperties = Get-RectangleProperties -Length 5.5 -Width 4.2
$rectangleProperties
```

The following figure shows the output of the combined function:

```
PS C:\> $rectangleProperties = Get-RectangleProperties -Length 5.5 -Width 4.2
PS C:\> $rectangleProperties

Area  Perimeter
----  ---------
23.10     19.40
```

Figure 7.23: Results from executing the Get-RectangleProperties function

You do not need to combine every function you create with other functions. Choose those that make sense to combine carefully and leave them separate as required.

For example, combining our **Get-Greeting** and **Add-Age** functions may make sense if you need to return both sets of information regularly. If you did need to, then the function could look like:

```
function Get-UserGreetingWithAgeUpdate {
    param (
```

```
    [string]$Name,

    [int]$Age,

    [int]$YearsToAdd = 1
)


$NewAge = $Age + $YearsToAdd

$GreetingMessage = "Hello, $Name! You are currently $Age years old. In $YearsToAdd years, you will be $NewAge."


return $GreetingMessage
}


$Message = Get-UserGreetingWithAgeUpdate -Name "Kaylen" -Age 40 -YearsToAdd 12

Write-Output $Message
```

The following figure shows the function used to display the current age of **Kaylen**, and how old she will be in the number of years specified in the **YearsToAdd** parameter:

```
PS C:\> $Message = Get-UserGreetingWithAgeUpdate -Name "Kaylen" -Age 40 -YearsToAdd 12
PS C:\> Write-Output $Message
Hello, Kaylen! You are currently 40 years old. In 12 years, you will be 52.
```

Figure 7.24: Results from executing the Get- UserGreetingWithAgeUpdate function

The combined function still provides customization through parameters, allowing users to specify a name, current age, and the number of years to add, yet provides a unified output that incorporates the details of both original functions.

Combining functions in PowerShell scripts is the cornerstone of developing efficient, modular, and maintainable automation solutions. By consolidating functionalities, we enhance code readability, making it easier for the author and collaborators to understand the script's flow. This practice also promotes code reusability; instead of rewriting or copying code blocks, a single function call can invoke a suite of actions. It reduces the likelihood of errors, as there are fewer redundancies and a centralized location for making updates or fixes. Additionally, well-structured functions are easier to test, ensuring the reliability of the script. As scripts become complex, the modular approach of combining functions becomes even more critical, enabling developers to break down intricate operations into manageable pieces.

Conclusion

Understanding the fundamentals of creating functions is essential to PowerShell scripting. As we have seen, integrating well-defined functions enhances the modular nature of scripts, driving efficiency and maintainability. With their flexibility and depth, parameters strengthen your scripts, making them adaptable across various scenarios. We also reviewed the importance of data accuracy through types and default values, ensuring robust and error-resistant code. Advanced parameter attributes like validation and input masks act as gatekeepers, ensuring the integrity of input values. As we progressed, the art of passing and returning values interconnected functions, laying the groundwork for complex, multi-faceted scripts. As your PowerShell proficiency grows, you will confidently and efficiently tackle more complex tasks.

In the upcoming chapter, you will learn how to control the execution control, looping of data, and error handling.

Join our book's Discord space

Join the book's Discord Workspace for Latest updates, Offers, Tech happenings around the world, New Release and Sessions with the Authors:

https://discord.bpbonline.com

CHAPTER 8
Flow Control, Looping, and Error Handling

Introduction

This chapter explains looping, starting with an overarching view and then diving into the mechanics of the **ForEach-Object** command and **foreach** loops. You will then progress into using the **switch** command, offering you pathways based on conditions. You will then delve into the foundational principles of error handling, where you will learn its pivotal role in scripting and how to implement it within PowerShell. By the end of the chapter, you will be able to control the flow of PowerShell scripts, including errors.

Structure

In this chapter, we will cover the following topics:
- Overview of looping within PowerShell
- Reviewing the ForEach-Object command
- Reviewing foreach loops
- Reviewing the switch command
- Looping capabilities

- Understanding error handling basics
- Implement error handling to control the flow

Objectives

By the end of this chapter, you will clearly understand the concept of looping and its significance in automating repetitive tasks and navigating data structures. You will also learn about the specifics of the `ForEach-Object` command and `foreach` loops and how to iterate over collections efficiently. In addition to this, you will review the `switch` command and its use in conditional execution. Furthermore, you will learn about other looping techniques that broaden your toolkit for different scenarios. The chapter will conclude with a discussion on error handling and its importance in maintaining the integrity and robustness of scripts.

Overview of looping within PowerShell

Looping is a fundamental construct in almost any programming or scripting language. In PowerShell, loops execute commands repeatedly based on conditions or a specified number of times. This repetition helps with collections like arrays or lists, where you must apply an operation to each item. Different kinds of loops are available in PowerShell, each tailored for specific use cases:

- **ForEach loop**: This is often the go-to loop for PowerShell scripting, especially when processing each item in a collection sequentially.
- **While loops**: These loops execute as long as a specific condition remains true. They are beneficial when the number of iterations is unknown ahead of time.
- **Do-while and Do-until loops**: These are variations of the while loop but with a crucial difference. The loop's body executes consistently in these loops at least once before evaluating the condition.
- **For loops**: In other languages, programmers might recognize a more traditional loop; in PowerShell, they use the for loop when they know the number of iterations or want more control over the initialization, condition, and increment expressions.
- **Switch statements**: While the `switch` statement in PowerShell is not a loop in the traditional sense, it evaluates multiple conditions and executes code blocks based on the results.

Looping constructs are indispensable for automating tasks in PowerShell. Loops streamline tedious and time-consuming processes by iterating over data sets or repeating specific tasks until they meet a condition. Moreover, by understanding and effectively implementing loops, one can ensure that scripts are efficient and readable.

Reviewing the ForEach-Object command

The **ForEach-Object** command, often abbreviated to **%**, is one of PowerShell's most frequently used cmdlets when working with collections. This cmdlet operates on each item in a collection, be it an array, list, or any enumerable set. It is a pipeline command that takes each object passed to it and performs a specified operation.

At its simplest, the **ForEach-Object** command executes a single operation on every item within a collection. The following generates numbers from 1 to 5, which are then passed to **ForEach-Object** to print each number:

```
1..5 | ForEach-Object { Write-Output $_ }
```

This figure displays the printing numbers 1 to 5 within the **ForEach-Object** loop:

```
PS C:\> 1..5 | ForEach-Object { Write-Output $_ }
1
2
3
4
5
```

Figure 8.1: Print numbers from 1 to 5

With **ForEach-Object**, you can introduce more complex logic, allowing you to act conditionally based on the properties of the current item. This example introduces a conditional check to print only even numbers from 1 to 10, as shown:

```
1..10 | ForEach-Object {
    if ($_ % 2 -eq 0) {
        Write-Output $_
    }
}
```

The following figure displays the printing of all even numbers:

```
PS C:\> 1..10 | ForEach-Object {
>>     if ($_ % 2 -eq 0) {
>>         Write-Output $_
>>     }
>> }
2
4
6
8
10
```

Figure 8.2: Print even numbers from 1 to 10

In addition to operating on simple data types, **ForEach-Object** works well when manipulating more complex objects. The following example uses the command **Get-ChildItem** to retrieve items from a directory and uses **ForEach-Object** to filter and display only the names of files with the **.txt** extension (Update the **-Path** property to be the correct location you are using):

```
Get-ChildItem -Path "C:\Files" | ForEach-Object {
    if ($_.Extension -eq ".txt") {
        Write-Output $_.Name
    }
}
```

This figure displays all the files with a specific extension:

```
PS C:\> Get-ChildItem -Path "C:\Files" | ForEach-Object {
>>     if ($_.Extension -eq ".txt") {
>>         Write-Output $_.Name
>>     }
>> }
File.txt
Sample File 1.txt
Sample File 2.txt
Sample File 3.txt
```

Figure 8.3: List names of files with specific extensions

For more advanced scenarios, **ForEach-Object** loops can be nested within one another to manage multi-dimensional collections or complex object hierarchies. For example, you can build a 3x3 matrix (two-dimensional array) using nested **ForEach-Object** loops, printing each matrix element:

```
$matrix = @( @(1,2,3), @(4,5,6), @(7,8,9) )

$matrix | ForEach-Object {

    $row = $_

    $row | ForEach-Object {

        Write-Output $_

    }

}
```

The following figure shows how to process multiple values within arrays:

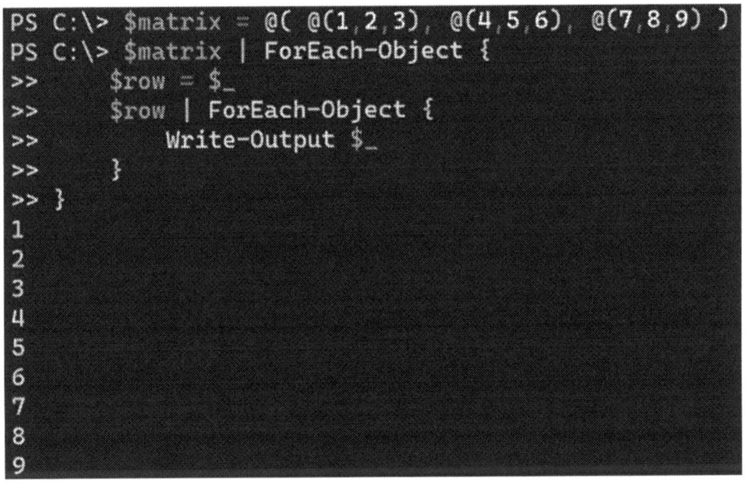

Figure 8.4: Process multi-dimensional arrays

The **ForEach-Object** command is a powerful tool in the PowerShell arsenal, proficient at handling various scenarios, from simple data processing to complex object manipulations.

Reviewing foreach loops

The **foreach** loop, distinct from the **ForEach-Object** cmdlet, is a staple of many programming languages, including PowerShell. It allows for iteration over collections, making it highly valuable for scripting and automation. Unlike **ForEach-Object**, which acts as a pipeline cmdlet, the **foreach** loop is a statement in PowerShell, giving it a more traditional loop structure. The standard pattern is simple: a block of code executes for each item in a collection. The following code iterates each color in the **$colors** array and prints them sequentially:

```
$colors = ("red", "blue", "green")
```

```
foreach ($color in $colors) {
    Write-Output $color
}
```

The following figure shows the output from iterating a basic array using a **foreach** loop:

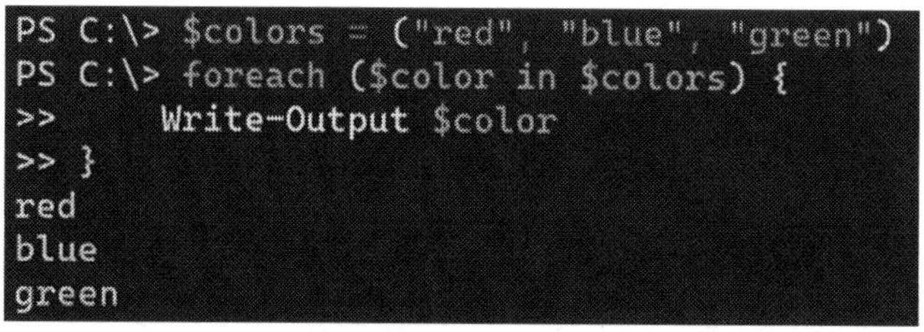

Figure 8.5: Basic Iteration over an Array

While simple data types benefit from **foreach**, the real power comes when working with complex objects, allowing for intricate data manipulations. For example, you can extract specific properties (Name and Age) from an array of hash tables and display them, as shown in the following example:

```
$users = @(
    @{Name="Alice"; Age=30},
    @{Name="Bob"; Age=25},
    @{Name="Charlie"; Age=28}
)
foreach ($user in $users) {
    Write-Output "Name: $($user.Name), Age: $($user.Age)"
}
```

The following figure shows the output from iterating an array of hash tables:

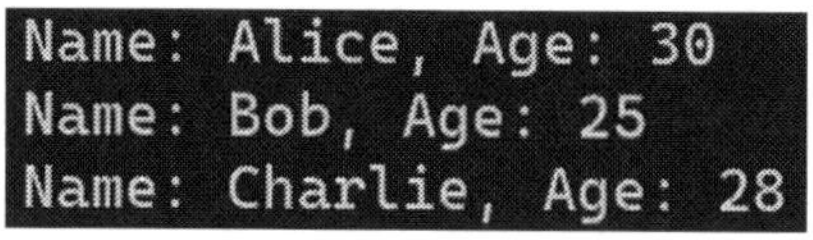

Figure 8.6: Extracting properties from objects

The **foreach** loop in PowerShell supports loop control keywords like break and continue. You can use it to exit the loop or skip to the next iteration prematurely. The following example breaks and exits once it encounters a number greater than five:

```
$numbers = 1..10

foreach ($number in $numbers) {

    if ($number -gt 5) {

        break

    }

    Write-Output $number

}
```

For multi-dimensional datasets or hierarchical data structures, foreach loops can be nested. For example, the following nested loop setup prints each student's name and their study subjects:

```
$students = @(

    @{Name="Alice"; Subjects=@("Math", "History")},

    @{Name="Bob"; Subjects=@("Physics", "Chemistry")}

)


foreach ($student in $students) {

    Write-Output "Name: $($student.Name)"

    foreach ($subject in $student.Subjects) {

        Write-Output "- Studying $subject"

    }

}
```

The following figure shows the output using nested loops to print out student and subject details:

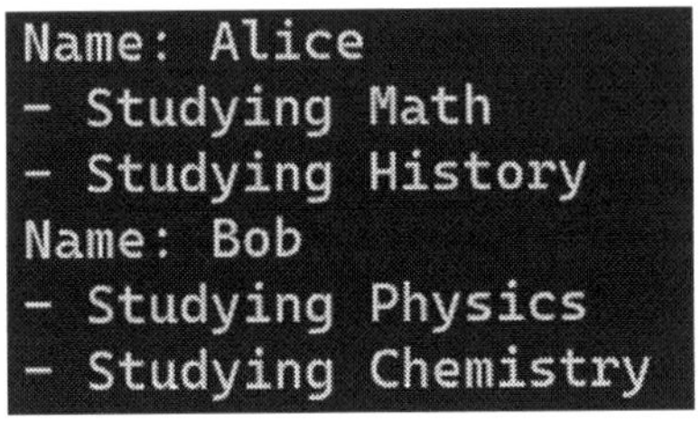

```
Name: Alice
- Studying Math
- Studying History
Name: Bob
- Studying Physics
- Studying Chemistry
```

Figure 8.7: Nested loop processing

When working with PowerShell scripting, **foreach** loops are a valuable tool to traverse collections and perform specific operations on each element. While the **ForEach-Object** cmdlet offers similar functionality, many prefer **foreach** loops for their distinct performance and style advantages that better suit particular situations. Knowing when and how to use **foreach** loops effectively instead of **ForEach-Object** is vital to becoming proficient in PowerShell scripting.

Reviewing the switch command

One of PowerShell's most versatile constructs for decision-making is the **switch** command. At its core, the switch provides a way to evaluate a single expression against multiple potential outcomes, making it a more compact and often more readable alternative to a series of nested if statements. The basis of the **switch** command lies in checking a value against a set of conditions and executing code based on the matching condition.

In this example, given that **$day** is **Wednesday**, the output would be **Hump day!**:

```
$day = "Wednesday"

switch ($day) {

    "Monday" { Write-Output "Start of the work week."}

    "Wednesday" { Write-Output "Hump day!"}

    "Friday" { Write-Output "Almost the weekend!"}

    default { Write-Output "A regular day."}

}
```

PowerShell's **switch** command can handle wildcard patterns, enabling pattern-based evaluations. For example, the script would recognize the filename and output **Word document**, as shown:

```
$filename = "document.docx"

switch -Wildcard ($filename) {

    "*.docx" { Write-Output "Word document" }

    "*.xlsx" { Write-Output "Excel spreadsheet" }

    default { Write-Output "Unknown file type"}

}
```

The following figure shows the output of the **switch** command when using wildcard values:

```
PS C:\> $filename = "document.docx"
PS C:\> switch -Wildcard ($filename) {
>>      "*.docx" { Write-Output "Word document" }
>>      "*.xlsx" { Write-Output "Excel spreadsheet" }
>>      default { Write-Output "Unknown file type"}
>> }
Word document
```

Figure 8.8: Using Wildcards in switch

Switch conditions can be more than static values or patterns; they can be script blocks for complex evaluations. For example, the output below would be **Teenager**, using a specific age:

$age = 18

switch ($age) {

    {$_ -lt 13} { Write-Output "Child" }

    {$_ -lt 20} { Write-Output "Teenager" }

    default { Write-Output "Adult"}

}

PowerShell's **switch** can also iterate over arrays, evaluating each element against the provided conditions. The following code evaluates and produces output for each color in the array:

$colors = @("red", "blue", "green")

switch ($colors) {

    "red" { Write-Output "Firetruck color" }

    "blue" { Write-Output "Sky color" }

    "green" { Write-Output "Grass color" }

}

The following figure shows the output of the **switch** command when using array values combined with the **switch** statement:

```
PS C:\> $colors = @("red", "blue", "green")
PS C:\> switch ($colors) {
>>      "red" { Write-Output "Firetruck color" }
>>      "blue" { Write-Output "Sky color" }
>>      "green" { Write-Output "Grass color" }
>> }
Firetruck color
Sky color
Grass color
```

Figure 8.9: Processing arrays with switch

PowerShell's `switch` command provides a powerful and flexible way of evaluating variables and deciding based on their values. It supports wildcards, script blocks, and arrays beyond traditional switch constructs in other programming languages. By mastering its usage, you can write cleaner, more efficient, and more readable scripts, mainly when dealing with multiple conditions. Whether you need to categorize data, filter input, or control the flow of your script, the `switch` command is an essential tool in your PowerShell toolkit.

Looping capabilities

In PowerShell, looping is an essential construct that facilitates the execution of a block of statements multiple times based on a condition or set of conditions. As you have seen from the previous sections, there are many ways to perform looping in PowerShell, such as using `ForEach-Object`, `foreach` loops, and even the `switch` command. By leveraging these tools, you can iterate over collections, process data sequentially, or repeat operations until you meet a specific condition.

Beyond the foundational loops, PowerShell offers several advanced looping mechanisms tailored for specific use cases:

- **While loops**: Executes a code block if a condition remains true.
- **Do-while and Do-until loops**: They ensure the code block runs at least once before evaluating the loop's condition.
- **For loops**: Offers precise control over the loop's initialization, condition checking, and iteration aspects.

The `while` loop checks a condition before executing the associated block of code. It continues to execute the block as long as the condition remains true. This `while` loop will print the values from 0 to 4:

```
$count = 0
```

```
while ($count -lt 5) {
    Write-Output "Current count value is: $count"
    $count++
}
```

The **Do-while** executes the code block at least once and then checks the condition, continuing as long as it remains true. This **Do-while** loop will print the numbers 10, 11, and 12:

```
$number = 10
do {
    Write-Output "Number is: $number"
    $number++
} while ($number -le 12)
```

The **Do-until** also ensures the code block runs at least once but continues until the condition becomes true. This **Do-until** loop will print the numbers 10, 11, and 12:

```
$number = 10
do {
    Write-Output "Number is: $number"
    $number++
} until ($number -gt 12)
```

The **for** loop offers a three-part loop control mechanism: Initialization, condition checking, and iteration. The following **for** loop will iterate five times, printing the iteration number from 0 to 4:

```
for ($i = 0; $i -lt 5; $i++) {
    Write-Output "Iteration number: $i"
}
```

Looping is a pivotal component of automation and data processing in PowerShell. By understanding and combining different looping constructs, you can efficiently tailor your scripts to handle varying complexities and data sets. Whether traversing multi-tiered data, processing files in a directory, or automating repetitive tasks, looping capabilities in PowerShell equip you with the tools to achieve your scripting objectives seamlessly.

Embracing advanced techniques, such as nested loops, loop controls, and integrated pipelines, will elevate your scripts, making them powerful and versatile.

Understanding error handling basics

Error handling is critical to any scripting or programming environment, and PowerShell is no exception. In PowerShell, error handling is not just about catching errors but also about managing and controlling the flow of script execution when errors occur. Understanding the basic principles of error handling in PowerShell can drastically reduce the time spent debugging and improve the reliability and robustness of your scripts.

There are two types of errors:

- **Terminating errors**: These serious errors stop the script's execution. For instance, trying to read a file that does not exist or calling a non-existent cmdlet would generate a terminating error.
- **Non-terminating errors**: These errors do not halt the script by default. Instead, they display an error message, and the script continues running. An example might be when trying to delete a non-existent file.

The `ErrorActionPreference` is a built-in variable in PowerShell that determines how the shell should handle errors, especially non-terminating errors. By setting or modifying its value, you influence the behavior of your scripts when encountering these errors. It allows for greater flexibility and control in managing errors during script execution. The primary function of `ErrorActionPreference` is to dictate the default behavior for how PowerShell handles errors across cmdlets and functions unless overridden by a specific cmdlet's `-ErrorAction` parameter. You can set the `ErrorActionPreference` variable for the entire session, a particular script, or even a single command. You can locally override the `ErrorActionPreference` for a single command using the `-ErrorAction` parameter. The valid values are:

- **Break:** Initiates debugger on error or exception.
- **Continue:** (Default) Shows the error and continues script execution.
- **Ignore:** Hides the error but continues. It is best for one-time command use, not a persistent preference.
- **Inquire:** Shows the error and asks if you would like to proceed.
- **SilentlyContinue:** Continues script without showing any error.
- **Stop:** Displays the error and halts script execution.
- **Suspend:** Pauses a workflow for investigation.

PowerShell also provides a built-in variable, **$Error**, which is an array that stores error objects (with the most recent error at index 0). It is beneficial when diagnosing problems, as it offers insights into the exact nature and origin of errors. You can also use **Try**, **Catch**, and **Finally**, code blocks for error handling:

- **Try**: Contains the script block in which an error might occur.
- **Catch**: Contains the executed script block if an error occurs in the Try block.
- **Finally**: This block runs after the Try and Catch blocks, regardless of whether there was an error.

You can also use the throw keyword, which allows you to generate your terminating errors. You can use it to signal unusual conditions and halt script execution if needed.

It is vital to always code with the forethought that errors may arise, enabling scripts to address unforeseen challenges smoothly. Messages must remain clear, concise, and insightful when composing custom errors. Additionally, in the event of errors, it is crucial to undertake cleanup measures, such as releasing resources, shutting files, or undoing changes, to maintain system stability.

Understanding error handling in PowerShell is fundamental to crafting resilient scripts. Predicting, capturing, and responding to errors ensures that scripts are robust and can handle unforeseen challenges. Proper error handling also provides informative feedback, which can be invaluable in development and production environments.

Implementing error handling to control the flow

Implementing error handling is unique to the type of script you are creating, the existing commands you are using, and your business or technical requirements. The most common and easiest option is to use the standard **Try-Catch** block. In the following example, you detect a potential error within a Try block and determine how to handle that error in the Catch block, which displays a message with the error:

```
Try {
    Get-Item "NonexistentPath" -ErrorAction Stop
}
Catch {
    Write-Host "An error occurred: $_"
}
```

The following figure displays the error message:

```
An error occurred: Cannot find path 'C:\NonexistentPath' because it does not exist.
```

Figure 8.10: Try the command and capture error

Sometimes, however, generated errors differ depending on the executed code, or you may have multiple generated errors and need to handle them differently. For example, you can handle each type separately by modifying the previous code to include another generated error, as shown:

```
Try {

    [int]$value = "TestString"

    Get-Item "NonexistentPath" -ErrorAction Stop

}

Catch [System.InvalidCastException] {

    Write-Host "Format issue detected: $_"

}

Catch {

    Write-Host "General error: $_"

}
```

The following figure displays the error messages for the invalid casting of a string value to an integer:

```
Format issue detected: Cannot convert value "TestString" to type "System.Int32"
. Error: "The input string 'TestString' was not in a correct format."
```

Figure 8.11: Try the commands and process each error

Of course, when using the **Try-Catch**, you can add the **Finally** option to act when the code is complete. Adding the **Finally** option displays the execution complete message:

```
Try {

    [int]$value = "TestString"

    Get-Item "NonexistentPath" -ErrorAction Stop

}

Catch [System.InvalidCastException] {
```

```
        Write-Host "Format issue detected: $_"
}
Catch {
        Write-Host "General error: $_"
}
Finally {
        Write-Host "Script execution completed!"
}
```

The following figure displays the error messages for the error from the **Catch** and the **Finally** message:

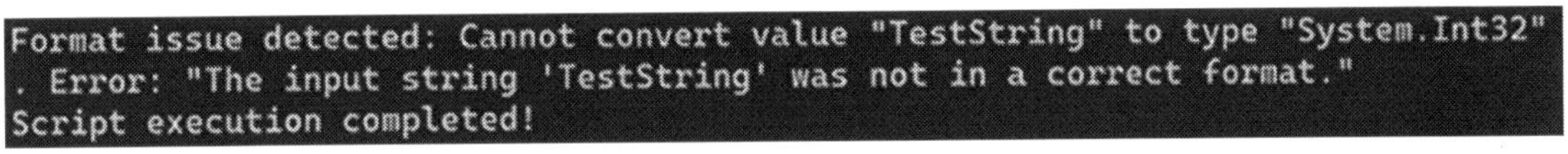

```
Format issue detected: Cannot convert value "TestString" to type "System.Int32"
. Error: "The input string 'TestString' was not in a correct format."
Script execution completed!
```

Figure 8.12: Try the Commands and Process the Error, including Displaying the Message

Sometimes, you do not want to manage the errors; you need the script to stop. Integrating **$ErrorActionPreference** to the previous script now halts when encountering an error:

```
$ErrorActionPreference = "Stop"
Try {
        Get-Item "NonexistentPath"
}
Catch [System.InvalidCastException] {
        Write-Host "Format issue detected: $_"
}
Catch {
        Write-Host "General error: $_"
}
Finally {
        Write-Host "Script execution completed!"
```

}

The following figure uses the **$ErrorActionPreference** variable to stop code execution when an error occurs:

```
General error: Cannot find path 'C:\NonexistentPath' because it does not exist.
Script execution completed!
```

Figure 8.13: Stop code execution when error raised

A best practice when implementing error handling is to log errors to a flat file or some other system, such as a database. You can modify the previous code using the **Out-File** command to write text files containing the error, as shown:

```
$ErrorActionPreference = "Stop"

Try {
    [int]$value = "TestString"
    Get-Item "NonexistentPath"
}
Catch [System.InvalidCastException] {
    Write-Host "Format issue detected: $_"
    "$_" | Out-File "errorlog.txt" -Append
}
Catch {
    Write-Host "General error: $_"
    "$_" | Out-File "errorlog.txt" -Append
}
Finally {
    Write-Host "Script execution completed!"
}
```

To enhance the script further and force the error handling code to execute, you can use the **Throw** option. Combined with **Try** and **Catch** blocks, Throw allows for structured error handling. You can **Throw** an error in one part of a script and then catch and handle that error in another part, providing a more graceful and user-friendly error resolution. You can modify the previous code to add an age check and throw an error, which the error handling code then captures:

```
$ErrorActionPreference = "Stop"


Try {
    $age = 15
    if ($age -lt 16) {
        throw "You must be at least 16 years old."
    }
    [int]$value = "TestString"
    Get-Item "NonexistentPath"
}
Catch [System.InvalidCastException] {
    Write-Host "Format issue detected: $_"
    "$_" | Out-File "errorlog.txt" -Append
}
Catch {
    Write-Host "General error: $_"
    "$_" | Out-File "errorlog.txt" -Append
}
Finally {
    Write-Host "Script execution completed!"
}
```

The following figure displays the thrown error message:

```
PS C:\> Try {
>>     $age = 15
>>     if ($age -lt 16) {
>>         throw "You must be at least 16 years old."
>>     }
>>     [int]$value = "TestString"
>>     Get-Item "NonexistentPath"
>> } Catch [System.InvalidCastException] {
>>     Write-Host "Format issue detected: $_"
>>     "$_" | Out-File "errorlog.txt" -Append
>> } Catch {
>>     Write-Host "General error: $_"
>>     "$_" | Out-File "errorlog.txt" -Append
>> } Finally {
>>     Write-Host "Script execution completed!"
>> }
General error: You must be at least 16 years old.
Script execution completed!
```

Figure 8.14: Stop code execution and display thrown error message

You could create the same code into a function and then support all error-handling approaches by passing various options and values to it, as shown:

```
function Invoke-DemonstrateErrors {

    param(

        [int]$AgeValue = 15,

        [string]$StringValue = "TestString",

        [string]$PathValue = "NonexistentPath"

    )


    $ErrorActionPreference = "Stop"


    Try {

        $age = $AgeValue

        if ($age -lt 16) {

            throw "You must be at least 16 years old."

        }
```

```
        [int]$value = $StringValue

        Get-Item $PathValue

    }

    Catch [System.InvalidCastException] {

        Write-Host "Format issue detected: $_"

        "$_" | Out-File "errorlog.txt" -Append

    }

    Catch {

        Write-Host "General error: $_"

        "$_" | Out-File "errorlog.txt" -Append

    }

    Finally {

        Write-Host "Script execution completed!"

    }

}
```

You can then call the function using the following options, knowing the code will capture the errors:

```
Invoke-DemonstrateErrors


Invoke-DemonstrateErrors -AgeValue 16 -StringValue "Test"


Invoke-DemonstrateErrors `

      -AgeValue 16 `

      -StringValue 15 `

      -PathValue "C:\Test"


Invoke-DemonstrateErrors `

      -AgeValue 16 `
```

```
    -StringValue 15 `

    -PathValue "C:\Files"
```

The following figure displays the varying errors based on the values assigned to the function parameters:

```
PS C:\> Invoke-DemonstrateErrors
General error: You must be at least 16 years old.
Script execution completed!

PS C:\> Invoke-DemonstrateErrors -AgeValue 16 -StringValue "Test"
Format issue detected: Cannot convert value "Test" to type "System.Int32". Error: "
The input string 'Test' was not in a correct format."
Script execution completed!

PS C:\> Invoke-DemonstrateErrors -AgeValue 16 -StringValue 15 -PathValue "C:\Test"
General error: Cannot find path 'C:\Test' because it does not exist.
Script execution completed!

PS C:\> Invoke-DemonstrateErrors -AgeValue 16 -StringValue 15 -PathValue "C:\Files"
Mode                 LastWriteTime         Length Name
----                 -------------         ------ ----
d----           9/26/2023   2:20 PM                Files
Script execution completed!
```

Figure 8.15: Error message outcomes

A structured approach to error handling allows you to effectively address multiple error scenarios, ensuring user-friendly and maintainable scripts.

Conclusion

Mastering flow control is essential to scripting in PowerShell. This chapter has provided an in-depth understanding of various looping mechanisms, ranging from **ForEach-Object** command to **foreach** loops, that enable iterative and repetitive tasks with precision. Learning about the **switch** command made you realize it is effortlessly adaptable in managing multiple conditions. Additionally, you have come to appreciate the significance of error handling. Your ability to create dynamic, flexible, and robust scripts will grow as you continue to learn.

The next chapter will explore creating PowerShell scripts containing multiple output paths.

CHAPTER 9
Scripts for Multiple Output Paths

Introduction

In this chapter, you will learn the fundamental concepts of PowerShell output redirection. You will understand how to effectively use output redirection operator methods to direct script output to various destinations. You will also learn how to pipe output to multiple destinations, a crucial technique for making your scripts more flexible and adaptable. Additionally, you will learn strategies for splitting output into different files, an essential skill for organizing and managing large volumes of data. You will further enhance this skill by learning to append results to existing files, ensuring your data collection is efficient and organized.

Structure

In this chapter, we will cover the following topics:
- Introduction to PowerShell output redirection
- Using output redirection operators
- Creating commands that produce multiple outputs
- Piping output to multiple destinations
- Splitting output into different files

- Appending results to existing files
- Customizing output destinations with conditional statements and loops
- Examples of scripts with multiple output paths

Objectives

By the end of this chapter, you will clearly understand PowerShell output redirection and how to use it in your scripts. The ability to create PowerShell commands that cater to multiple outputs will be within your grasp, along with the proficiency to pipe these outputs to varied destinations seamlessly. The chapter will teach you to customize output destinations with unprecedented precision and flexibility. You will also work with real-world script examples that present these concepts into actionable knowledge, preparing you to understand and apply PowerShell's versatile output redirection capabilities.

Introduction to PowerShell output redirection

It is essential for every PowerShell user, whether enthusiast or professional, to understand the concept of PowerShell Output Redirection. It refers to the ability to control where the output of your scripts, including errors, results, and other data, is sent and stored. Using PowerShell Output Redirection, you can keep your PowerShell environment organized and ensure that the generated data is easily accessible, readable, and manageable. A range of operators and cmdlets achieves PowerShell output redirection by directing the output of your script to the desired destination. These destinations can include the PowerShell console, various types of files, or even null, which discards the output.

Depending on the complexity and requirements of your scripts, you have different options for redirecting output. You can choose to capture standard output while ignoring errors, or you can explore more advanced options where each output type is carefully captured and redirected based on the specific needs of your tasks. Output redirection closely links to PowerShell pipelines. They work as channels that transfer data smoothly from one cmdlet to another, with each cmdlet performing its operation before passing it on. This data coordination is essential to PowerShell's design, ensuring that data is processed, directed, stored, and managed effectively.

Using output redirection operators

PowerShell output redirection operators efficiently direct script output to various destinations. These operators are not just about redirecting output; they are about control, precision, and customization, ensuring that each piece of data finds its way to the appropriate location.

PowerShell employs a variety of operators for managing the redirection of standard outputs. People commonly use the **>** operator to redirect the standard output to a file. If the file does not exist, the operator creates it; if it does, the operator overwrites it. The following example retrieves the output of **Get-Process** and redirects it to a file named **Processes.txt** located in the C drive:

```
Get-Process > "C:\Processes.txt"
```

For errors, PowerShell uses **2>** to redirect error output. It is handy for capturing errors for later analysis while keeping the console uncluttered. This example tries to get a process that does not exist and redirects the resulting error message to an **Errors.txt** file:

```
Get-Process -Name NonExistentProcess 2> "C:\Errors.txt"
```

The **>>** operator is used when you want to append output to an existing file instead of overwriting it, ensuring that previous data is not lost. The following example appends the list of services to the **Services.txt** file, preserving the existing content:

```
Get-Service >> "C:\Services.txt"
```

Combining operators allows for simultaneous redirection of standard and error outputs, offering enhanced flexibility. This example ensures that the standard output goes to **Output.txt** while capturing errors in **Errors.txt**:

```
Get-Item "Path" > "C:\Output.txt" 2> "C:\Errors.txt"
```

You can also use **2>&1**, redirecting the error output to standard output. Here, **2** refers to the error stream, and **1** refers to the standard output stream in PowerShell's redirection operations.

```
Get-ChildItem "NonExistentPath" 2>&1
```

So, **2>&1** means **redirect all errors (2) to the standard output stream (1)**. This can be particularly useful when capturing standard and error outputs together, for example, in a single log file.

At times, you might want to discard the output, and this is where null redirection comes into play, utilizing the **$null** variable. This example discards the output, ensuring the console remains clean and uncluttered:

```
Get-Process -Name NonExistentProcess > $null
```

Understanding and effectively utilizing these operators allows for scripts that are not only efficient but also clean and manageable. It ensures that every piece of data, whether an output or an error, is captured, stored, and managed effectively. This example lists all files and directories in the C drive, redirecting the output to **Files.txt** and any errors encountered (like access denied errors) to **Errors.txt**:

```
Get-ChildItem -Path C:\ -Recurse > "C:\Files.txt" 2> "C:\Errors.txt"
```

PowerShell's output redirection operators work silently behind the scenes, ensuring that data flows seamlessly to the correct destinations, that errors are captured and not lost, and that your scripts are as efficient and effective as they are clean and manageable. Implementing these operators will become integral to your scripting, enhancing control and precision.

Creating commands that produce multiple outputs

Creating PowerShell commands capable of producing multiple outputs is critical as you make your scripts. This capability is highly beneficial when generating various types of information from a single command or script, enabling more comprehensive data analysis and reporting.

Let us begin with a basic example. Consider a scenario where you want to retrieve the list of running processes and services on a system. You can achieve this by emitting multiple outputs within a single function. In this example, calling **Get-SystemInfo** will display the running processes and services on the console:

```
function Get-SystemInfo {

    Get-Process

    Get-Service

}

Get-SystemInfo
```

While the previous example is functional, there might be more user-friendly options. You can enhance readability by categorizing the outputs, making them clearer and more organized. You have added labels and used the **Select-Object** cmdlet to limit the output, making it more manageable and clearer, as shown:

```
function Get-SystemInfo {

    "Processes:"

    Get-Process | Select-Object -First 5
```

```
"`nServices:"
    Get-Service | Where-Object Status -eq 'Running' | Select-Object -First 5
}
Get-SystemInfo
```

The following figure displays the returned output from executing the custom function **Get-SystemInfo** using custom labels:

```
PS C:\> function Get-SystemInfo {
>>     "Processes:"
>>         Get-Process | Select-Object -First 5
>>     "`nServices:"
>>         Get-Service | Where-Object Status -eq 'Running' | Select-Object -First 5
>> }
PS C:\> Get-SystemInfo
Processes:

 NPM(K)    PM(M)     WS(M)    CPU(s)       Id  SI ProcessName
 ------    -----     -----    ------       --  -- -----------
     10     2.46      7.19      1.88     5168   0 AggregatorHost
      9     1.57      4.81      0.03     1556   0 AppVShNotify
     14     7.15     14.81      0.12     2500   0 audiodg
     28     6.27      9.36     19.44    13352   2 AuthManSvr
     31    16.66      1.62      0.36     4948   2 backgroundTaskHost

Services:

Status      : Running
Name        : AIPScanner
DisplayName : Azure Information Protection Scanner


Status      : Running
Name        : Appinfo
DisplayName : Application Information
```

Figure 9.1: Output returned from Get-SystemInfo function using labels

You can take this further by creating custom objects to hold and organize the outputs effectively. In this version, you store the results in variables and then load them into a custom object, leading to an organized, structured output:

```
function Get-SystemInfo {
    $processes = Get-Process | Select-Object -First 5
    $services = Get-Service | Where-Object Status -eq 'Running' | Select-
```

```
Object -First 5

    [PSCustomObject]@{

        Processes = $processes

        Services = $services

    }

}
Get-SystemInfo
```

Adding parameters to the function makes the command more flexible, allowing users to specify the type of output they want. In this example, users can request specific information, making the command more targeted and efficient:

```
function Get-SystemInfo {

    param (

        [string]$InfoType

    )

    if ($InfoType -eq "Processes") {

        Get-Process | Select-Object -First 5

    } elseif ($InfoType -eq "Services") {

        Get-Service | Where-Object Status -eq 'Running' | Select-Object -First 5

    } else {

        Write-Host "Invalid InfoType specified"

    }

}
Get-SystemInfo
```

The following figure displays the execution of the **Get-SystemInfo** function to retrieve different outputs:

```
PS C:\> Get-SystemInfo -InfoType 'Services'

Status   Name                  DisplayName
------   ----                  -----------
Running  AIPScanner            Azure Information Protection Scanner
Running  Appinfo               Application Information
Running  AppXSvc               AppX Deployment Service (AppXSVC)
Running  AudioEndpointBuil…    Windows Audio Endpoint Builder
Running  Audiosrv              Windows Audio

PS C:\> Get-SystemInfo -InfoType 'Processes'

 NPM(K)    PM(M)    WS(M)   CPU(s)      Id  SI ProcessName
 ------    -----    -----   ------      --  -- -----------
     10     2.46     7.19     1.88    5168   0 AggregatorHost
      9     1.57     4.81     0.03    1556   0 AppVShNotify
     14     7.07    14.75     0.12    2500   0 audiodg
     28     6.27     9.36    19.44   13352   2 AuthManSvr
     31    16.66     1.62     0.36    4948   2 backgroundTaskHost
```

Figure 9.2: Executing Get-SystemInfo function and choosing the output

You can also incorporate output redirection operators to channel the outputs to specific destinations, such as a file. This addition ensures that reviewers can review, share, or analyze the results later. In this example, you can use the **Out-File** cmdlet and the **-FilePath** and **-Append** parameters to redirect the command outputs to a specific file. The **-Append** parameter ensures the file adds each new output instead of overwriting the previous content. The function now not only retrieves the desired information based on the specified parameter but also saves this information to a file for future reference, further analysis, or sharing, as shown:

```
function Get-SystemInfo {

    param (

        [string]$InfoType

    )


    $outputPath = "C:\SystemInfo.txt"


    if ($InfoType -ieq "Processes") {
```

```
        Get-Process | Select-Object -First 5 | Out-File -FilePath
        $outputPath -Append

        "Processes info has been saved to $outputPath"
    } elseif ($InfoType -ieq "Services") {

        Get-Service | Where-Object Status -ieq 'Running' | Select-Object
        -First 5 | Out-File -FilePath $outputPath -Append

        "Services info has been saved to $outputPath"
    } else {

        Write-Host "Invalid InfoType specified" | Out-File -FilePath
        $outputPath -Append

        "Error message has been logged to $outputPath"
    }
}

Get-SystemInfo -InfoType 'Services'
```

The following figures display the execution of the updated **Get-SystemInfo** function to retrieve different outputs and show the use of output redirection operators:

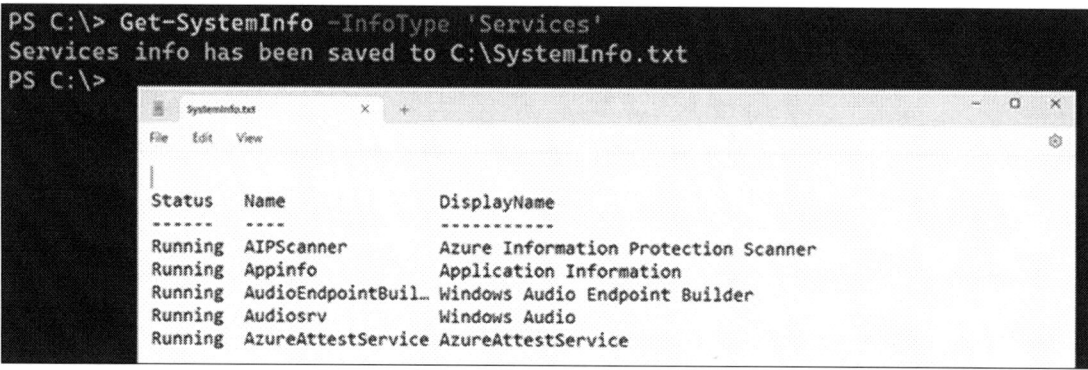

Figure 9.3: *Executing the Get-SystemInfo function to show output redirection operators for services*

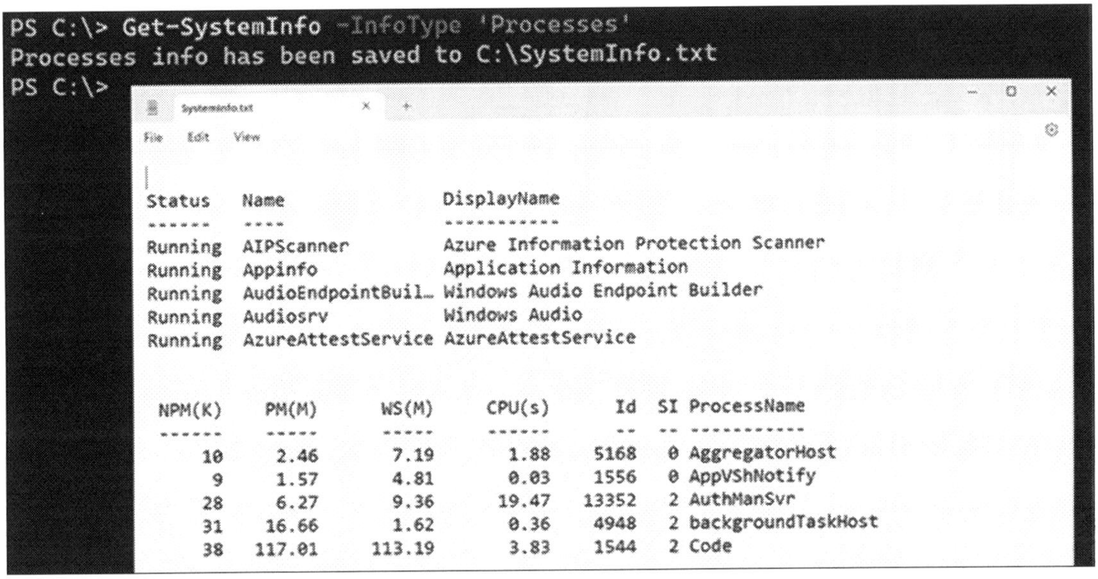

Figure 9.4: Executing the Get-SystemInfo function to show output redirection operators for processes

Producing multiple outputs in PowerShell commands enables flexibility and efficiency, especially in scenarios where diverse data sets are essential for comprehensive analysis. By incrementally enhancing the structure, readability, and flexibility of commands, you ensure it is functional, user-friendly, and adaptable to various needs and scenarios.

Piping output to multiple destinations

PowerShell's piping ability is one of its most compelling features. It allows the result of one command to be used as the input for another, creating a seamless flow of data manipulation. PowerShell also supports sending the data to multiple destinations, enhancing the versatility of data handling and reporting. To achieve this, cmdlets like **Tee-Object** play a fundamental role. The **Tee-Object** cmdlet is particularly handy, as it sends the output of a command to both the console and a file (or a variable), effectively splitting the output stream. It is instrumental in scenarios where you need to log the output of a script for audit purposes while simultaneously processing the data for other operations.

This example retrieves the list of processes and displays them in the console. Simultaneously, it saves a list copy to a text file named **Processes.txt** on the C: drive:

```
Get-Process | Tee-Object -FilePath "C:\Processes.txt"
```

You can also redirect the output directly to a variable. The following adjustment pipes the output of running services to the console and stores it in a variable **RunningServices** using the **-Variable** parameter of the **Tee-Object** cmdlet:

```
$Services = Get-Service | Where-Object { $_.Status -eq 'Running' } | Tee-Object -Variable RunningServices
```

The following figure displays the values stored within the **$RunningServices** variable:

```
PS C:\> $Services = Get-Service | Where-Object { $_.Status -eq 'Running' } | Tee-Object -Variable RunningServices
PS C:\> $RunningServices

Status   Name                 DisplayName
------   ----                 -----------
Running  AIPScanner           Azure Information Protection Scanner
Running  Appinfo              Application Information
Running  AudioEndpointBuil…   Windows Audio Endpoint Builder
Running  Audiosrv             Windows Audio
Running  AzureAttestService   AzureAttestService
Running  BFE                  Base Filtering Engine
Running  BrokerInfrastruct…   Background Tasks Infrastructure Servi…
Running  camsvc               Capability Access Manager Service
Running  cbdhsvc_13f185c0     Clipboard User Service_13f185c0
Running  CDPSvc               Connected Devices Platform Service
```

Figure 9.5: Display the values within the $RunningServices variable

You can also extend it and add further pipeline actions. The following update reads the content of **Example.txt**, creating a backup named **ExampleBackup.txt**, and then pipes the content to the **Measure-Object** cmdlet to count the file's lines, words, and characters:

```
Get-Content "C:\Example.txt" | Tee-Object -FilePath "C:\ExampleBackup.txt" | Measure-Object -Line -Word -Character
```

This example extracts error entries from the Security event log, saves them to a text file, and pipes them to **Out-GridView** for an interactive display. It is an illustration of real-time monitoring coupled with logging for post-analysis:

```
Get-EventLog -LogName Security | Where-Object { $_.EntryType -eq 'Error' } | Tee-Object -FilePath "C:\SecurityErrors.txt" | Out-GridView
```

The following figure displays the grid view from the executed command:

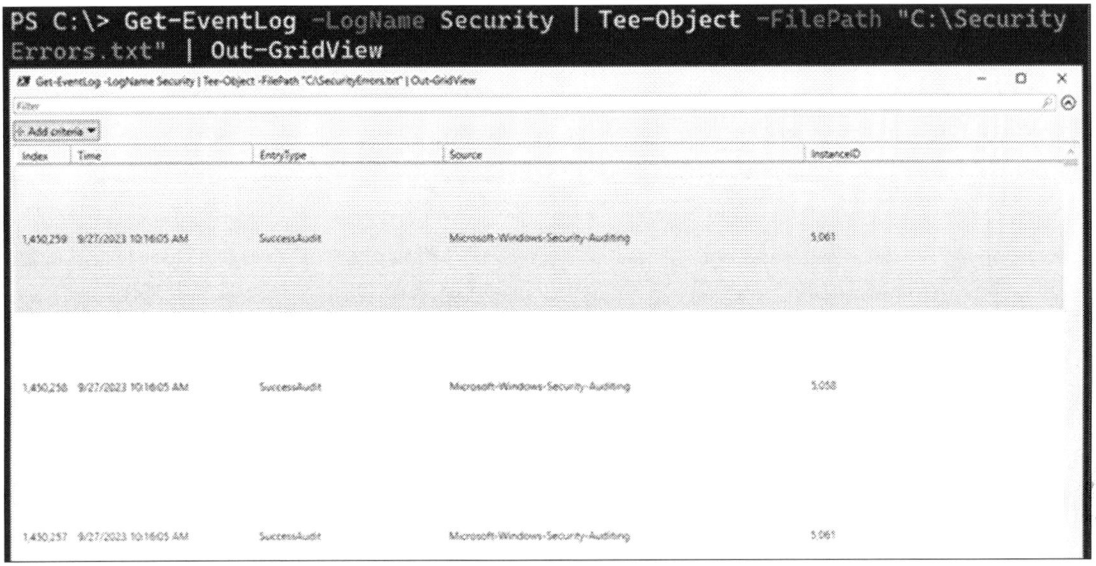

Figure 9.6: Display the grid view

Understanding and effectively utilizing the capability to direct outputs to multiple destinations is vital in making your PowerShell scripts versatile and adaptable to various operational requirements.

Splitting output into different files

Using PowerShell, splitting outputs into different files helps organize data, work with large datasets, and manage outputs tailored to various audiences or purposes. You can accomplish this by using cmdlets and output redirection operators to separate outputs based on specific criteria or logic. This example segregates processes into two distinct files based on CPU usage. The system stores processes consuming more than ten CPU units in **HighCPUProcesses.txt** and the others in **LowCPUProcesses.txt** files:

```
Get-Process | Where-Object {$_.CPU -gt 10} | Out-File "C:\HighCPUProcesses.txt"

Get-Process | Where-Object {$_.CPU -le 10} | Out-File "C:\LowCPUProcesses.txt"
```

The following figure displays the two created files:

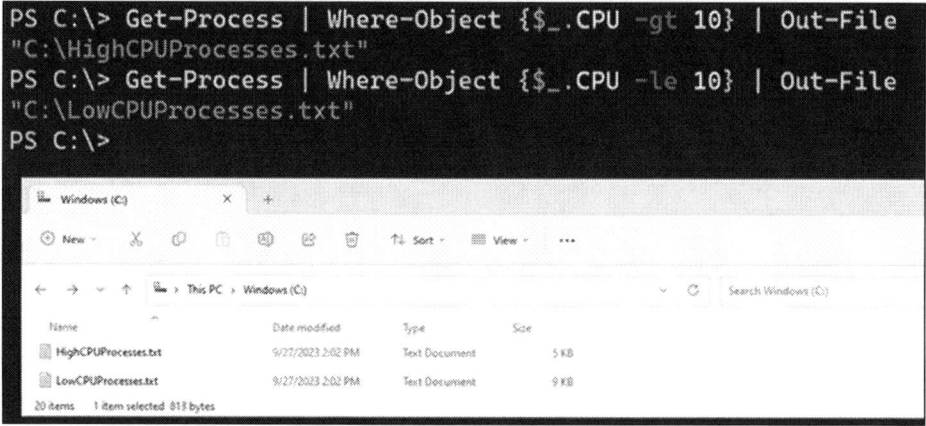

Figure 9.7: Output files

The following example separates the application logs into two distinct files depending on their entry type: **Error** or **Information**:

```
Get-EventLog -LogName Application | Where-Object { $_.EntryType -eq 'Error' } | Out-File "C:\ErrorLogs.txt"

Get-EventLog -LogName Application | Where-Object { $_.EntryType -eq 'Information' } | Out-File "C:\InfoLogs.txt"
```

In the following example, users are divided into separate CSV files based on their department attribute, segregating Sales, and HR department users:

```
Get-ADUser -Filter * | Where-Object {$_.Department -eq 'Sales'} | Export-Csv "C:\SalesUsers.csv" -NoTypeInformation

Get-ADUser -Filter * | Where-Object {$_.Department -eq 'HR'} | Export-Csv "C:\HRUsers.csv" -NoTypeInformation
```

If you modify the previous example, you can utilize other commands, such as the **ForEach-Object**, to create a single command that retrieves and exports based on the same logic:

```
Get-ADUser -Filter * | Where-Object { $_.Department -eq 'Sales' -or $_.Department -eq 'HR' } |

ForEach-Object {
    if ($_.Department -eq 'Sales') { $_ | Export-Csv "C:\SalesUsers.csv" -NoTypeInformation -Append }
```

        elseif ($_.Department -eq 'HR') { $_ | Export-Csv "C:\HRUsers.csv"
-NoTypeInformation -Append }
}

Imagine a situation where you have a significant amount of data to retrieve, filter, and split into different files based on specific criteria, such as user roles. The following example includes a loop that allows you to iterate over user roles, execute a query to retrieve the corresponding users, and then export the results to separate CSV files:

$roles = 'Admin', 'Editor', 'Viewer'

foreach ($role in $roles) {

    Get-ADUser -Filter * |

    Where-Object {$_.Description -eq $role} |

    Export-Csv -Path "C:\Users\$role-users.csv" -NoTypeInformation
}

Using PowerShell to manage and split outputs into different files efficiently is a skill that enhances organization and data handling.

Appending results to existing files

Appending results to existing files is a crucial log management, monitoring, and auditing feature. It allows adding new data to the end of an existing file, ensuring that you can continuously update files with further information while retaining the original data. Each time the below command runs, it appends the current list of processes to **Processes.txt**, thus creating a log over time:

Get-Process | Out-File "C:\Processes.txt" -Append

This script captures error logs from the Application log and appends them to **ErrorLogs.txt**, allowing for a historical view of errors:

Get-EventLog -LogName Application | Where-Object { $_.EntryType -eq 'Error' } | Out-File "C:\ErrorLogs.txt" -Append

The following example retrieves users created within the last week and appends them to a CSV file, ensuring a continually updated list of new users:

Get-ADUser -Filter * | Where-Object {$_.Created -ge (Get-Date).AddDays(-7)} | Export-Csv "C:\NewUsers.csv" -NoTypeInformation -Append

The following is a more complex example: the system filters users based on their departments and appends the results to the respective department's CSV files. Using the **-Append** parameter ensures that new data gets added to the existing file, preventing overwriting and data loss. It is beneficial for incremental data updates where tracking changes over time is essential:

```
$departments = 'Sales', 'HR', 'Engineering'
foreach ($dept in $departments) {
    Get-ADUser -Filter * |
    Where-Object {$_.Department -eq $dept} |
    Export-Csv -Path "C:\Users\$dept-users.csv" -NoTypeInformation -Append
}
```

Understanding how to manage the output by splitting it into different files or appending it to existing ones increases the versatility and precision of your PowerShell scripts. It enables more organized, strategic, and systematic data storage, management, and retrieval, which is essential in comprehensive data handling and reporting.

Customizing output destinations with conditional statements and loops

PowerShell allows customizing output destinations using conditional statements and loops, enhancing data organization, and directing information precisely where needed for more dynamic data handling.

Sorting and redirecting data based on specific criteria can be a daunting task. However, conditional statements such as **if**, **else**, and **switch**, and looping constructs such as **foreach** and **while** can easily automate this process. You can sort and store the data based on attributes such as date, size, type, or any other definable parameter.

To explain in practical terms, you can write a script that checks each data item's attributes and then, based on conditional logic, decides where to send that data. For example, you can send log files older than a week to an archive folder, while more recent ones go to a folder for immediate review. In another scenario, data with errors can be redirected to a specific error log file, while successful data entries append to a separate success log.

Looping constructs are useful for iterating over large datasets, checking each item against specific conditions, and directing them to the appropriate output destination. This automation enhances efficiency, accuracy, and speed in managing data, reducing the need for manual labor and the potential for human error.

The following example sorts files into two separate output destinations depending on their sizes. Files larger than 1MB are written to **LargeFiles.txt**, while others go to **SmallFiles.txt**:

```
Get-ChildItem "C:\Files" | ForEach-Object {
    if ($_.Length -gt 1MB) {
        $_ | Out-File "C:\LargeFiles.txt" -Append
    } else {
        $_ | Out-File "C:\SmallFiles.txt" -Append
    }
}
```

The following figure shows both output files opened and side by side for comparison:

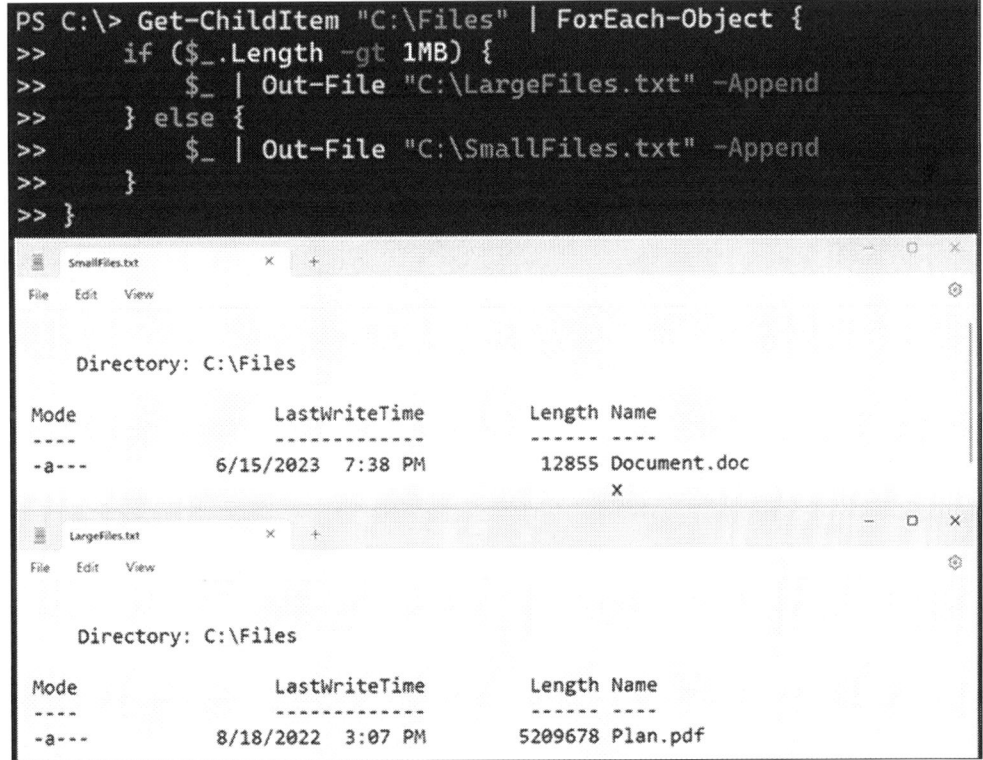

Figure 9.8: Side by side comparison

In the following example, the script validates a list of user directories and divides the output into two separate files that indicate whether each user directory exists:

```
$users = Get-Content "C:\UsersList.txt"
foreach ($user in $users) {
    $status = Test-Path "C:\Users\$user"
    $output = "$user exists: $status"
    if ($status) {
        $output | Out-File "C:\ExistingUsers.txt" -Append
    } else {
        $output | Out-File "C:\NonExistingUsers.txt" -Append
    }
}
```

Loop constructs allow for data manipulation and execution control within PowerShell scripts. The example below uses a switch statement within a loop to categorize files by their extensions and directs them to corresponding output files:

```
$items = Get-ChildItem "C:\Files"
foreach ($item in $items) {
    switch ($item.Extension) {
        ".txt" { $item | Out-File "C:\TextFiles.txt" -Append }
        ".log" { $item | Out-File "C:\LogFiles.txt" -Append }
        default { $item | Out-File "C:\OtherFiles.txt" -Append }
    }
}
```

Combining loops, conditions, and multiple output paths ensures that your scripts are efficient and intelligent in segregating and directing data outputs.

Examples of scripts with multiple output paths

The following three PowerShell scripts show varying combinations of constructs when using multiple output paths.

The first example is handy for system administrators who must separate logs based on their types and send them to different directories:

```
$errorLogPath = "C:\Logs\ErrorLogs\"

$infoLogPath = "C:\Logs\InfoLogs\"

Get-Content "C:\Logs\AllLogs.log" | ForEach-Object {

    if ($_ -match "ERROR") {

        Add-Content -Path ($errorLogPath + "errors.log") -Value $_

    } elseif ($_ -match "INFO") {

        Add-Content -Path ($infoLogPath + "info.log") -Value $_

    }

}
```

The second example exports user data to separate CSV files based on their departments:

```
$users = Get-ADUser -Filter *

$users | ForEach-Object {

    $department = $_.Department

    if ($department) {

        $_ | Export-Csv "C:\Users\$department-users.csv" -NoTypeInformation
        -Append

    } else {

        $_ | Export-Csv "C:\Users\NoDepartment-users.csv"
        -NoTypeInformation -Append

    }
```

}

The final example helps sort files in a directory into separate folders based on their file extensions:

```
$srcDir = "C:\UnsortedFiles\"

$fileTypes = @("*.txt", "*.jpg", "*.pdf")

$fileTypes | ForEach-Object {
    $files = Get-ChildItem -Path $srcDir -Filter $_
    $fileType = $_.TrimStart('*')
    $destDir = "C:\SortedFiles\$fileType"

    if (!(Test-Path $destDir)) {
        New-Item -ItemType Directory -Path $destDir
    }

    $files | Move-Item -Destination $destDir
}
```

Each example demonstrates how to utilize multiple output paths effectively in real-world scenarios using PowerShell. They help organize and manage data efficiently, promoting cleaner and more structured data handling.

Conclusion

This chapter explained how to precisely and flexibly direct and manipulate script outputs. You also learned to use output redirection operators to create commands that produce varied outputs. You also reviewed combining piping with output redirection operators, techniques directing outputs to multiple destinations, and methods of splitting and appending outputs. Lastly, you utilized conditional statements and loops to customize output destinations, offering a tailored approach to handling script results.

The next chapter will explore PowerShell Remoting using **Windows Remote Management (WinRM)** and the Invoke-Command PowerShell cmdlet.

CHAPTER 10
PowerShell Remoting, WinRM, and the Invoke-Command

Introduction

This chapter will teach you about PowerShell remoting for managing and scripting remote computers. You begin by exploring what PowerShell remoting is. You will then dive into **Windows Remote Management (WinRM)**, illustrating its role within PowerShell remoting. You will review the configurations, functionalities, and implications and understand the security implications of PowerShell remoting. You will step through the configuration for remoting in both Windows and Linux environments. Once completed, you will learn how to use `New-PSSession` and `Enter-PSSession` to remotely connect to both Windows and Linux systems seamlessly. Lastly, you will review using the Invoke-Command in executing commands on remote computers.

Structure

In this chapter, we will cover the following topics:
- What is PowerShell remoting?
- Understanding WinRM and its role in PowerShell remoting
- Understanding the security implications of PowerShell remoting
- Configure remoting within Windows

- Configure remoting within Linux
- Creating and using a remote session with New-PSSession and Enter-PSSession
- Remotely connect to Windows and Linux using PowerShell
- Using Invoke-Command to execute commands on remote computer

Objectives

By the end of this chapter, you will have reviewed PowerShell remoting, a vital skill set for system administration and automation. You will gain knowledge of WinRM and understand its architecture, configuration, and security implications. You will also have learned about managing and optimizing remote sessions with **New-PSSession** and **Enter-PSSession**, as well as using the **Invoke-Command**. This chapter will explain and help you understand PowerShell remoting.

What is PowerShell remoting?

For network administration and system management, efficiency and scalability are two pivotal elements defining any administrative operation's success. PowerShell remoting is significant because it allows remote management of Windows computers from a command-line interface. This feature can simplify system administration, configuration management, and troubleshooting tasks. PowerShell remoting will enable administrators to execute PowerShell commands on a remote machine or a set of remote machines. It is like having the ability to be everywhere at once, ensuring that systems, irrespective of their location, are operating optimally and are configured correctly. You can establish a session with a remote machine by creating a communication channel to send and execute commands and return their results to the initiating machine.

The cornerstone of PowerShell remoting is its communication protocol. Within Windows, this is called WinRM. WinRM is a firewall-friendly protocol PowerShell remoting uses to negotiate connections and transport data. It is a Microsoft implementation of WS-Management Protocol, based on **Simple Object Access Protocol (SOAP)**. Secure Shell or **Secure Socket Shell (SSH)** is available for Linux and Windows platforms and provides a multiplatform PowerShell remoting where WinRM is unavailable. The seamless integration across various platforms boosts the versatility of PowerShell, making it a tool for Windows administrators and administrators of heterogeneous environments.

Stringent security protocols enclose every command executed during each session to ensure confidentiality, integrity, and availability. The pursuit of efficiency and scalability does not compromise security. Configuring PowerShell Remoting is relatively straightforward. It involves setting up both the initiating and receiving machines to ensure they have the appropriate protocol and permissions. It ensures that only authorized personnel can execute remote commands, adding a layer of security.

Utilizing PowerShell remoting extends beyond singular command execution. It involves creating scripts to execute remotely. You can use these scripts for many administrative tasks, including system updates, configuration changes, and so on. The power to execute complex administrative tasks from a central location eliminates the need for physical presence, saving time and resources. The interactive sessions offered by PowerShell Remoting are another aspect worth noting. Administrators can create a session with a remote machine and execute commands interactively, allowing real-time administration. It is vital for tasks requiring immediate feedback, ensuring administrators can make informed decisions promptly. Despite the complexity of its operations and the security protocols it adheres to, using PowerShell Remoting is intuitive. The commands are straightforward, and the feedback is immediate, ensuring that novice or experienced administrators can confidently execute remote commands.

Some everyday use cases for using PowerShell remoting are:

- **System updates and patch management**: PowerShell remoting can automate updating Windows operating systems across a network. Administrators can initiate, monitor, and complete updates remotely, ensuring that all systems use the latest security patches and feature updates.
- **Configuration management:** On the Linux front, PowerShell remoting can modify configuration files, adjust system settings, or tune application configurations remotely, ensuring that every system adheres to the desired configurations and standards.
- **Real-time monitoring and reporting:** Admins can employ PowerShell remoting to gather real-time data on system performance, application behavior, and user activity across multiple Windows systems.
- **User and permission management:** User management tasks like adding, modifying, or deleting users and groups and setting permissions can be performed on multiple Linux systems simultaneously using PowerShell remoting, ensuring uniform access controls.
- **Automated deployments:** Deploying software and applications across a fleet of Windows machines is streamlined with PowerShell remoting. Admins can push installation commands, configure software, and validate installations remotely.

Understanding WinRM and its role in PowerShell remoting

Windows Remote Management (WinRM) is an essential component of the Microsoft model for managing and maintaining Windows-based machines remotely. It operates as a protocol that facilitates remote management, allowing system administrators to interact with remote systems efficiently, executing commands and managing configuration across a network. This powerful tool stems from implementing the WS-Management protocol, a standard SOAP-based, firewall-friendly protocol developed to ensure hardware and operating systems interoperability.

The role of WinRM in PowerShell remoting is vital. It acts as the communication gateway between the local machine and the remote server. With the facilitation of WinRM, administrators can invoke PowerShell commands on remote machines, making it an essential tool for managing a network of Windows-based systems.

Security is a cornerstone in the design and operation of WinRM. It supports various authentication mechanisms, including Basic, Digest, Certificate, and Kerberos authentication, offering flexibility while ensuring the secure execution of commands. The integration of encryption ensures that data transmitted between the local and remote machine is safeguarded against unauthorized access, enhancing the security posture of remote management.

WinRM is typically pre-installed on most modern Windows operating systems. However, it requires configuration to be functional. Enabling WinRM is often as simple as executing a single command that starts the service and sets it up to start automatically with the system. This ease of setup simplifies preparing a Windows machine for remote management. With WinRM, the scalability and manageability of IT infrastructures are profoundly enhanced. System administrators can script commands and automate routine tasks across numerous machines from a central location. This capability not only saves time but also ensures consistency in the execution of commands, configuration management, and system updates. Avoiding manual and per-machine management reduces the risk of errors and enhances operational efficiency.

Furthermore, WinRM is not limited to PowerShell scripting alone. It provides an interface for other management protocols and scripting languages. This versatility ensures that it caters to various administrative needs and preferences. Whether it is a simple task of retrieving system information or a complex configuration management routine, WinRM is a reliable and flexible tool.

The integration of WinRM and PowerShell is seamless. When you initiate a PowerShell remote command, WinRM facilitates the communication between the local machine and the remote server. It provides secure and efficient delivery of commands and the return of results. This integration ensures the power and flexibility of PowerShell to extend not just to the local machine but across a network of systems.

WinRM also plays a vital role in enabling session connectivity in PowerShell. With sessions, administrators can establish persistent connections to remote machines, allowing for the execution of multiple commands over the same connection. This functionality is particularly beneficial for tasks that require numerous command executions, as it enhances efficiency and reduces the overhead associated with establishing new connections for each command. Its security, efficiency, and flexibility make it a staple for Windows system administrators.

Understanding the security implications of PowerShell remoting

When delving into PowerShell remoting, addressing the security aspects surrounding this powerful functionality is paramount. Security is an inherent concern, given that PowerShell remoting entails executing commands and scripts on remote machines, possibly across vast networks. The ability to control systems remotely necessitates robust security protocols to mitigate potential vulnerabilities and unauthorized access. One of the primary security facets of PowerShell remoting is authentication. Authentication ensures that the individual or system initiating the remote session is verified and authorized to access the target machine. PowerShell remoting supports various authentication protocols, including Kerberos, NTLM, and SSL, each offering different levels of security and operational characteristics that align with diverse network environments and security requirements. Let us take a look at them:

- **Kerberos** is a network authentication protocol that uses secret-key cryptography to securely verify the identities of users, services, or devices in a computer network.
- **New Technology LAN Manager** (**NTLM**) is a suite of Microsoft security protocols intended to provide authentication, integrity, and confidentiality to users.
- **Secure Sockets Layer** (**SSL**) is a technology that encrypts data sent between websites and applications, ensuring secure and private communication.

The most secure authentication protocol for PowerShell remoting is Kerberos. Kerberos uses mutual authentication, which means the client and remote computers must prove their identity to each other. It uses a trusted third party called a **Key Distribution Center** (**KDC**). If Kerberos is not available, PowerShell remoting will use NTLM authentication. NTLM is less secure than Kerberos because it does not use mutual authentication. However, in most cases, NTLM is still a secure way to authenticate users. You can also use Secure Shell or Secure Socket Shell authentication for PowerShell remoting. SSH is a secure protocol often used for remote access to Linux and Unix systems. However, Kerberos or NTLM are more common for PowerShell remoting than SSH. Once a user has authenticated, they can run PowerShell commands on the remote computer as if sitting in front of it.

PowerShell remoting ensures secure transmission of data and commands by incorporating encryption protocols. Networks are susceptible to interception and eavesdropping, which can compromise sensitive data. Encryption in PowerShell remoting obfuscates the data, making it unintelligible to unauthorized entities. It encrypts all communication between the client and remote computers to enhance security. Kerberos or NTLM authentication enables encryption by default. However, SSH authentication does not have encryption enabled by default. To enable encryption for SSH authentication, use the `-UseSSL` parameter when connecting to the remote computer.

Authorization is crucial in defining what authenticated users can do once they gain access. It ensures that users have specific permissions aligned with their roles and responsibilities. This granular control ensures that users can only execute actions within their defined scope, reducing the risk of misuse or accidental system disruptions.

Role-Based Access Control (RBAC) further enhances the security landscape of PowerShell remoting. It allows administrators to assign roles to users based on their job requirements. Each role has specific permissions and restrictions, ensuring users can execute only the tasks aligned with their roles. RBAC provides a structured and manageable approach to controlling access and permissions across complex network environments.

PowerShell remoting also enforces security through logging and auditing. It logs every action executed via remoting, providing a trail of activities. These logs are instrumental in auditing, where administrators can review actions to ensure compliance with organizational policies. During security incidents, logs provide insights into actions, facilitating efficient incident response and resolution.

PowerShell execution policies are another layer of defense. Execution policies determine the conditions under which PowerShell scripts are allowed to run. By setting restrictive policies, administrators can prevent the execution of unauthorized or potentially harmful scripts, adding an extra layer of security to the remoting environment. It is important to note that security concerns also impact the configuration of WinRM. Properly securing WinRM is crucial, given its role in enabling remote access. It involves limiting the IP addresses that can initiate remote sessions and using secure communication protocols.

Security in PowerShell remoting is not just about technological controls. Training and awareness among users and administrators are pivotal. Understanding the potential risks, best practices, and appropriate use of remoting ensures that human factors do not become the weak link in the security chain. Education empowers users to act as additional layers of defense, enhancing the overall security posture. Understanding the security implications of PowerShell remoting provides a foundation for its safe and effective use. By considering authentication, encryption, authorization, role-based access control, logging, and execution policies, you can create a secure environment for remoting.

Configure remoting within Windows

PowerShell remoting is an essential feature that allows administrators to manage Windows machines remotely, executing commands and scripts as if they were physically on the machine. Enabling remoting is a straightforward process, but it needs to be approached with a clear understanding of the involved steps and potential security implications to ensure a safe and secure configuration.

The first step in configuring PowerShell remoting on a Windows machine is to ensure the **Windows Remote Management (WinRM)** service is installed and running. It plays a pivotal role in creating and managing remoting sessions.

To enable PowerShell remoting on a Windows Client such as Windows 10 or 11, execute **Enable-PSRemoting**. The execution of **Enable-PSRemoting** runs the **Set-WSManQuickConfig** command which performs the required tasks. To see this, you can execute **Set-WSManQuickConfig**.

The following figure displays the configuration steps performed as part of the **Set-WSManQuickConfig** configuration:

```
WinRM Quick Configuration
Running the Set-WSManQuickConfig command has significant security implications, as it enables remote
management through the WinRM service on this computer.
This command:
    1. Checks whether the WinRM service is running. If the WinRM service is not running, the service is
 started.
    2. Sets the WinRM service startup type to automatic.
    3. Creates a listener to accept requests on any IP address. By default, the transport is HTTP.
    4. Enables a firewall exception for WS-Management traffic.
    5. Enables Kerberos and Negotiate service authentication.
Do you want to enable remote management through the WinRM service on this computer?
```

Figure 10.1: Execution of Set-WSManQuickConfig and displaying options

If you are using a firewall, you must open port 5985 (TCP) for incoming traffic.

Check if WinRM is enabled by executing **Get-Service WinRM**.

It is important to note that for the **Enable-PSRemoting** and **Set-WSManQuickConfig** to complete successfully, the network connection type needs setting to either domain or private, not public. You can do this within Windows itself using inbuilt network adapter tools or using PowerShell. If the client machine or server is part of a domain then this is not a problem. To check the current setting, you can execute

Get-NetConnectionProfile which displays the current setting.

The following figure displays the current network connection profile:

```
Name                        : Network
InterfaceAlias              : Ethernet
InterfaceIndex              : 6
NetworkCategory             : Public
DomainAuthenticationKind    : None
IPv4Connectivity            : Internet
IPv6Connectivity            : NoTraffic
```

Figure 10.2: Current network connection profile

You set the connection profile by executing the following command:

`Set-NetConnectionProfile -InterfaceAlias Ethernet -NetworkCategory Private`

With the profile set correctly, you can then execute **Enable-PSRemoting** successfully.

The following figure displays the status of the WinRM service after the successful execution of **Enable-PSRemoting**:

```
PS C:\> Get-Service WinRM

Status   Name        DisplayName
------   ----        -----------
Running  WinRM       Windows Remote Management (WS-Managem...
```

Figure 10.3: Viewing status of the WinRM service

If it did not work and is showing is not enabled, activate it using the following command:

`Enable-PSRemoting -Force`

The **-Force** parameter ensures that the action proceeds without prompting for confirmation, making the process seamless. This command starts the WinRM service and sets it to auto-start with your system.

The next phase is configuring the listener. A listener is essential to accept requests from the remote machines. By default, PowerShell remoting allows connections from machines in the same domain. To enable cross-domain connections, you must configure the listener to accept requests from other domains, ensuring that the necessary firewall rules are in place to allow traffic through. You can check the existing listeners using:

`winrm e winrm/config/listener`

If you have not configured a listener to meet your requirements, you can create one using the following command:

`winrm quickconfig`

This command starts the service, sets it to auto-start, and creates a listener on HTTP. Remember, you do not need to create the listener if you use domain-joined clients and servers. With the infrastructure in place, you need to consider who has permission to connect remotely. By default, only members of the administrators group have this ability. You can add users to this group, or if you prefer a more granular approach, use the **Set-PSSessionConfiguration** cmdlet to allow specific users to create remote sessions.

To test the configuration, you can use the **Enter-PSSession** cmdlet, specifying the computer name of the remote machine. For example, **Enter-PSSession -ComputerName Computer** will initiate a remote session with **Computer**:

Enter-PSSession -ComputerName locahost

The following figure displays the connected prompt for the local computer after connecting using PowerShell remoting:

```
PS C:\> Enter-PSSession -ComputerName localhost
[localhost]: PS C:\>
```

Figure 10.4: Connecting to the local computer using PowerShell remoting

Beyond individual machines, configuring remoting in a network or domain environment can also be accomplished with Group Policy. It allows administrators to manage the configurations centrally, ensuring uniformity and compliance across all machines in the network or domain.

Configure remoting within Linux

PowerShell remoting in Linux operates differently than in Windows, but it still provides the powerful capability to execute commands and scripts on remote Linux machines. This feature is crucial for admins and developers who manage cross-platform environments, aiding in seamless operations and maintenance. PowerShell remoting in Linux uses SSH, a protocol granting secure access to remote machines.

The first step to enable PowerShell remoting within Linux involves installing PowerShell. If not installed, this can be done by accessing the releases on GitHub or using package managers like APT or YUM, depending on your Linux distribution. You must install PowerShell to execute the subsequent steps. Next, it is essential to have SSH installed and configured on your system. SSH is a protocol used for secure communications over an unsecured network. You can use the command **ssh -V** to verify SSH installation, which should return the installed version of SSH. If you do not have SSH, use the package manager pertinent to your Linux distribution to install it. The following commands install SSH services within Ubuntu Linux:

sudo apt update

```
sudo apt install openssh-server

sudo systemctl status ssh

sudo systemctl start ssh

sudo systemctl enable ssh

sudo ufw allow ssh
```

The following figure displays installing SSH on Ubuntu Linux:

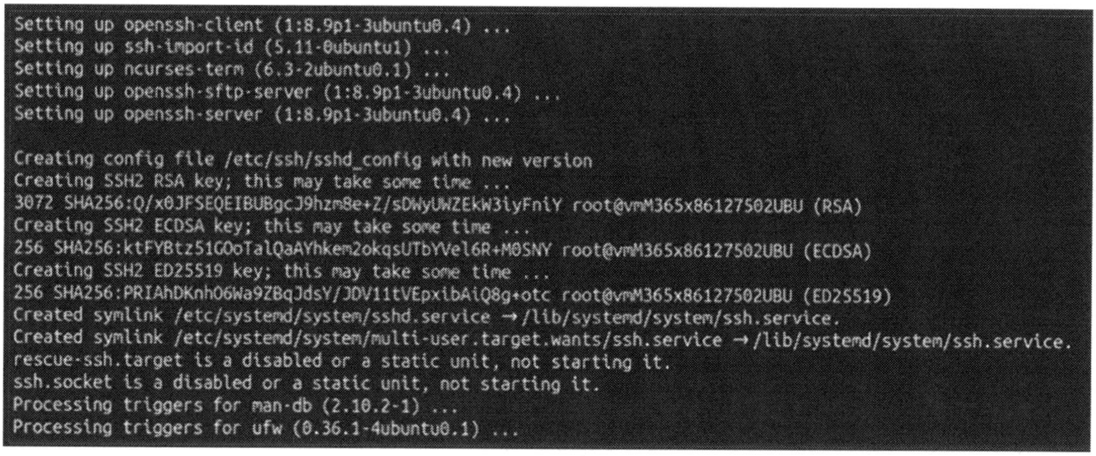

Figure 10.5: Installing SSH on Ubuntu Linux

SSH configuration involves editing the SSHD config file to allow remote access. This process may vary depending on the Linux distribution in use. However, generally, you will need to open and edit the SSH daemon's config file to ensure that password authentication and other necessary settings are enabled. Permission management is another critical aspect to consider. Ensure to add the users who need remote access to the SSH **allowed** list. It can typically be done by editing the **sshd_config** file, ensuring that users who require access are permitted, thus enabling a secure yet flexible access mechanism. The fifth step is to restart the SSH service to apply the changes made in the configuration. The exact command may vary, but typically, it could be **systemctl restart sshd** or **service ssh restart**. It ensures all configurations are set and ready for secure remote connections:

```
systemctl restart sshd

service ssh restart
```

The **Enter-PSSession** cmdlet initiates a remote session, like Windows. Since Linux uses SSH, you will need to specify the SSH parameters, including the remote machine's username and hostname/IP address. For example:

```
Enter-PSSession -HostName <IP> -UserName <UserName> -SSHTransport
```

The following figure displays connecting to Ubuntu Linux over SSH:

```
PS C:\> Enter-PSSession -HostName "40.76.211.20" -UserName "_m365x86127502adm" -SSHTransport
_m365x86127502adm@40.76.211.20's password:
[40.76.211.20]: PS /home/_m365x86127502adm>
```

Figure 10.6: Connecting to Ubuntu Linux over SSH

When the remoting is over SSH, the **-SSHTransport** parameter is crucial as it tells PowerShell to use SSH for the remoting transport. It contrasts with Windows remoting, which utilizes WinRM. Ensuring this parameter is included is vital for successful PowerShell remoting in Linux environments.

Testing the configuration is always a good practice. Try executing a few commands to ensure the remoting session is functional and the commands return the expected outputs. A simple **Get-Process** can confirm the accuracy of the processes fetched from the remote machine. Security should be at the forefront of any remote operation:

```
Get-Process
```

The following figure displays running processes within a PowerShell remote session:

```
[40.76.211.20]: PS /home/_m365x86127502adm> Get-Process

NPM(K)    PM(M)     WS(M)     CPU(s)      Id  SI ProcessName
------    -----     -----     ------      --  -- -----------
     0     0.00      5.30       0.00   16009 ..08 (sd-pam)
     0     0.00      5.30       0.00   16561 ..60 (sd-pam)
     0     0.00      9.05       0.10     651 651 accounts-daemon
     0     0.00      2.25       0.01     707 707 agetty
     0     0.00      1.78       0.00     728 728 agetty
     0     0.00      0.00       0.00      82   0 ata_sff
     0     0.00      2.20       0.00     686 686 atd
     0     0.00      2.00       0.03    2783 ..83 audispd
     0     0.00      2.18       0.04    2265 ..65 auditd
     0     0.00      0.00       0.00    2769   0 audit_prune_tre
     0     0.00     13.93       0.05   16085 ..85 bash
     0     0.00     13.97       0.04   16507 ..07 bash
     0     0.00      0.00       0.00      80   0 blkcg_punt_bio
     0     0.00      0.56       0.00     275   0 bpfilter_umh
     0     0.00      2.57       0.43     682 681 chronyd
     0     0.00      0.19       0.00     717 681 chronyd
     0     0.00      0.00       0.00      17   0 cpuhp/0
     0     0.00      0.00       0.00      18   0 cpuhp/1
     0     0.00      2.71       0.00     659 659 cron
     0     0.00      0.00       0.00     245   0 cryptd
     0     0.00     13.27       0.45     660 660 dbus-daemon
     0     0.00      0.00       0.00      88   0 devfreq_wq
     0     0.00      0.00       0.00      94   0 ecryptfs-kthrea
     0     0.00      0.00       0.00      84   0 edac-poller
     0     0.00      0.00       0.00     136   0 ext4-rsv-conver
     0     0.00      0.00       0.00     611   0 ext4-rsv-conver
     0     0.00      0.00       0.04     122   0 hv_balloon
     0     0.00      3.09       0.75     280 280 hv_kvp_daemon
     0     0.00      0.00       0.00      86   0 hv_pri_chan
```

Figure 10.7: Executing Get-Process within Linux using PowerShell Remoting

With SSH, you benefit from built-in encryption, ensuring secure data in transit. However, it is also wise to keep the SSH and PowerShell versions updated to mitigate vulnerabilities and enhance the security stature of the remote environment.

Creating and using a remote session with New-PSSession and Enter-PSSession

PowerShell remoting allows administrators to manage remote systems efficiently, executing scripts and commands on remote servers and computers. Two critical cmdlets enabling this capability are **New-PSSession** and **Enter-PSSession**. They facilitate creating and managing remote sessions, necessary in today's diverse and distributed computing environments.

The **New-PSSession** cmdlet has parameters that streamline new remoting sessions' creation. The **-ComputerName** parameter, akin to its counterpart in **Enter-PSSession**, designates the target computer. The **-Credential** parameter adeptly handles user authentication, while the **-Authentication** parameter empowers users to select an appropriate authentication protocol, with Negotiate being the default. For users keen on organization and easy identification, the **-Name** parameter allows the allocation of distinct names to sessions. In environments where managing multiple connections is a norm, the **-ThrottleLimit** parameter caps the number of concurrent connections, ensuring optimal performance and manageability. With **New-PSSession**, you can establish a persistent connection to a remote machine. This cmdlet creates a session, also referred to as a **PSSession**, on a local or remote computer. The session contains the environment wherein PowerShell runs an essential foundation for executing commands remotely. The initial command to create a new session could look like **New-PSSession -ComputerName Computer**. It initiates a session, but it is essential to understand each part of this cmdlet to utilize it effectively. The following code creates a new PowerShell remote session to the target computer:

```
$credential = Get-Credential

New-PSSession -ComputerName Computer -Credential $credential
```

The following figure displays the creation of a new PowerShell remote session:

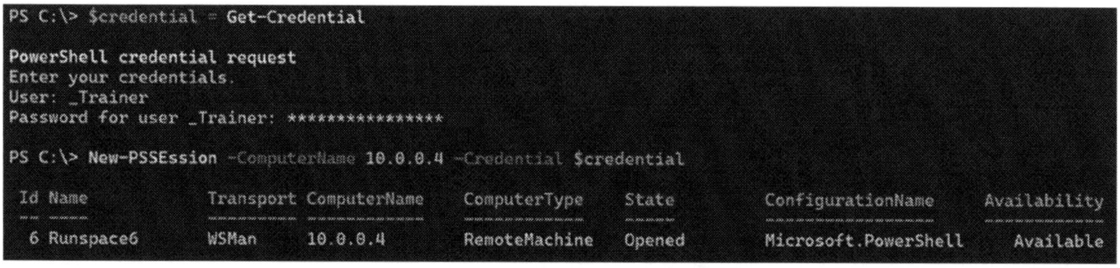

Figure 10.8: Create a new remote PowerShell session

The **-ComputerName** parameter specifies the remote computer. You can input the computer's name or IP address. It is not just a placeholder but a parameter that directs the session to the exact machine required, allowing you to target specific systems in your network.

Now, having created a session, you would want to enter it. That is where **Enter-PSSession** comes in. This cmdlet allows you to enter an interactive session with the remote machine. The **Enter-PSSession** cmdlet is integral for initiating a PowerShell remoting session, and it comes equipped with a set of useful parameters to tailor the session according to the user's needs. The **-ComputerName** parameter is pivotal, accepting the name or IP address of the target machine to establish a connection. For secure access, the **-Credential** parameter allows the incorporation of username and password, ensuring authenticated entry into the session. Users with an existing session can swiftly re-enter using the **-Session** parameter, while the **-Name** parameter offers the convenience of assigning a friendly identifier to each session for easy navigation. Executing the following command will let you enter the interactive session:

```
$credential = Get-Credential

Enter-PSSession -ComputerName Computer -Credential $credential
```

The following figure displays entering a PowerShell remote session:

```
PS C:\> $credential = Get-Credential

PowerShell credential request
Enter your credentials.
User: _Trainer
Password for user _Trainer: ****************

PS C:\> Enter-PSSession -ComputerName 10.0.0.4 -Credential $credential
[10.0.0.4]: PS C:\Users\_Trainer\Documents>
```

Figure 10.9: Enter a remote PowerShell session

In the following example, a new session to a remote computer named **Computer** is created and stored in the **$session** variable:

```
$session = New-PSSession -ComputerName "Computer"
```

To ensure security, you can create an interactive remoting session to **Computer**, prompting the user for credentials:

```
Enter-PSSession `
    -ComputerName "Computer" `
    -Credential (Get-Credential)
```

You also can set the protocol used for the remote connection. Using the Negotiate authentication protocol with the following code, you can create a new session:

```
$session = New-PSSession `
    -ComputerName "Computer" `
    -Authentication Negotiate `
    -Credential (Get-Credential)
```

Now you are connected and inside the environment, ready to execute commands as if you were physically at the machine. You can remotely manage, configure, and administer various systems simultaneously across multiple computers using PowerShell Remoting. To manage multiple sessions, **Get-PSSession** can list all active sessions, as shown:

```
Get-PSSession
```

The following figure displays existing active PowerShell remote sessions:

```
PS C:\> Get-PSSession

Id Name        Transport ComputerName  ComputerType  State   ConfigurationName     Availability
-- ----        --------- ------------  ------------  -----   -----------------     ------------
 6 Runspace6   WSMan     10.0.0.4      RemoteMachine Opened  Microsoft.PowerShell     Available
 9 Runspace9   WSMan     10.0.0.4      RemoteMachine Opened  Microsoft.PowerShell     Available
10 Runspace10  WSMan     10.0.0.4      RemoteMachine Opened  Microsoft.PowerShell     Available
12 Runspace11  SSH       40.76.211.20  RemoteMachine Opened  DefaultShell             Available
```

Figure 10.10: List active remote sessions

It gives you an overview, ensuring you are aware of all connections enhancing manageability and security. You can filter and select sessions based on criteria like computer name or ID. This feature is handy in environments with numerous ongoing sessions, aiding the organization and selection process.

With an established connection, executing commands is straightforward. Whether fetching a directory listing with **Get-ChildItem** or stopping a specific service, it is as if you are running the commands on the local machine. **Enter-PSSession** facilitates real-time interaction. Every command executes in real-time, and the system immediately relays the responses, offering a live, interactive experience. Use a simple

Exit-PSSession command to exit the session. It ensures that the session is closed correctly, maintaining the integrity and security of the remote machine. Every session created with **New-PSSession** is reusable. You can disconnect and reconnect to the sessions, a handy feature for ongoing tasks or managing long-term connections. The **Disconnect-PSSession** cmdlet helps in disconnecting from the session without entirely terminating it. It allows for reconnection, making it a flexible option for intermittent tasks.

Security is integral in remoting. The system authenticates every session and checks permissions. Utilizing secure connections ensures the integrity and confidentiality of the data exchanged. PowerShell supports several authentication mechanisms to ensure only authorized personnel can create and enter sessions, underscoring the security foundation integral to remoting. You can script the PowerShell remoting commands. Automation scripts can initiate, manage, and close sessions, driving efficiency and reducing the manual overhead involved in remote system management. Understanding **New-PSSession** and **Enter-PSSession** is fundamental to leveraging PowerShell's remoting capabilities.

Remotely connecting to Windows and Linux using PowerShell

Being able to manage both Windows and Linux systems remotely is a vital skill for administrators. PowerShell provides powerful tools to accomplish this task. With PowerShell's remoting feature, administrators can execute commands and scripts on remote systems as if they were local. This feature is not limited to Windows but extends to Linux systems, making PowerShell an extremely versatile tool for cross-platform administration.

The simplest way to initiate a remote PowerShell session to a Windows machine is by using the **Enter-PSSession** cmdlet, followed by the **-ComputerName** parameter to specify the target machine:

```
Enter-PSSession `
    -ComputerName "Computer" `
    -Credential (Get-Credential)
```

Alternatively, you can create a new session using the **New-PSSession** cmdlet and then enter the session. This two-step process is beneficial for managing multiple sessions:

```
$session = New-PSSession `
        -ComputerName "Computer" `
    -Credential (Get-Credential)
Enter-PSSession -Session $session
```

For easier management, you can assign a friendly name to your sessions using the **-Name** parameter when creating a new session:

```
New-PSSession `
```

```
    -ComputerName "Computer" `

    -Name "Session" `

    -Credential (Get-Credential)
```

`Enter-PSSession -Name "Session"`

The following figure connects to a specific Windows PowerShell remote session by name:

```
PS C:\> $session = New-PSSession -ComputerName 10.0.0.4 -Credential $credential
PS C:\>
PS C:\> $session

Id Name            Transport ComputerName    ComputerType    State    ConfigurationName     Availability
-- ----            --------- ------------    ------------    -----    -----------------     ------------
14 Runspace14      WSMan     10.0.0.4        RemoteMachine   Opened   Microsoft.PowerShell     Available

PS C:\>
PS C:\> Enter-PSSession -Session $session
[10.0.0.4]: PS C:\Users\_Trainer\Documents>
```

Figure 10.11 Create and then connect to the PowerShell Remote Session

The **-ComputerName** parameter can also accept IP addresses, offering another way to connect if the hostname is unavailable:

```
Enter-PSSession `

    -ComputerName "192.168.1.101" `

    -Credential (Get-Credential)
```

There are multiple ways to connect to a Windows system through PowerShell remoting. Each of these methods has its own set of benefits. PowerShell has covered whether you need simplicity, better management, or alternative addressing methods. PowerShell is cross-platform and even supports Linux, thanks to SSH support integration. The cmdlets used in this case are like those for Windows. However, there are additional parameters that are specific to SSH.

Using **Enter-PSSession** with the **-SSHTransport** parameter facilitates a direct connection via SSH:

```
Enter-PSSession `

    -HostName "Linux" `

    -UserName "root" `

    -SSHTransport
```

When using **New-PSSession** with SSH, transport is a versatile option for Linux and allows passing or a username for the connection:

```
$session = New-PSSession `

        -HostName "Linux" `

        -UserName "root" `

        -SSHTransport

Enter-PSSession -Session $session
```

The following figure connects to a specific Linux PowerShell remote session by name:

```
PS C:\> $session = New-PSSession -HostName "40.76.211.20" -UserName "_m365x86127502adm" -SSHTransport
_m365x86127502adm@40.76.211.20's password:
PS C:\>
PS C:\> $session

 Id Name            Transport ComputerName  ComputerType   State    ConfigurationName    Availability
 -- ----            --------- ------------  ------------   -----    -----------------    ------------
 19 Runspace18      SSH       40.76.211.20  RemoteMachine  Opened   DefaultShell            Available

PS C:\>
PS C:\>
PS C:\> Enter-PSSession -Session $session
[40.76.211.20]: PS /home/_m365x86127502adm>
```

Figure 10.12: Create and then connect to the PowerShell Remote Session

To ensure a successful connection, you can specify a different SSH port with the **-Port** parameter:

```
$session = Enter-PSSession `

        -HostName "Linux" `

        -UserName "root" `

        -Port 2222 `

        -SSHTransport

Enter-PSSession -Session $session
```

The following figure connects to a specific Linux PowerShell remote with a specified port:

```
PS C:\> $session = New-PSSession -HostName "40.76.211.20" -UserName "_m365x86127502adm" -SSHTransport -Port 2222
_m365x86127502adm@40.76.211.20's password:
PS C:\>
PS C:\>
PS C:\> $session

 Id Name            Transport ComputerName  ComputerType   State    ConfigurationName    Availability
 -- ----            --------- ------------  ------------   -----    -----------------    ------------
 30 Runspace29      SSH       40.76.211.20  RemoteMachine  Opened   DefaultShell            Available

PS C:\>
PS C:\>
PS C:\> Enter-PSEssion -Session $session
[40.76.211.20]: PS /home/_m365x86127502adm>
```

Figure 10.13: Connect to the PowerShell Remote Session over SSH with a specific port

Like Windows systems, Linux systems can also connect using IP addresses:

```
Enter-PSSession `
    -HostName "192.168.1.102" `
    -UserName "root" `
    -SSHTransport
```

A practical application of PowerShell remoting in Windows is retrieving detailed system information remotely. The **Invoke-Command** cmdlet is perfect for this task:

```
$credential = Get-Credential

Invoke-Command `
    -ComputerName "Computer" `
    -ScriptBlock {Get-ComputerInfo} `
    -Credential $credential
```

The following figure connects to a Remote Windows Computer and Retrieve Computer Information:

```
PS C:\> Invoke-Command -ComputerName 10.0.0.4 -ScriptBlock {Get-ComputerInfo} -Credential $credential

PSComputerName                            : 10.0.0.4
RunspaceId                                : 24f4032a-efc4-4a48-89df-b5cc9db5510d
WindowsBuildLabEx                         : 20348.1.amd64fre.fe_release.210507-1500
WindowsCurrentVersion                     : 6.3
WindowsEditionId                          : ServerTurbine
WindowsInstallationType                   : Server
WindowsInstallDateFromRegistry            : 9/8/2023 2:11:03 PM
WindowsProductId                          : 00446-90000-00000-AA276
WindowsProductName                        : Windows Server 2022 Datacenter Azure Edition
WindowsRegisteredOrganization             :
WindowsRegisteredOwner                    :
WindowsSystemRoot                         : C:\Windows
WindowsVersion                            : 2009
OSDisplayVersion                          : 21H2
BiosCharacteristics                       : {3, 9, 15, 16...}
BiosBIOSVersion                           : {VRTUAL - 1, Hyper-V UEFI Release v4.1, Microsoft - 100032}
BiosBuildNumber                           :
BiosCaption                               : Hyper-V UEFI Release v4.1
BiosCodeSet                               :
BiosCurrentLanguage                       :
BiosDescription                           : Hyper-V UEFI Release v4.1
BiosEmbeddedControllerMajorVersion        : 255
BiosEmbeddedControllerMinorVersion        : 255
BiosFirmwareType                          : Uefi
BiosIdentificationCode                    :
BiosInstallableLanguages                  :
BiosInstallDate                           :
BiosLanguageEdition                       :
BiosListOfLanguages                       :
BiosManufacturer                          : Microsoft Corporation
BiosName                                  : Hyper-V UEFI Release v4.1
BiosOtherTargetOS                         :
BiosPrimaryBIOS                           : True
```

Figure 10.14: Connect to a Remote Windows Computer and retrieve computer information

In a Linux environment, listing all active processes on the system is a common task. PowerShell remoting via SSH makes this task straightforward:

```
Invoke-Command `
    -HostName "Linux" `
    -UserName "root" `
    -SSHTransport `
    -ScriptBlock {ps aux}
```

The following figure connects to a Remote Linux Computer and retrieve running processes:

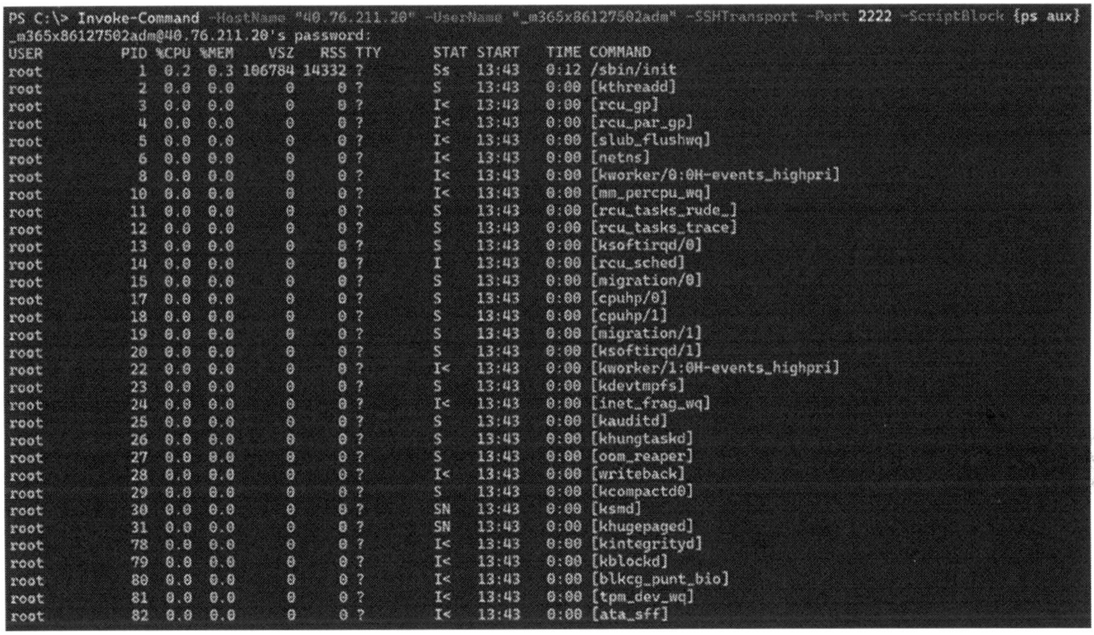

Figure 10.15: Connect to a remote Linux computer and retrieve running processes

These examples highlight the adaptability and versatility of PowerShell remoting across different operating systems. You can execute various tasks on remote machines by leveraging the appropriate cmdlets and parameters, enhancing productivity and system management efficiency.

Using Invoke-Command to execute commands on remote computer

The **Invoke-Command** cmdlet is a cornerstone of PowerShell remoting, enabling administrators to execute scripts or commands on remote computers seamlessly. With a syntax that supports flexibility and adaptability, **Invoke-Command** caters to various scenarios, offering streamlined solutions for complex remote management tasks. It is crucial to understand the set of parameters that accompany **Invoke-Command**. Parameters like **-ComputerName**, **-ScriptBlock**, and **-Credential** play a vital role in the **Invoke-Command**. They determine the target machine, execute the commands, and establish the authentication mechanisms.

For example, the following command fetches the process list from a remote Windows server. The **-ComputerName** parameter identifies the target, and **-ScriptBlock** encapsulates the command for remote execution:

```
Invoke-Command `
    -ComputerName "Server" `
    -ScriptBlock {Get-Process} `
    -Credential (Get-Credential)
```

The **-ScriptBlock** parameter is pivotal, especially when paired with the **Invoke-Command** cmdlet for remote sessions. Understanding its intricacies, uses, and capabilities is essential to leverage PowerShell remoting effectively.

A script block in PowerShell consists of a collection of statements or expressions used as a single unit. Enclosed in curly braces **{}**, a script block can contain valid PowerShell commands. When used with **Invoke-Command**, the **-ScriptBlock** parameter specifies the commands that run on the remote machine, turning it into a powerful tool for executing complex operations remotely.

The beauty of **-ScriptBlock** lies in its ability to execute dynamically. It does not just hold static commands; it encapsulates an entire miniature script that runs on the remote machine. This feature allows administrators to execute complex, multi-line operations remotely, enabling intricate task executions without being physically present on the remote machine.

The following example remotely retrieves a list of all installed services on a remote machine and filters to show only those currently running:

```
Invoke-Command -ComputerName RemoteServer -ScriptBlock {
```

```
    Get-Service | Where-Object {$_.Status -eq 'Running'}
}
```

The following figure displays running services from a remote machine:

```
PS C:\> Invoke-Command -ComputerName 10.0.0.4 -Credential $credential -ScriptBlock {
>>      Get-Service | Where-Object {$_.Status -eq 'Running'}
>> }

Status   Name                DisplayName                            PSComputerName
------   ----                -----------                            --------------
Running  AppXSvc             AppX Deployment Service (AppXSVC)      10.0.0.4
Running  BFE                 Base Filtering Engine                  10.0.0.4
Running  BrokerInfrastruct…  Background Tasks Infrastructure Servi… 10.0.0.4
Running  camsvc              Capability Access Manager Service      10.0.0.4
Running  cbdhsvc_e959d       Clipboard User Service_e959d           10.0.0.4
Running  CDPSvc              Connected Devices Platform Service     10.0.0.4
Running  CDPUserSvc_e959d    Connected Devices Platform User Servi… 10.0.0.4
Running  CertPropSvc         Certificate Propagation                10.0.0.4
Running  CoreMessagingRegi…  CoreMessaging                          10.0.0.4
Running  CryptSvc            Cryptographic Services                 10.0.0.4
Running  DcomLaunch          DCOM Server Process Launcher           10.0.0.4
Running  Dhcp                DHCP Client                            10.0.0.4
Running  DiagTrack           Connected User Experiences and Teleme… 10.0.0.4
Running  DispBrokerDesktop…  Display Policy Service                 10.0.0.4
Running  dmwappushservice    Device Management Wireless Applicatio… 10.0.0.4
Running  Dnscache            DNS Client                             10.0.0.4
Running  DPS                 Diagnostic Policy Service              10.0.0.4
Running  EventLog            Windows Event Log                      10.0.0.4
Running  EventSystem         COM+ Event System                      10.0.0.4
Running  fdPHost             Function Discovery Provider Host       10.0.0.4
Running  FDResPub            Function Discovery Resource Publicati… 10.0.0.4
Running  FontCache           Windows Font Cache Service             10.0.0.4
Running  gpsvc               Group Policy Client                    10.0.0.4
Running  iphlpsvc            IP Helper                              10.0.0.4
Running  KeyIso              CNG Key Isolation                      10.0.0.4
Running  LanmanServer        Server                                 10.0.0.4
Running  LanmanWorkstation   Workstation                            10.0.0.4
Running  lmhosts             TCP/IP NetBIOS Helper                  10.0.0.4
Running  LSM                 Local Session Manager                  10.0.0.4
```

Figure 10.16: Remotely retrieving a list of services filtered to show only those currently running

Integrating variables within a script block amplifies its potential. The **$using** scope modifier allows the use of local variables within a script block during remote execution. This feature ensures dynamic data can be processed and manipulated remotely, fostering adaptability and precision.

The following code remotely creates a folder on a remote machine using a local variable to specify the folder name:

```
$folderName = "PowerShell-is-Great"

Invoke-Command -ComputerName RemoteServer -ScriptBlock {
```

```
    New-Item -Path "C:\Users\Public\$using:folderName" -ItemType Directory

    Write-Host "Folder: $using:foldername created on 10.0.0.4"

}
```

The following figure displays the folder creation on a remote machine using a local variable to specify the folder name:

```
PS C:\> $folderName = "PowerShell-is-Great"
PS C:\> Invoke-Command -ComputerName 10.0.0.4 -Credential $credential -ScriptBlock {
>>     New-Item -Path "C:\Users\_Trainer\Documents\$using:folderName" -ItemType Directory
>>     Write-Host "Folder: $using:foldername created on 10.0.0.4"
>> }

    Directory: C:\Users\_Trainer\Documents

Mode                LastWriteTime         Length Name                                    PSComputerName
----                -------------         ------ ----                                    --------------
                                                                                         10.0.0.4
Folder: PowerShell-is-Great created on 10.0.0.4
```

Figure 10.17: Remotely creating a folder on a Remote Machine using a local variable to specify the folder name

It supports conditional statements, loops, functions, and other advanced PowerShell features. This adaptability ensures that complex tasks, from file manipulations to system diagnostics, can be accomplished remotely, offering versatility and control.

The following code remotely checks disk space and returns a custom object with formatted results:

```
Invoke-Command -ComputerName RemoteServer -ScriptBlock {

    $disk = Get-WmiObject Win32_LogicalDisk `

-Filter "DeviceID='C:'"

[PSCustomObject]@{

        FreeSpaceGB = [math]::Round(($disk.FreeSpace / 1GB), 2)

        TotalSpaceGB = [math]::Round(($disk.Size / 1GB), 2)

        UsedSpaceGB = [math]::Round((($disk.Size - $disk.FreeSpace) / 1GB), 2)

    }

}
```

The following figure displays formatted results from checking disk space:

```
PS C:\> Invoke-Command  -ComputerName 10.0.0.4 -Credential $credential -ScriptBlock {
>>     $disk = Get-WmiObject Win32_LogicalDisk `
>> -Filter "DeviceID='C:'"
>> [PSCustomObject]@{
>>         FreeSpaceGB = [math]::Round(($disk.FreeSpace / 1GB), 2)
>>         TotalSpaceGB = [math]::Round(($disk.Size / 1GB), 2)
>>         UsedSpaceGB = [math]::Round((($disk.Size - $disk.FreeSpace) / 1GB), 2)
>>     }
>> }

FreeSpaceGB    : 115.03
TotalSpaceGB   : 126.45
UsedSpaceGB    : 11.42
PSComputerName : 10.0.0.4
RunspaceId     : 615279f6-3fe7-4f2d-a908-2a809e03b6ce
```

Figure 10.18: Remotely checking disk space and returning a custom object with formatted results

Like Windows, local variables can be leveraged in the Linux environment using the **$using** scope modifier. The following example code displays the contents of a folder within Linux:

$directory = "/etc"

Invoke-Command `

    -HostName "Linux" `

    -UserName "root" `

    -SSHTransport `

    -ScriptBlock {ls $using:directory}

Here, the directory to be listed is specified in a local variable, marking a seamless integration of local and remote command executions.

The following figure displays folder contents by passing the required folder as a variable into the **Invoke-Command** within Linux:

```
PS C:\> $directory = "/etc"
PS C:\> Invoke-Command `
>> -HostName "40.76.211.20" `
>> -UserName "_m365x86127502adm" `
>> -SSHTransport `
>> -Port 2222 `
>> -ScriptBlock {ls $using:directory}
_m365x86127502adm@40.76.211.20's password:
ModemManager
NetworkManager
PackageKit
X11
aadpasswd
adduser.conf
alternatives
apparmor
apparmor.d
apport
apt
at.deny
audisp
audit
bash.bashrc
bash_completion
bash_completion.d
bindresvport.blacklist
binfmt.d
byobu
ca-certificates
ca-certificates.conf
ca-certificates.conf.dpkg-old
calendar
chrony
cifs-utils
```

Figure 10.19: Display the content of a folder within Linux

The **Invoke-Command** supports simple and complex scripting. For example, you could retrieve system information and Active Directory users, create a file with the retrieved information, save it locally on the remote machine, and then save the created file back to the local machine. The **Invoke-Command** is a crucial command for PowerShell remoting, bridging the gap between local and remote execution environments seamlessly. Every parameter, especially **-ScriptBlock**, provides versatility in orchestrating remote tasks.

Conclusion

This chapter explained the complexities of PowerShell remoting. You reviewed Windows Remote Management, learning about its use and security protocols for safeguarding integrity and confidentiality during remote operations. You also configured remoting in Windows and Linux. Then, you utilized the **New-PSSession** and **Enter-PSSession** cmdlets to create remote sessions and use Invoke-Command to execute commands on remote computers precisely and efficiently.

In the next chapter, you will learn how to manage on-premises services using PowerShell.

CHAPTER 11
Managing On-premises Services

Introduction

This chapter provides an in-depth understanding of managing on-premises services using PowerShell. First, you will explore PowerShell commands designed explicitly for on-premises management. Secondly, you will learn to configure and manage Active Directory, user, and group management, making everyday administrative tasks more manageable. Furthermore, you will focus on Active Directory roles and features and understand how to use PowerShell to manage **Domain Name Service (DNS)** and **Dynamic Host Configuration Protocol (DHCP)** services. Additionally, you will learn how to use PowerShell to create and manage file shares and certificates within Windows Server.

Structure

In this chapter, we will cover the following topics:
- Introduction to PowerShell for on-premises management
- Configuring and managing Active Directory
- User and group management
- Managing domain controllers
- Managing DNS and DHCP services

- Creating and managing file shares
- Managing certificates
- Managing server roles and features

Objectives

After reading this chapter, you will have the skills to manage on-premises services through PowerShell. You will learn to configure and manage Active Directory, including user and group management for consistent policies and streamlining administrative tasks. In addition, you will learn to manage DNS and DHCP services, which are essential for network communication. Creating and managing file shares will also be covered, enabling more efficient data access. Lastly, you will learn to manage server roles and features for your on-premises servers, including certificate management.

Introduction to PowerShell for on-premises Management

Since its beginning, PowerShell has revolutionized how IT professionals approach scripting and automation, especially in on-premises environments. It simplifies managing local resources, and its extensible nature ensures you can scale its functionalities per your enterprise needs.

PowerShell is not just a command-line interface; it is a powerful scripting environment. When working with on-premises servers, it offers tools to perform tasks ranging from simple ones, like creating a new user, to complex operations, like configuring domain controllers, all with a few lines of code. It does this by providing modules that enhance its native capabilities. A module is a set of related cmdlets (commands) packaged together. Windows comes with several modules designed explicitly for on-premises management. Administrators can seamlessly integrate their scripts with various Windows Server roles and features by utilizing these modules.

One of the fundamental modules available is the **ActiveDirectory** module. This module makes tasks such as user creation, group management, and **Organizational Unit (OU)** structuring almost effortless. If you have ever tried to manage an extensive directory without automation, you will instantly appreciate the efficiency this module brings. Another essential module is **DnsServer**. Given that DNS is integral to the proper functioning of internet services in an enterprise, having a tool that allows for easy management and configuration of DNS records is indispensable. For those working with DHCP, the **DhcpServer** module comes to the rescue. This module facilitates the management of IP addresses in a network, ensuring devices communicate effectively without IP conflicts.

When combined with the **NetTCPIP** module, configuring IP settings on Windows, viewing, and setting IP addresses, gateways, DNS servers, and more become easier.

For file system management, the **Storage** module is available. This module is all-encompassing regarding on-premises storage management, from managing disks and partitions, to configuring storage spaces. Beyond these are several other modules, such as **ServerManager** for roles and feature management, **WebAdministration** for IIS management, and many more. These modules highlight the adaptability of PowerShell. By using these modules, administrators can set their on-premises environment just as they desire.

These purpose-built toolsets, designed for specific tasks, provide you, the IT professional, with a powerful and efficient way to oversee and shape your on-premises environment.

Configuring and managing Active Directory

Setting up Active Directory using PowerShell involves several steps, starting with the installation of the required role and features, and moving through the post-installation configuration steps.

First, you must ensure you configure your server with a static IP address, which is crucial for an Active Directory Domain Controller. You then start by installing the **Active Directory Domain Services** (**AD DS**) role. You can achieve this by using the `Install-WindowsFeature` cmdlet:

```
Install-WindowsFeature -Name AD-Domain-Services -IncludeManagementTools
```

Once installed, you must promote the server to a domain controller. You can use the `Install-ADDSDomainController` cmdlet to achieve this. This cmdlet requires several parameters:

- `DomainName:` Specifies the name of the domain.
- `InstallDns:` Installs the DNS server role.
- `CreateDnsDelegation:` Indicates whether to create a DNS delegation that references the new DNS server you are installing along with the domain controller.
- `DatabasePath`, `-SysvolPath`, `-LogPath:` Specify paths for the AD DS database, log files, and SYSVOL folder.
- `NoRebootOnCompletion:` Upon completion, do not restart the server.
- `Force:` Skips confirmation prompts during the installation.-`SafeModeAdministratorPassword:` Specifies the password for the AD restore mode.

An example of executing these commands is:

```
$SafeModePassword = ConvertTo-SecureString 'Pass@word1' -AsPlainText -Force

Install-ADDSDomainController `
    -DomainName "example.local" `
    -InstallDns `
    -DatabasePath "C:\Windows\NTDS" `
    -SysvolPath "C:\Windows\SYSVOL" `
    -LogPath "C:\Windows\NTDS\Logs" `
    -NoRebootOnCompletion $true `
    -SafeModeAdministratorPassword $SafeModePassword `
    -Force
```

If you are setting up a new forest instead of adding a domain to an existing forest, use **Install-ADDSForest** instead of **Install-ADDSDomainController**. The parameters would be similar, but there would be some differences. A basic example could be:

```
Install-ADDSForest -DomainName "example.local" -InstallDNS
```

A more complex example, such as, executing the **Install-ADDSDomainController** is:

```
$HashArguments = @{
    CreateDNSDelegation = $false
    DatabasePath = "C:\Windows\NTDS"
    DomainMode = "WinThreshold"
    DomainName = "example.local"
    DomainNetbiosName = "EXAMPLE"
    ForestMode = "WinThreshold"
    InstallDns = $true
```

```
    LogPath = "C:\Windows\NTDS\Logs"

    SysvolPath = "C:\Windows\SYSVOL"

    SafeModeAdministratorPassword = $SafeModePassword

    Force = $true
}
Install-ADDSForest @HashArguments
```

The following figure displays the output after installing a new Active Directory Forest and executing **Get-ADForest**:

```
ApplicationPartitions  : {DC=ForestDnsZones,DC=example,DC=local, DC=DomainDnsZones,DC=example,DC=local}
CrossForestReferences  : {}
DomainNamingMaster     : vmM365x86127502.example.local
Domains                : {example.local}
ForestMode             : Windows2016Forest
GlobalCatalogs         : {vmM365x86127502.example.local}
Name                   : example.local
PartitionsContainer    : CN=Partitions,CN=Configuration,DC=example,DC=local
RootDomain             : example.local
SchemaMaster           : vmM365x86127502.example.local
Sites                  : {Default-First-Site-Name}
SPNSuffixes            : {}
UPNSuffixes            : {}
```

Figure 11.1: Displays the output after executing the Get-ADForest

With an Active Directory and domain controller created, you can use PowerShell to manage it easily. Before diving into the capabilities, you need to ensure you have the Active Directory Module for PowerShell installed. It is a part of the **Remote Server Administration Tools** (**RSAT**). You can install it via Windows Features or, for newer Windows versions, directly from the Microsoft Store. Use the following PowerShell command to install the module:

Install-WindowsFeature -Name RSAT-AD-PowerShell

Once installed, you can import the module using the following command:

Import-Module ActiveDirectory

With the module in place, you can start using cmdlets tailored for Active Directory. One of the primary cmdlets `is Get-ADForest`. This cmdlet retrieves information about the current forest:

Get-ADForest | Select-Object *

The following figure displays the output from executing the **Get-ADForest** command:

```
ApplicationPartitions    : {DC=ForestDnsZones,DC=example,DC=local, DC=DomainDnsZones,DC=example,DC=local}
CrossForestReferences    : {}
DomainNamingMaster       : vmM365x86127502.example.local
Domains                  : {example.local}
ForestMode               : Windows2016Forest
GlobalCatalogs           : {vmM365x86127502.example.local}
Name                     : example.local
PartitionsContainer      : CN=Partitions,CN=Configuration,DC=example,DC=local
RootDomain               : example.local
SchemaMaster             : vmM365x86127502.example.local
Sites                    : {Default-First-Site-Name}
SPNSuffixes              : {}
UPNSuffixes              : {}
PropertyNames            : {ApplicationPartitions, CrossForestReferences, DomainNamingMaster, Domains…}
AddedProperties          : {}
RemovedProperties        : {}
ModifiedProperties       : {PartitionsContainer}
PropertyCount            : 13
```

Figure 11.2: Display details about the Active Directory Forest

Another essential command in the Active Directory module is **Get-ADDomain**. This command retrieves information about a specific domain or the domain of the current user:

Get-ADDomain -Identity "example.local"

The following figure displays the output from executing the **Get-ADDomain** command:

```
AllowedDNSSuffixes              : {}
ChildDomains                    : {}
ComputersContainer              : CN=Computers,DC=example,DC=local
DeletedObjectsContainer         : CN=Deleted Objects,DC=example,DC=local
DistinguishedName               : DC=example,DC=local
DNSRoot                         : example.local
DomainControllersContainer      : OU=Domain Controllers,DC=example,DC=local
DomainMode                      : Windows2016Domain
DomainSID                       : S-1-5-21-2786483157-1564416545-4049087456
ForeignSecurityPrincipalsContainer : CN=ForeignSecurityPrincipals,DC=example,DC=local
Forest                          : example.local
InfrastructureMaster            : vmM365x86127502.example.local
LastLogonReplicationInterval    :
LinkedGroupPolicyObjects        : {CN={31B2F340-016D-11D2-945F-00C04FB984F9},CN=Policies,CN=System,DC=example,DC=loc
                                  al}
LostAndFoundContainer           : CN=LostAndFound,DC=example,DC=local
ManagedBy                       :
Name                            : example
NetBIOSName                     : EXAMPLE
ObjectClass                     : domainDNS
ObjectGUID                      : 7bde087e-8947-46c9-9fce-774aa8c81059
ParentDomain                    :
PDCEmulator                     : vmM365x86127502.example.local
PublicKeyRequiredPasswordRolling : True
QuotasContainer                 : CN=NTDS Quotas,DC=example,DC=local
ReadOnlyReplicaDirectoryServers : {}
ReplicaDirectoryServers         : {vmM365x86127502.example.local}
RIDMaster                       : vmM365x86127502.example.local
SubordinateReferences           : {DC=ForestDnsZones,DC=example,DC=local, DC=DomainDnsZones,DC=example,DC=local,
                                  CN=Configuration,DC=example,DC=local}
SystemsContainer                : CN=System,DC=example,DC=local
UsersContainer                  : CN=Users,DC=example,DC=local
```

Figure 11.3: Display details about the Active Directory Domain

Managing OUs is another important aspect of Active Directory administration. To create a new Organizational Unit, use the **New-ADOrganizationalUnit** cmdlet:

`New-ADOrganizationalUnit -Name "Example" -Path "DC=example, DC=local"`

Once created, you can retrieve information about the Organizational Unit by using the **Get-ADOrganizationalUnit** cmdlet:

`Get-ADOrganizationalUnit -Filter 'Name -like "*Example*"'`

The following figure displays details about the newly created OU:

```
City                      :
Country                   :
DistinguishedName         : OU=Example,DC=example,DC=local
LinkedGroupPolicyObjects  : {}
ManagedBy                 :
Name                      : Example
ObjectClass               : organizationalUnit
ObjectGUID                : 64d4771c-5d3a-4c48-9a09-97956ef925f6
PostalCode                :
State                     :
StreetAddress             :
```

Figure 11.4: Display details about the Organizational Unit (OU)

You can also manage **Group Policy Object (GPO)** using PowerShell. While the cmdlets might not be in the Active Directory module, they remain pivotal for Active Directory administrators. The **Get-GPO** cmdlet, for instance, fetches details about GPOs. To use these commands, you need to install the GPO PowerShell module using:

`Install-WindowsFeature -Name GPMC`

With the feature added, you then import the required module:

`Import-Module GroupPolicy`

Now you can, for example, list all GPOs using the following command:

`Get-GPO -All`

This figure displays information about existing GPOs:

```
DisplayName      : Default Domain Policy
DomainName       : example.local
Owner            : EXAMPLE\Domain Admins
Id               : 31b2f340-016d-11d2-945f-00c04fb984f9
GpoStatus        : AllSettingsEnabled
Description      :
CreationTime     : 10/25/2023 4:56:38 PM
ModificationTime : 10/25/2023 5:02:08 PM
UserVersion      :
ComputerVersion  :
WmiFilter        :

DisplayName      : Default Domain Controllers Policy
DomainName       : example.local
Owner            : EXAMPLE\Domain Admins
Id               : 6ac1786c-016f-11d2-945f-00c04fb984f9
GpoStatus        : AllSettingsEnabled
Description      :
CreationTime     : 10/25/2023 4:56:38 PM
ModificationTime : 10/25/2023 4:56:38 PM
UserVersion      :
ComputerVersion  :
WmiFilter        :
```

Figure 11.5: Display details about existing Group Policy Objects (GPOs)

With PowerShell's Active Directory module, the ability to automate and script administrative tasks becomes more manageable. Well-crafted scripts can fetch details about your infrastructure and make significant changes. PowerShell's integration with Active Directory simplifies complex tasks and offers exceptional control and flexibility. It bridges the gap between GUI-based operations and the need for automation, making Active Directory management a more streamlined and efficient process.

User and group management

PowerShell provides cmdlets to manage local users in the **Microsoft.PowerShell.LocalAccounts** module. Before any operations, ensure you are running PowerShell with administrative privileges. As with most PowerShell modules, there are commands for creating, modifying, and removing items.

The first task in managing local users and groups is to create a local user account. To do this, you use the **New-LocalUser** cmdlet:

```
$Password = Read-Host -AsSecureString
```

```
New-LocalUser 'ExampleLocalUser1' -Password $Password -FullName 'Example
Local User1' -Description 'Example Local User'
```

Once the account is created, you can execute **Get-LocalUser** to retrieve the details:

```
Get-LocalUser -Name 'ExampleLocalUser1' | Select-Object *
```

This figure displays information about the newly created user account:

```
AccountExpires          :
Description             : Example Local User
Enabled                 : True
FullName                : Example Local User1
PasswordChangeableDate  : 11/21/2023 10:09:06 PM
PasswordExpires         : 1/1/2024 10:09:06 PM
UserMayChangePassword   : True
PasswordRequired        : False
PasswordLastSet         : 11/20/2023 10:09:06 PM
LastLogon               :
Name                    : ExampleLocalUser1
SID                     : S-1-5-21-1930361551-2360079863-3637753127-1000
PrincipalSource         : Local
ObjectClass             : User
```

Figure 11.6: Display details about the newly created user account

You can modify any available user account properties using the **Set-LocalUser** cmdlet. The following command updates the account description:

```
Set-LocalUser -Name 'ExampleLocalUser1' -Description 'Modified: Example Local
User'
```

Like users, you can manage local groups using cmdlets from the same module. To create a new local group named **ExampleLocalGroup1**, use the following:

```
New-LocalGroup -Name 'ExampleLocalGroup1' -Description 'Example Local Group'
```

The **Get-LocalGroup** cmdlet retrieves details about a specific group:

```
Get-LocalGroup -Name 'ExampleLocalGroup1' | Select-Object *
```

This figure displays information about the newly created group:

```
Description     : Example Local Group
Name            : ExampleLocalGroup1
SID             : S-1-5-21-1930361551-2360079863-3637753127-1001
PrincipalSource : Local
ObjectClass     : Group
```

Figure 11.7: Display details about the newly created group

You can add or remove users to the groups using the **Add-LocalGroupMember** or **Remove-LocalGroupMember**. The following commands show an example for each command:

Add-LocalGroupMember -Group 'ExampleLocalGroup1' -Member 'ExampleLocalUser1'

Remove-LocalGroupMember -Group 'ExampleLocalGroup1' -Member 'ExampleLocalUser1'

Most organizations do not use local users as they usually have an Active Directory for storing all accounts and groups. Managing domain users cannot be done using the **Microsoft.PowerShell.LocalAccounts** module. It requires the Active Directory module for PowerShell. You need to check it is installed and loaded using **Import-Module ActiveDirectory.**

With the module loaded, you can add domain users using the **New-ADUser** command. The syntax for this command is significantly different than the **New-LocalUser** command. Let us compare the two commands, **New-LocalUser** and **New-ADUser**, are used to create users on local machines and in Active Directory. **New-LocalUser** is typically used on standalone machines or machines not joined to a domain. It is handy for setting up local administrative accounts, kiosk accounts, or other local machine-specific users. **New-ADUser** is essential for enterprise environments where centralized management of user accounts is required.

While both cmdlets offer parameters to specify details about the user, they differ in the parameters available due to the distinct nature of local versus domain accounts:

New-LocalUser:

    -Name: The account name.

    -Description: A brief description of the account.

    -NoPassword: Indicates that the account does not have a password.

    -Password: Secure string for the account password.

    -UserMayNotChangePassword: Password-related flag.

    -UserMustChangePassword: Password-related flag.

New-ADUser:

    -SamAccountName: The SAM account name.

    -Name: The full name of the user.

    -GivenName: First name.

    -Surname: Last name.

- **-UserPrincipalName**: The UPN associated with the account.
- **-Path**: Organizational unit (OU) where you will create the user.
- **-AccountPassword**: Secure string for the account password.

New-ADUser also provides more parameters related to Active Directory domain-specific attributes, such as **-Title**, **-Department**, **-Manager**, and so on.

With **New-LocalUser**, management is often limited to the individual machine. If you need to change or apply policies, you do so on that machine. **New-ADUser** integrates into the broader Active Directory ecosystem. Once a user is created using this cmdlet, they can be managed via various other AD tools and utilities. The lifecycle of domain users, including group memberships, permissions, and policies, is often managed centrally. While both **New-LocalUser** and **New-ADUser** serve the purpose of creating user accounts, their scope and use cases are different. The choice between the two depends on the specific requirements of your setup and the scope of user management you are aiming for.

To create a domain account, you can use the following command:

```
$Password = Read-Host -AsSecureString
```

```
New-ADUser -SamAccountName 'DomainUser1' -GivenName 'Domain' -Surname 'User1' -Name 'Domain User1' -Enabled $true -ChangePasswordAtLogon $true -AccountPassword $Password
```

To retrieve the account, you use **Get-ADUser**:

```
Get-ADUser -Identity 'DomainUser1' -Properties *
```

This figure displays information about the newly created Active Directory User account:

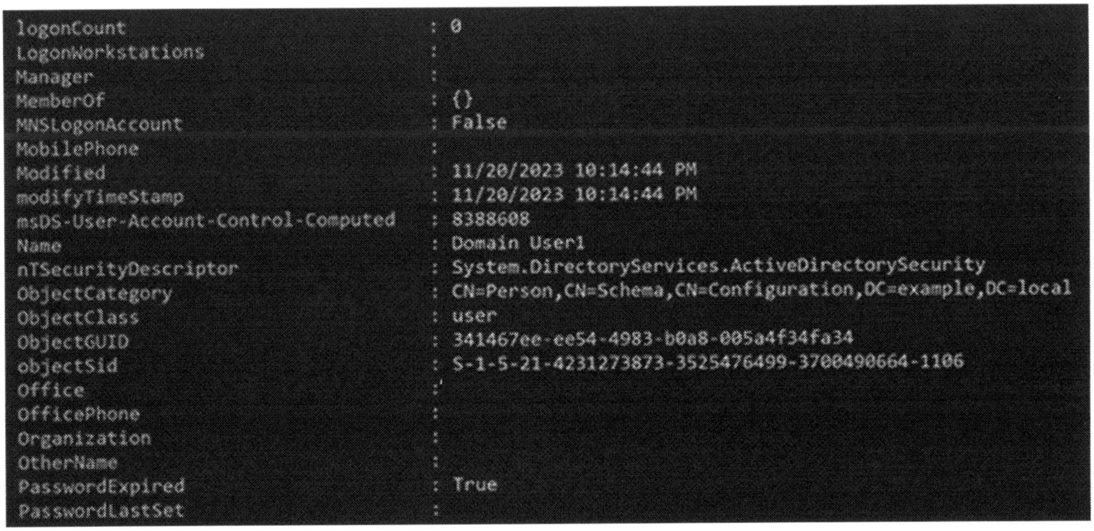

Figure 11.8: Display details about the newly created Active Directory User account

Modifying domain users also follows the same pattern as the local users. To update a domain account, you use **Set-ADUser**:

```
Set-ADUser -Identity 'DomainUser1' -Office 'HQ'
```

Like managing local groups, you can similarly manage domain security groups. To add a new domain security group, you use the **New-ADGroup** command:

```
New-ADGroup -Name 'DomainGroup1' -GroupScope Global -PassThru
```

When creating a group within the Active Directory, it is essential to choose the correct scope. The **GroupScope** property determines the extent or range within which a group is recognized and can be applied in the Active Directory domain hierarchy. Here is a breakdown of the **Group Scope** property:

- **Universal (GroupScope 'Universal'):** Universal groups are available in a domain that is part of a forest and is recognizable across the entire forest. These groups can have members from any domain within the forest. It is often used in large organizations with multiple domains, allowing for centralized group management.
- **Global (GroupScope 'Global'):** Global groups are used to group users based on business needs or roles within a domain. These groups can be added as members of other global groups or universal groups within the same domain but not from different domains. These global groups can then be added to domain local or universal groups, where they are assigned permissions to resources.
- **Domain Local (GroupScope 'DomainLocal'):** Domain local groups are specific to a domain and can have members from any domain in the forest. The critical aspect of domain local groups is that you can assign permissions to resources (like shared folders or printers) within that specific domain using these groups. If you want to give a set of users (that might come from different domains) access to a particular resource in one domain, you will typically add those users or their global groups to a local domain group and then assign the necessary permissions to that domain local group.

To retrieve a domain group, you can use the **Get-ADGroup** command:

```
Get-ADGroup -Identity 'DomainGroup1'
```

This figure displays information about the newly created Active Directory Group:

```
DistinguishedName : CN=DomainGroup1,CN=Users,DC=example,DC=local
GroupCategory     : Security
GroupScope        : Global
Name              : DomainGroup1
ObjectClass       : group
ObjectGUID        : 6fe73889-d5d2-4a1a-9640-e1b6c3a10a62
SamAccountName    : DomainGroup1
SID               : S-1-5-21-4231273873-3525476499-3700490664-1107
```

Figure 11.9: Display details about the newly created Active Directory Group

You can also add users to the domain groups like the local groups. You use the **Add-ADGroupMember** to add users and the **Remove-ADGroupMember** to remove users from the group. The following shows both commands:

`Add-ADGroupMember -Identity 'DomainGroup1' -Members 'DomainUser1'`

`Remove-ADGroupMember -Identity 'DomainGroup1' -Members 'DomainUser1'`

PowerShell simplifies local and domain user/group management, increasing productivity in larger environments.

Beyond creating, updating, and removing users and groups or adding members to groups, there are many other management tasks in Active Directory and local systems where PowerShell can help. Here is a list of a few of those tasks with brief explanations:

- **Resetting user passwords**: Administrators can quickly reset passwords using PowerShell.
- **Force password change at next logon**: You can require users to change their password the next time they sign in.
- **Identify locked out accounts**: Quickly pinpoint locked accounts due to repeated incorrect password attempts.
- **Unlock accounts**: Unlock user accounts that have been automatically locked.
- **Enable/disable accounts**: You can deactivate or activate user accounts.
- **Setting logon hours**: Restrict the hours a user can log into the domain.
- **Set expiry date for accounts**: Useful for temporary accounts like contractors.
- **Nesting groups**: Understand and manage the hierarchy of groups within groups.
- **Enumerate effective group membership**: Determine all groups a user is a member of, including nested groups.
- **Query group membership**: List all members of a particular group.

- **Manage fine-grained password policies**: Implement different password policies for different sets of users within the same domain.
- **Manage OUs**: Create, delete, or move OUs.
- **Set home folders and script paths**: Assign home directories or logon scripts to users.
- **Managing roaming profiles**: Set or update roaming profile paths for users.
- **Auditing and reporting**: Find the last time a user logged into the domain. Identify user accounts or computer accounts that have not been used.
- **Log off users:** Terminate user sessions.

The previous list shows the possible user and group management tasks using PowerShell in Active Directory and local systems. Administrators leveraging PowerShell can efficiently handle various tasks, from day-to-day operations to complex setups and configurations.

Managing domain controllers

Domain controllers (DCs) are:

- Essential servers in the Active Directory infrastructure.
- Store a copy of the directory database.
- Handle authentication.
- Govern interactions within the domain.

PowerShell provides a robust environment to manage and automate tasks related to domain controllers.

Before managing domain controllers, knowing how to promote a server to become a domain controller using PowerShell is essential. It is achieved using the

`Install-ADDSForest`, `Install-ADDSDomain`, and `Install-ADDSDomainController` cmdlets:

```
Install-WindowsFeature -Name AD-Domain-Services
```

```
Install-ADDSDomainController -DomainName "example.local"
```

In an Active Directory environment, DCs play separate roles based on their functionality and services. These are the types of domain controllers that you can add to an Active Directory domain:

- **Primary Domain Controller (PDC) Emulator**: In Active Directory, all domain controllers are peers. However, the PDC Emulator role still exists for backward compatibility. It takes on specific tasks in an Active Directory domain, such as time synchronization and being the default target for password updates if the original update fails.

- **Global catalog (GC) server**: A Global Catalog server contains a full copy of all objects in its host domain and a partial copy of all objects in other domains in the forest. It allows for forest-wide searches in Active Directory. Having a GC on a site can speed up logon processes and searches, as it provides universal group membership information for user logons.

- **Read-only Domain Controller (RODC)**: Introduced in Windows Server 2008, an RODC hosts a read-only replica of the domain database. The design suit's locations that may be physically insecure, such as a branch office that needs a secure DC.

- **Bridgehead server**: In replication, a bridgehead server is a domain controller designated to receive and send directory updates across a site link. When there is more than one domain controller in a site, the **Knowledge Consistency Checker (KCC)** selects one of those DCs as the bridgehead to manage replication to domain controllers in other sites.

- **Child domain controller**: When you add a new domain to an existing AD tree, the domain controllers in this new domain would technically be part of the child domain. It is more about domain hierarchy than a specific domain controller type.

When planning your AD deployment or expansion, it is essential to understand these roles and design the placement and type of your domain controllers according to your organizational needs, infrastructure topology, and security requirements. Although Active Directory works in a multi-master replication model, where multiple domain controllers can accept changes, one domain controller can only manage specific roles or functions at a time for integrity and consistency. **Flexible Single Master Operations (FSMO)** roles are available to match the type of domain controller you need, which will help you. The forest-wide roles are:

- **Schema master**: The domain controller holding this role manages all updates and modifications to the Active Directory schema. The schema defines object classes and attributes within AD.

- **Domain naming master**: This role controls the addition and removal of domains in an AD forest. If you wish to add a new domain or remove an existing one, the domain controller with this role is responsible for that operation.

The domain-wide roles are:

- **Relative ID (RID) Master**: When an object, like a user or group, is created, it is assigned a **Security Identifier (SID)**. This SID comprises a domain SID (common for all SIDs) and a unique RID for each object. The RID master allocates RID pools to each domain controller to ensure uniqueness.

- **Primary Domain Controller (PDC) Emulator**: This role is a remnant of the era of Windows NT 4.0, where the PDC was the Primary Domain Controller, with others being **Backup Domain Controllers** (**BDC**). Today, in AD environments, the PDC Emulator receives preference in certain operations, such as password changes or account lockouts. It acts as a tiebreaker and synchronizes the latest changes, ensuring consistency.
- **Infrastructure master**: This role manages cross-domain object references. It handles references between objects in different domains correctly.

It is possible to manage and transfer FSMO roles using PowerShell. Commands like `Get-ADForest` and `Get-ADDomain` allow you to identify which domain controller currently holds each FSMO role. For transferring roles, you would use commands like `Move-ADDirectoryServerOperationMasterRole`.

For example, if you needed to set a domain controller as the **Primary Domain Controller (PDC) Emulator**, you would use the following command:

```
Move-ADDirectoryServerOperationMasterRole `
    -Identity "EXAMPLEDC" `
    -OperationMasterRole PDCEmulator
```

To convert a domain controller to a **Global Catalog**, you would use the following command:

```
Add-ADDSReadOnlyDomainControllerAccount `
    -DomainControllerAccountName "EXAMPLEDC" `
    -DomainName "example.local" `
    -DelegatedAdministratorAccountName "EXAMPLE\Admin" `
    -SiteName "Default-First-Site-Name"
```

If required, you can also transfer multiple FSMO roles to single domain controllers using PowerShell. The following example moves the `OperationMasterRole`, `SchemaMaster`, and `DomainNamingMaster` roles to a single domain controller, as shown:

```
Move-ADDirectoryServerOperationMasterRole `
    -Identity "EXAMPLEDC" `
    -OperationMasterRole SchemaMaster, DomainNamingMaster
```

Sometimes, you might need to retrieve the list of domain controllers and filter the list to those that serve as **Global Catalog** servers. The `Get-ADDomainController` command helps you to do this:

```
Get-ADDomainController -Filter {IsGlobalCatalog -eq $true}
```

The following figure displays all Global Catalog Servers:

```
ComputerObjectDN          : CN=vmDC,OU=Domain Controllers,DC=example,DC=local
DefaultPartition          : DC=example,DC=local
Domain                    : example.local
Enabled                   : True
Forest                    : example.local
HostName                  : vmDC.example.local
InvocationId              : cf305159-36cd-4e94-b0e1-84a2d4d2cc1f
IPv4Address               : 10.0.0.4
IPv6Address               :
IsGlobalCatalog           : True
IsReadOnly                : False
LdapPort                  : 389
Name                      : vmDC
OperatingSystemVersion    : 10.0 (20348)
OperationMasterRoles      : {SchemaMaster, DomainNamingMaster, PDCEmulator, RI[
Partitions                : {DC=ForestDnsZones,DC=example,DC=local, DC=DomainD
ServerObjectDN            : CN=vmDC,CN=Servers,CN=Default-First-Site-Name,CN=S
ServerObjectGuid          : e580504d-97f3-4664-8d94-845c988084d8
Site                      : Default-First-Site-Name
SslPort                   : 636
```

Figure 11.10: Displays all global catalog servers

There may come a time when a domain controller needs removal from service. PowerShell allows for clean demotion:

```
Uninstall-ADDSDomainController -DemoteOperationMasterRole
```

Active Directory replicates information between the serves that make up the entire forest and domain. Using the `Get-ADReplicationFailure` command, you can administrators spot any replication issues:

```
Get-ADReplicationFailure -Scope SITE -Target default
```

You can also modify replication information, such as adding a new subnet to a site, as shown:

```
Get-ADReplicationSite -Filter *

New-ADReplicationSubnet -Name "10.10.0.0/24" -Site "SITE"
```

Managing Domain Controllers is complex and requires consideration when making any changes. PowerShell provides excellent capabilities, allowing you to make configuration updates and changes quickly and with minimal impact.

Managing DNS and DHCP services

Managing DNS and DHCP are integral to network administration, ensuring efficient and effective network communication. PowerShell provides a comprehensive set of cmdlets to manage these services, enhancing automation and precision.

DNS is a hierarchical and decentralized naming system for computers, services, or any resource connected to the Internet or a private network. With PowerShell, you can automate the management of DNS settings, records, and zones.

Before managing DNS through PowerShell, ensure you have installed the DNS role on your server. You can install it using the **Install-WindowsFeature** cmdlet:

```
Install-WindowsFeature -Name DNS -IncludeManagementTools
```

You can add several types of DNS records using PowerShell. For example, to add an A record:

```
Add-DnsServerResourceRecordA `
    -Name "ExampleHost" `
    -ZoneName "example.local" `
    -IPv4Address "10.10.0.4"
```

To view DNS records in a zone, use the **Get-DnsServerResourceRecord** cmdlet:

```
Get-DnsServerResourceRecord -ZoneName "example.local"
```

The following figure displays all the DNS entries for the specified zone:

HostName	RecordType	Type	RecordData
@	A	1	10.0.0.4
@	NS	2	vmdc.example.local.
@	SOA	6	[21][vmdc.example.local.][hostmaster
_msdcs	NS	2	vmdc.example.local.
_gc._tcp.Default-First-S...	SRV	33	[0][100][3268][vmdc.example.local.]
_kerberos._tcp.Default-F...	SRV	33	[0][100][88][vmdc.example.local.]
_ldap._tcp.Default-First...	SRV	33	[0][100][389][vmdc.example.local.]
_gc._tcp	SRV	33	[0][100][3268][vmdc.example.local.]
_kerberos._tcp	SRV	33	[0][100][88][vmdc.example.local.]
_kpasswd._tcp	SRV	33	[0][100][464][vmdc.example.local.]
_ldap._tcp	SRV	33	[0][100][389][vmdc.example.local.]
_kerberos._udp	SRV	33	[0][100][88][vmdc.example.local.]
_kpasswd._udp	SRV	33	[0][100][464][vmdc.example.local.]
DomainDnsZones	A	1	10.0.0.4
_ldap._tcp.Default-First...	SRV	33	[0][100][389][vmdc.example.local.]
_ldap._tcp.DomainDnsZones	SRV	33	[0][100][389][vmdc.example.local.]
ExampleHost	A	1	10.10.0.4
ForestDnsZones	A	1	10.0.0.4
_ldap._tcp.Default-First...	SRV	33	[0][100][389][vmdc.example.local.]
_ldap._tcp.ForestDnsZones	SRV	33	[0][100][389][vmdc.example.local.]
vmBDC	A	1	10.0.0.8
vmdc	A	1	10.0.0.4

Figure 11.11: All DNS entries for the specified zone

Modifying DNS records is done by removing the old record and adding a new one. Here is an example of modifying an A record:

```
Remove-DnsServerResourceRecord `
    -ZoneName "example.local" `
    -Name "ExampleHost" `
    -RRType "A"

Add-DnsServerResourceRecordA `
    -Name "ExampleHost" `
    -ZoneName "example.local " `
    -IPv4Address "10.10.0.4"
```

DHCP is a network management protocol that automates configuring devices on IP networks. PowerShell allows you to manage DHCP scopes, leases, reservations, and options. To manage DHCP, ensure you install the DHCP role:

Install-WindowsFeature -Name DHCP -IncludeManagementTools

You can create a new DHCP scope using PowerShell:

```
Add-DhcpServerv4Scope `
    -Name "Scope1" `
    -StartRange "10.10.0.1" `
    -EndRange "10.10.0.100" `
    -SubnetMask 255.255.255.0
```

Creating a DHCP reservation ensures a device always receives the same IP address:

```
Add-DhcpServerv4Reservation `
    -ScopeId "10.10.0.0" `
    -IPAddress "10.10.0.50" `
    -ClientId "00:1A:2B:3C:4D:5E"
```

You can use PowerShell to monitor and troubleshoot both DNS and DHCP services. For instance, to list all active leases in a DHCP scope:

```
Get-DhcpServerv4Lease -ScopeId "10.10.0.0"
```

For DNS, you can test the resolution for a specific record:

```
Resolve-DnsName -Name "examplehost.example.local"
```

The following figure displays the resolution of a DNS address:

Name	Type	TTL	Section	IPAddress
examplehost.example.local	A	3600	Answer	10.10.0.4

Figure 11.12: Resolve a DNS name

Managing DNS and DHCP through PowerShell provides the flexibility to script and automate tasks and offers a level of detail and control that might not be as easily accessible through GUI-based tools. This approach is particularly beneficial in larger environments, where batch processing and scripting can save considerable time and reduce the likelihood of human error.

Creating and managing file shares

Creating and managing file shares is common for network and system administrators. PowerShell provides a powerful and flexible set of cmdlets to manage file shares, offering more control and automation capabilities than traditional GUI-based tools.

People use file shares in Windows to share files and folders across the network. PowerShell can create, configure, and manage these shares efficiently, allowing for batch processing and advanced configuration options. Before setting up file shares, ensure you have installed the File Server role on your server. You can do this via PowerShell, as shown:

`Install-WindowsFeature -Name FS-FileServer`

You can create a new file share using the **New-SmbShare** cmdlet. This command creates a new share named **MyPowerShell** with the path **C:\PowerShell** and gives full access to everyone:

```
New-SmbShare `
    -Name "MyPowerShell" `
    -Path "C:\PowerShell" `
    -FullAccess "Everyone"
```

The following figure displays creating a new file share for a specific path and assigning everyone within permission:

```
Name           ScopeName  Path          Description
----           ---------  ----          -----------
MyPowerShell   *          C:\PowerShell
```

Figure 11.13: Create a new FileShare

While the **New-SmbShare** cmdlet can set basic permissions, more detailed control can be achieved using Windows **Access Control Lists** (**ACLs**). PowerShell allows you to modify these ACLs:

$Acl = Get-Acl "C:\PowerShell"

$AccessRule = New-Object System.Security.AccessControl.FileSystemAccessRule(

    "Domain\User",

    "Modify",

    "ContainerInherit, ObjectInherit",

    "None",

    "Allow")

$Acl.SetAccessRule($AccessRule)

Set-Acl "C:\PowerShell" $Acl

To view all shares on a server, use the **Get-SmbShare** cmdlet:

Get-SmbShare

The following figure returns all file shares within the Windows Server:

```
Name          ScopeName  Path                                                  Description
----          ---------  ----                                                  -----------
ADMIN$        *          C:\Windows                                            Remote Admin
C$            *          C:\                                                   Default share
D$            *          D:\                                                   Default share
IPC$          *                                                                Remote IPC
MyPowerShell  *          C:\PowerShell
NETLOGON      *          C:\Windows\SYSVOL\sysvol\example.local\SCRIPTS        Logon server share
SYSVOL        *          C:\Windows\SYSVOL\sysvol                              Logon server share
```

Figure 11.14: Display all FileShares on the Windows Server

You can change the properties of an existing share using the **Set-SmbShare** cmdlet. For instance, to change the description of a share:

Set-SmbShare `

        -Name "MyPowerShell" `

        -Description "New Share Description"

To check who has access to a share, use the **Get-SmbShareAccess** cmdlet:

Get-SmbShareAccess -Name "MyPowerShell"

The following figure shows the current permissions for the names file share:

```
Name           ScopeName  AccountName  AccessControlType  AccessRight
----           ---------  -----------  -----------------  -----------
MyPowerShell   *          Everyone     Allow              Full
```

Figure 11.15: Display file share permissions

When no longer needed, you can remove a share with the **Remove-SmbShare** cmdlet:

Remove-SmbShare -Name "MyPowerShell" -Force

If you need to limit the amount of data stored in a share, you can use **File Server Resource Manager (FSRM)** cmdlets to set quotas:

Install-WindowsFeature -Name FS-Resource-Manager -IncludeManagementTools

Import-Module FileServerResourceManager

Set-FsrmQuota -Path "C:\PowerShell" -Size 100GB

For more advanced scenarios, such as configuring BranchCache or access-based enumeration, PowerShell offers additional cmdlets like **Set-SmbShare** and **Set-SmbBranchCache**. These cmdlets provide further customization and optimization options for your file shares. Managing file shares with PowerShell is a highly efficient approach. It allows for scripting and automation, significantly streamlining configuring and maintaining file shares, especially in larger or more complex environments. PowerShell's integration with Windows ACLs and FSRM further enhances this capability, allowing for detailed permission control and storage management.

Managing certificates

Managing certificates is crucial to ensuring secure communications and transactions in any network environment. PowerShell provides a comprehensive set of cmdlets for certificate management, enabling administrators to automate certificate provisioning, renewal, and revocation tasks. Certificates are used to validate the identity of a server or user and to secure data transmission. Through its **Public Key Infrastructure (PKI)** module, PowerShell offers an array of commands for managing these certificates.

You can list all certificates in a certificate store using the **Get-ChildItem** cmdlet. For instance, to list certificates in the local machine's store:

```
Get-ChildItem -Path Cert:\LocalMachine\My
```

The following figure displays all current certificates within the local machine store:

```
Thumbprint                                Subject                        EnhancedKeyUsageList
----------                                -------                        --------------------
994ED12ECF9DBAB757F1787FBB997833D59B04    DC=Windows Azure CR...
```

Figure 11.16: Display all local machine certificates

You might need to create a self-signed certificate for testing purposes or internal use. PowerShell simplifies this with the **New-SelfSignedCertificate** cmdlet:

```
New-SelfSignedCertificate `
    -DnsName "www.example.local" `
    -CertStoreLocation "cert:\LocalMachine\My"
```

The following figure creates a new self-signed certificate:

```
Thumbprint                                Subject                  EnhancedKeyUsageList
----------                                -------                  --------------------
F12EE0945F7C3875F23E2D5A18DACD0FD2760186  CN=www.example.local     {Client Authentication, Server Authentication}
```

Figure 11.17: Create a self-signed certificate

Exporting a certificate, with its private key, is a common requirement. It is achieved using the **Export-Certificate** and **Export-PfxCertificate** cmdlets:

```
$cert = Get-ChildItem `
    -Path Cert:\LocalMachine\My | `
    Where-Object {$_.Subject -like "*www.example.local*"}
Export-Certificate -Cert $cert -FilePath "C:\PowerShell\exportedCert.cer"
```

To import a certificate into a store, use the **Import-Certificate** cmdlet:

```
Import-Certificate `
    -FilePath "C:\PowerShell\certificate.cer" `
    -CertStoreLocation Cert:\LocalMachine\My
```

If a certificate is no longer needed or is compromised, you can remove it:

```
$cert = Get-ChildItem `
    -Path Cert:\LocalMachine\My | `
    Where-Object {$_.Subject -like "*www.example.local*"}
Remove-Item -Path $cert.PSPath
```

In an environment with a certificate authority, you can request a new certificate using the **certreq** tool in conjunction with PowerShell. While PowerShell does not have a native cmdlet for this, it can be used to automate the process:

```
certreq -new -f "C:\PowerShell\request.inf" "C:\PowerShell\output.req"
```

You can search for certificates with specific properties, such as subject name, issuer name, or expiration date:

```
Get-ChildItem `
    -Path Cert:\LocalMachine\My | `
    Where-Object {$_.NotAfter -lt (Get-Date).AddYears(1)}
```

While PowerShell does not directly provide a cmdlet for renewing certificates, it can be done by requesting a new certificate using the old certificate's details:

```
$dnsName = ($cert.DnsNameList).Unicode
New-SelfSignedCertificate `
    -CloneCert $cert -DnsName $dnsName
```

For more complex scenarios, such as managing **Certificate Revocation Lists (CRLs)**, interacting with AD CS, or automating certificate deployment, PowerShell scripts can be combined with command-line tools and the Windows API to provide comprehensive solutions. Managing certificates using PowerShell provides the flexibility and scripting capability to handle various certificate-related tasks efficiently and automatically. Whether for an enterprise PKI or managing self-signed certificates, PowerShell's PKI module, combined with its scripting capabilities, offers a robust solution for certificate management.

Managing server roles and features

Managing server roles and features is a fundamental task for system administrators. PowerShell provides a powerful and efficient way to manage this, especially when dealing with multiple servers. PowerShell simplifies the management of server roles and features, allowing administrators to automate repetitive tasks and manage servers remotely. The **ServerManager** module is beneficial for this purpose.

Internet Information Services (IIS) is a widely used web server on Windows servers. To install IIS using PowerShell:

`Install-WindowsFeature -Name Web-Server -IncludeManagementTools`

After installation, you can manage various aspects of IIS. For instance, to create a new website:

```
Import-Module IISAdministration

$siteName = "MyPowerShell"

$bindingInformation = "*:80:www.example.local"

$physicalPath = "C:\inetpub\wwwroot\MyPowerShell"


if (-not (Test-Path $physicalPath)) {

    New-Item -Path $physicalPath -Type Directory

}


New-IISSite `

    -Name $siteName `

    -BindingInformation $bindingInformation `

    -PhysicalPath $physicalPath
```

The following figure displays creating a new website within Internet Information Server, running on port 80, with a specific path:

Name	ID	State	Physical Path	Bindings
MyPowerShell	2	Started	C:\inetpub\wwwroot\MyPowerShell	http *:80:www.example.local

Figure 11.18: Create a new website

Monitoring disk usage is a vital part of managing file services. PowerShell allows you to gather this information quickly:

`Get-PSDrive -PSProvider FileSystem`

For organizations that rely on printing, managing print services efficiently is essential. To install print services:

`Install-WindowsFeature -Name Print-Services -IncludeManagementTools`

After installation, you can add printers and manage print queues. Here is how you can list all printers:

`Get-Printer`

One of PowerShell's strengths is its ability to execute commands on multiple servers, making it ideal for environments with many servers. For example, to install a role on numerous servers, you can use:

```
$servers = @("Server1", "Server2", "Server3")

Invoke-Command `
    -ComputerName $servers `
    -ScriptBlock { Install-WindowsFeature `
        -Name Web-Server -IncludeManagementTools }
```

PowerShell scripts can be written to automate the deployment of roles and features based on specific criteria, such as server function or location. This level of automation helps in maintaining consistency across the IT infrastructure. Whether you are managing a web server, configuring file shares, overseeing print services, or setting up remote desktop services, PowerShell provides the functionality needed to perform these tasks efficiently.

Conclusion

This chapter explained various techniques, and methodologies for effectively managing on-premises services with PowerShell. You started by exploring how to configure and administer Active Directory, a crucial component of many IT environments. You also discussed user and group management, which helps ensure streamlined administrative procedures. Furthermore, we delved into managing DNS and DHCP services, which form the backbone of network communications. You also reviewed configuring file shares for easy data accessibility and sharing. Finally, we went through managing certificates within Windows Server using PowerShell. In the next chapter, you will focus on using PowerShell to troubleshoot Windows issues and optimize performance.

Chapter 12
Troubleshooting Windows and Performance Optimization

Introduction

In this chapter, you will learn how to use PowerShell commands to analyze system resources, such as CPU, memory, disk, and network usage. You will also learn how to identify potential performance issues and diagnose and resolve performance bottlenecks that may affect the responsiveness and reliability of your Windows system. Additionally, you will learn how to troubleshoot network connectivity issues using PowerShell commands such as ping, traceroute, DNS lookup, and firewall configuration. You will also learn how to identify and remediate security vulnerabilities, such as scanning for malware, updating Windows Defender, and applying security patches. You will also learn how to analyze and filter event logs using PowerShell commands to find errors, warnings, and critical events that may indicate system problems. Lastly, you will learn about the common pitfalls and challenges in using PowerShell for Windows troubleshooting, such as handling errors, exceptions, and permissions.

Structure

In this chapter, we will cover the following topics:

- Analyzing system resources
- Diagnosing and resolving performance bottlenecks

- Troubleshooting network connectivity issues
- Identifying and remediating security vulnerabilities
- Analyzing and filtering event logs
- Challenges in using PowerShell for Windows troubleshooting

Objectives

After reading this chapter, you will have learned how to utilize PowerShell to troubleshoot various issues on Windows systems. With PowerShell, you can analyze system resources and identify the components that consume the most CPU, memory, disk, or network resources. You will also learn how to diagnose and resolve performance bottlenecks, optimize the system for faster and smoother operation, and troubleshoot network connectivity issues. In addition, you will be able to identify and remediate security vulnerabilities by scanning the system for malware, unauthorized access, or misconfigured settings. Furthermore, you will learn how to analyze and filter event logs with PowerShell and extract useful information from the system's records of events, errors, and warnings. This chapter will provide you with best practices, tips for practical scripting, and guidance on avoiding common pitfalls and challenges in using PowerShell for Windows troubleshooting.

Analyzing system resources

Analyzing system resources is a crucial part of troubleshooting and optimizing performance in Windows. PowerShell provides a robust toolkit for this purpose. PowerShell offers a range of cmdlets and functionalities to monitor and analyze system resources such as CPU usage, memory, disk space, and network activity. These tools are essential for diagnosing performance issues and ensuring the smooth operation of Windows systems.

You can use the **Get-Counter** cmdlet to get an overview of CPU usage. It can retrieve performance data from performance counters – system diagnostics tools that monitor various aspects of system performance. The following command displays the total CPU usage percentage, helping you identify if high CPU usage is a concern:

```
Get-Counter -Counter "\Processor(_Total)\% Processor Time"
```

The following figure displays the total CPU usage percentage:

Figure 12.1: Displays the total CPU usage percentage

You can also sample the performance counter data and then format it into a table using PowerShell. The following example samples the processor counter and returns a formatted table, as shown:

```
Get-Counter `
    -Counter "\Processor(_Total)\% Processor Time" `
    -SampleInterval 1 `
    -MaxSamples 5 | `
        Select-Object -ExpandProperty CounterSamples | `
            Select-Object `
                -Property Timestamp, CookedValue | `
                    Format-Table -AutoSize
```

The following figure samples the processor counter and returns a formatted table:

```
Timestamp                  CookedValue
---------                  -----------
11/27/2023 8:25:46 AM             3.37
11/27/2023 8:25:47 AM             2.68
11/27/2023 8:25:48 AM             0.02
11/27/2023 8:25:49 AM             0.38
11/27/2023 8:25:50 AM             1.76
```

Figure 12.2: Displays the sampled processor counter as a table

You can also use the **Get-Counter** cmdlet to retrieve various system information, such as the memory on the server. The following example displays the amount of free memory and the percentage of memory used:

```
Get-Counter -Counter "\Memory\Available MBytes"

Get-Counter `
    -Counter "\Memory\Available MBytes" `
    -SampleInterval 1 `
    -MaxSamples 5 | `
        Select-Object -ExpandProperty CounterSamples | `
            Select-Object `
                -Property Timestamp, CookedValue | `
                    Format-Table -AutoSize
```

The following figure displays the amount of free memory and the percentage of memory used:

```
Timestamp                    CookedValue
---------                    -----------
11/27/2023 8:26:47 AM          10513.00
11/27/2023 8:26:48 AM          10507.00
11/27/2023 8:26:49 AM          10507.00
11/27/2023 8:26:50 AM          10506.00
11/27/2023 8:26:51 AM          10507.00
```

Figure 12.3: Displays the sampled memory counter as a table

Disk management is a core administration task for any system administrator. PowerShell also provides the ability to check the disk performance. To display each disk with its used and available disk space, you can use the **Get-Counter** or the dedicated **Get-PSDrive** command:

Get-Counter -Counter "\LogicalDisk(*)\Free Megabytes"

Get-PSDrive -PSProvider FileSystem

The following figure displays the amount of free disk storage:

```
Name   Used (GB)   Free (GB) Provider   Root
----   ---------   --------- --------   ----
C          36.25      219.03 FileSystem C:\
D                           FileSystem D:\
Temp       36.25      219.03 FileSystem C:\Users\liamcleary\AppData\Local\…
```

Figure 12.4: Displays disks free storage

The performance of disks is found in the read/write speeds and queue length. You can retrieve this information again using the **Get-Counter** command and the **LogicalDisk** counter option:

Get-Counter -Counter "\LogicalDisk(*)\Disk Read Bytes/sec"

Get-Counter -Counter "\LogicalDisk(*)\Disk Write Bytes/sec"

Get-Counter -Counter "\LogicalDisk(*)\Current Disk Queue Length"

You can combine the counter queries into a single query instead of executing three commands:

Get-Counter `
            -Counter "\LogicalDisk(*)\Disk Read Bytes/sec",
                    "\LogicalDisk(*)\Disk Write Bytes/sec",
                    "\LogicalDisk(*)\Current Disk Queue Length"

Analyzing network usage is vital, especially in diagnosing network-related performance issues. You can query the **Network Interface** counter to view network traffic information for each interface:

```
Get-Counter -Counter "\Network Interface(*)\Bytes Total/sec"
```

The following example samples the network traffic and returns the results as a formatted table:

```
Get-Counter -Counter "\Network Interface(*)\Bytes Total/sec" `
            -SampleInterval 1 `
            -MaxSamples 5 | `
                Select-Object -ExpandProperty CounterSamples | `
                    Select-Object `
                            -Property Timestamp,
                            CookedValue, Path | `
                                For-
mat-Table -AutoSize
```

The following figure displays disk information from querying three disk counters:

```
Timestamp                 CookedValue   Path
---------                 -----------   ----
11/27/2023 8:30:55 AM           0.00   \\helloitsliamwin\network
11/27/2023 8:30:56 AM           0.00   \\helloitsliamwin\network
11/27/2023 8:30:57 AM           0.00   \\helloitsliamwin\network
11/27/2023 8:30:58 AM         215.32   \\helloitsliamwin\network
11/27/2023 8:30:59 AM         216.94   \\helloitsliamwin\network
```

Figure 12.5: Displays network interface counter information

As with other components within PowerShell, there are dedicated cmdlets for accessing network adapter and interface information. You can use **Get-NetAdapterStatistics** to retrieve similar information to the network performance counters:

```
Get-NetAdapterStatistics

Get-NetAdapterStatistics | `
    Select-Object -Property Name, ReceivedBytes, SentBytes
```

The following figure displays network information after executing the dedicated PowerShell cmdlet:

```
Name       ReceivedBytes   SentBytes
----       -------------   ---------
Ethernet       394194233    13014679
```

Figure 12.6: Displays network interface information

You can also use the **Get-NetAdapter** to retrieve specific network adapter details like what you would retrieve from the other commands but targeted to the adapters:

```
Get-NetAdapter | Select-Object -Property Name, LinkSpeed, Status
```

Combining both commands, you can retrieve the adapter details and network statistics:

```
Get-NetAdapter | Get-NetAdapterStatistics | `
    Select-Object -Property Name, ReceivedBytes, SentBytes
```

Another essential counter to review within servers is running processes. Identifying resource-intensive processes is often the first step in troubleshooting. You can list all running processes along with their CPU and memory usage using the following commands:

```
Get-Counter -Counter "\Process(*)\% Processor Time"
```

```
Get-Counter -Counter "\Process(*)\Working Set - Private"
```

You can use the **Get-Counter** command to query the **Process** counter, or you can use the dedicated **Get-Process** cmdlet. The following example uses the **Get-Process** cmdlet:

```
Get-Process
```

```
Get-Process | Select-Object -Property ProcessName, CPU, WorkingSet
```

The following figure displays process information:

```
ProcessName                        CPU  WorkingSet
-----------                        ---  ----------
AggregatorHost                    0.12     9158656
ApplicationFrameHost              0.20    44384256
backgroundTaskHost                0.12    32129024
Code                              0.30    91377664
Code                              0.31   109555712
Code                              0.05    31047680
Code                              5.83    93405184
Code                              0.31    94941184
Code                           1060.14   253366272
Code                              2.69   108060672
Code                             86.36   131293184
Code                              0.22    85245952
Code                              0.91    42967040
Code                             31.78   278540288
Code                              0.44    82317312
Code                              4.11   254689280
coherence                         0.03     7319552
coherence                         0.03     9641984
conhost                           0.23     8630272
csrss                             0.53     7036928
csrss                             2.36    72728576
```

Figure 12.7: Display process information

Establishing a performance baseline can be vital for ongoing system health monitoring. With PowerShell, you can collect and store performance data regularly, which you can use for comparison in future troubleshooting. The first task is to combine the counter queries into a counter set to execute in a single command:

```
$counterSet = @(
    "\Processor(_Total)\% Processor Time",
    "\Memory\% Committed Bytes In Use",
    "\PhysicalDisk(_Total)\Disk Read Bytes/sec")
```

You can then query the counters within the counter set and export the details to an XML file:

```
$performanceData = Get-Counter `
    -Counter $counterSet `
    -SampleInterval 2 `
    -MaxSamples 60


$performanceData | Export-Clixml `
    -Path "C:\PowerShell\PerformanceBaseline.xml"
```

The following figure displays the exported XML file with the counter details:

Figure 12.8: Display counter set information within the exported XML

By regularly analyzing these aspects of your system, you can identify and troubleshoot performance issues more effectively. PowerShell's flexibility in scripting allows for automating these checks, which can be particularly useful in larger environments or for routine maintenance tasks.

Diagnosing and resolving performance bottlenecks

Performance bottlenecks can cause significant issues in Windows environments, leading to slow response times, decreased productivity, and system crashes. Identifying and resolving these bottlenecks is crucial to ensure the optimal functioning of the system. PowerShell, a powerful command-line tool, provides extensive tools and cmdlets designed explicitly for practical performance analysis and troubleshooting. These tools allow for in-depth analysis of system performance, resource usage, and application behavior, enabling administrators to pinpoint the root cause of any performance issues and take appropriate corrective actions. By leveraging PowerShell's performance diagnostics capabilities, administrators can ensure their Windows environments' stability, reliability, and efficiency.

A performance bottleneck occurs when a component reduces system performance. PowerShell identifies bottlenecks by monitoring system resources.

For example, we can simulate excessive memory by executing the following PowerShell:

```
$end = (Get-Date).AddMinutes(2)
while ((Get-Date) -lt $end) {
    [math]::Sqrt((Get-Random -Min 1 -Max 100))
}
```

This command generates random square root numbers for 2 minutes. To see the effect on the CPU, you can then execute the following command:

```
Get-Process | `
    Sort-Object -Property CPU -Descending | `
        Select-Object -First 10 -Property Id, ProcessName, CPU
```

The following figure displays the most CPU-intensive processes running on the Windows server:

```
                 Id ProcessName          CPU
                 --  -----------        ------
               8860 Code              1087.62
               1256 dwm                405.17
               3424 MsMpEng            297.88
               9392 Code                90.62
                  4 System             61.64
               1896 pwsh                43.89
               9856 Code                32.02
               5000 explorer            30.73
              10764 Code                22.66
               2364 svchost             19.80
```

Figure 12.9: Displays CPU intensive processes

You can use PowerShell to simulate other intensive memory processes. Execute the following example code, which allocates significant memory over time:

```
function Consume-Memory {

    param (

        [int]$MB

    )

    $bytes = New-Object byte[] ($MB * 1024 * 1024)

    $random = New-Object Random

    $random.NextBytes($bytes)

}


$startTime = Get-Date

$duration = New-TimeSpan -Minutes 5

$chunkSizeMB = 10


while ((Get-Date) -lt $startTime.Add($duration)) {

    Write-Host "Allocating $chunkSizeMB MB of memory." -ForegroundColor Red

    Consume-Memory -MB $chunkSizeMB

    Start-Sleep -Seconds 10
```

}

To see the effect on the memory, you can then execute the following command:

```
Get-Process | `
    Sort-Object -Property WS -Descending | `
        Select-Object -First 10 -Property Id, ProcessName, WS
```

The following figure displays the **pwsh** process running on the Windows server:

```
   Id ProcessName              WS
   -- -----------              --
 5000 explorer           442171392
 6036 SearchHost         331198464
 1896 pwsh               285376512
 9856 Code               279756800
10764 Code               268431360
 8860 Code               268320768
 3424 MsMpEng            252461056
13652 pwsh               241209344
 9728 msedge             206098432
 7328 GitHubDesktop      202121216
```

Figure 12.10: Displays memory intensive process (pwsh)

Sometimes, specific services can cause bottlenecks. You can execute the following command to check the status and performance of all running services. The command returns the services, their internal processes, and CPU and memory usage:

```
Get-Service | `
    Where-Object -FilterScript { $_.Status -eq "Running" } | `
        ForEach-Object -Process { Get-Process } | `
            Select-Object -Property ProcessName, CPU, WorkingSet | `
            Sort-Object -Property CPU -Descending | `
            Format-Table -AutoSize
```

This query type provides a static snapshot of running services and processes you can manually review to identify potential bottlenecks. After identifying the bottleneck, resolution might involve terminating a process, adding more resources, or changing system configurations. For instance, you could execute the following command to stop a high-resource-consuming process:

```
Stop-Process -Id 2376 -Force
```

Regular monitoring and analysis can prevent performance bottlenecks. Automate the monitoring process using scheduled tasks in PowerShell and log the results for trend analysis. You can use scheduled Windows tasks that regularly check the server for potential issues:

```
$scriptBlock = {

$monitoringData = @()

$cpuUsage = Get-Counter `

    -Counter "\Processor(_Total)\% Processor Time" `

    -ErrorAction SilentlyContinue

$monitoringData += [PSCustomObject]@{

    ResourceType = "CPU Usage"

    Value = "$($cpuUsage.CounterSamples.CookedValue)%"

}


$memoryUsage = Get-Counter `

    -Counter "\Memory\Available MBytes" `

    -ErrorAction SilentlyContinue

    $monitoringData += [PSCustomObject]@{

    ResourceType = "Available Memory"

    Value = "$($memoryUsage.CounterSamples.CookedValue) MB"

}


$diskUsage = Get-PSDrive -PSProvider FileSystem

foreach ($disk in $diskUsage) {

$monitoringData += [PSCustomObject]@{

    ResourceType = "Disk Space on Drive $($disk.Name)"

    Value = "Used - $($disk.Used / 1GB) GB, Free - $($disk.Free / 1GB) GB"

}
```

```
}

$networkTraffic = Get-Counter `
    -Counter "\Network Interface(*)\Bytes Total/sec" `
    -ErrorAction SilentlyContinue
foreach ($interface in $networkTraffic.CounterSamples) {
$monitoringData += [PSCustomObject]@{
    ResourceType = "Network Traffic on $($interface.InstanceName)"
    Value = "$($interface.CookedValue) Bytes/sec"
}
}

$monitoringData | Export-Clixml -Path "C:\PowerShell\MonitoringData.xml"
}

$scriptPath = "C:\PowerShell\MonitoringData.ps1"
$scriptBlock | Out-File -FilePath $scriptPath

$trigger = New-ScheduledTaskTrigger `
    -AtStartup -RandomDelay (New-TimeSpan -Minutes 30)

$action = New-ScheduledTaskAction `
    -Execute "`"C:\Program Files\PowerShell\7\pwsh.exe`"" `
    -Argument "-File `"$scriptPath`""

Register-ScheduledTask `
    -TaskName "SystemPerformanceMonitoring" `
    -Trigger $trigger `
    -Action $action `
```

    -Description "System Performance Monitoring Task"

By regularly using these PowerShell tools and techniques, administrators can avoid performance issues, ensuring that the Windows environment remains stable and efficient.

Troubleshooting network connectivity issues

Troubleshooting network connectivity issues is a common task for system administrators. PowerShell provides various tools and cmdlets that can help diagnose and resolve network-related problems. Network issues range from simple misconfigurations to complex problems involving multiple network components. PowerShell offers cmdlets like **Test-Connection**, **Get-NetIPAddress**, and **Test-NetConnection** for diagnosing these issues.

To begin troubleshooting, start with a basic ping test to check connectivity. The **Test-Connection** cmdlet works like the traditional ping command. This command checks the connectivity to **www.example.local**:

`Test-Connection -ComputerName www.example.local`

For more detailed diagnostics, **Test-NetConnection** is a versatile tool. You can use it to test a specific port. This example tries the connection to port **80** on **www.example.local**:

```
Test-NetConnection `
    -ComputerName www.example.local `
    -Port 80
```

You can also view the current IP configuration of your machine's network adapter, including viewing the DNS servers currently used:

`Get-NetIPAddress`

`Get-NetIPAddress | Select-Object IPAddress`

The following example excludes all IP version 6 addresses and returns IP version 4 addresses plus the current DNS Server entries:

```
Get-NetAdapter | `
Select-Object `
    -Property Name, LinkSpeed, Status,
        @{ Name="IPv4 Address";Expression={ (Get-NetIPAddress -InterfaceIndex
        $_.ifIndex -AddressFamily IPv4).IPAddress }},
```

```
@{ Name="IPv4 DNS Servers";Expression={ (Get-DnsClientServerAddress
-InterfaceIndex $_.ifIndex -AddressFamily IPv4).ServerAddresses }} |
Format-Table -AutoSize
```

The following figure displays the IP version 4 addresses and the currently configured DNS servers:

Figure 12.11: Displays IP Addresses and DNS Servers

DNS problems can prevent access to network resources. To check DNS resolution, you can use the **Resolve-DnsName** cmdlet. This command resolves the DNS name to an IP address:

Resolve-DnsName www.example.local

Incorrect routing can lead to connectivity issues. To view the network route table and check for correct routes, you execute **Get-NetRoute**. This command shows the route entries in the system:

Get-NetRoute

The **Get-NetRoute** does not directly tell us whether a route is **working** in the sense of successfully routing packets to its destination. It only provides the configured routes. You typically send a network request (like a ping) to test a route's functionality to the destination:

```
$routeEntries = Get-NetRoute | Where-Object { $_.DestinationPrefix -notmatch
"^127\.0\.0\." -and $_.AddressFamily -eq 2 }


foreach ($route in $routeEntries) {

    $destination = ($route.DestinationPrefix -split '/')[0]

    if ($destination -eq "0.0.0.0" -or $destination -eq $route.NextHop) {
    continue }

    Write-Host "Testing route to destination: $destination"

    $result = Test-Connection -ComputerName $destination -Count 1 -Quiet

    if ($result) {
```

```
        Write-Host "Route to $destination is working." -ForegroundColor Green
    } else {
        Write-Host "Route to $destination failed." -ForegroundColor Red
    }
}
```

The following figure displays testing each route from the **Get-NetRoute** command:

```
Testing route to destination: 255.255.255.255
Route to 255.255.255.255 failed.
Testing route to destination: 255.255.255.255
Route to 255.255.255.255 failed.
Testing route to destination: 224.0.0.0
Route to 224.0.0.0 failed.
Testing route to destination: 224.0.0.0
Route to 224.0.0.0 failed.
Testing route to destination: 127.255.255.255
Route to 127.255.255.255 failed.
Testing route to destination: 10.211.55.255
Route to 10.211.55.255 failed.
Testing route to destination: 10.211.55.3
Route to 10.211.55.3 is working.
Testing route to destination: 10.211.55.0
Route to 10.211.55.0 failed.
```

Figure 12.12: Testing each route from Get-NetRoute

For bandwidth issues, you should test the network speed. While PowerShell does not have a built-in cmdlet for speed tests, you use the **Test-Connection** cmdlet:

```
$computerName = "www.example.local"

$port = 80


$tcpTestResult = Test-NetConnection `

    -ComputerName $computerName `

    -Port $port `

    -InformationLevel Detailed


$pingTestResult = Test-Connection `

    -ComputerName $computerName -Count 1
```

```
$result = [PSCustomObject]@{

    ComputerName = $tcpTestResult.ComputerName

    RemoteAddress = $tcpTestResult.RemoteAddress

    RemotePort = $tcpTestResult.RemotePort

    InterfaceAlias = $tcpTestResult.InterfaceAlias

    InterfaceDescription = $tcpTestResult.InterfaceDescription

    TcpTestSucceeded = $tcpTestResult.TcpTestSucceeded

    Latency = $pingTestResult.Latency

    PingSucceeded = $pingTestResult.StatusCode -eq 0

    PingReplyDetails = $pingTestResult

}

$result | Format-Table -AutoSize
```

The following figure displays the network return details from testing a network connection using its DNS name:

Figure 12.13: Testing results using test-connection

You can also create a script to automate the diagnostics and run it regularly or when issues are detected. The following example combines multiple troubleshooting commands and then exports the results into a text file:

```
$scriptBlock = {

$outputFile = "C:\PowerShell\OutputFile.txt"


Test-Connection  -ComputerName  www.example.local  |  Out-File  -FilePath $outputFile -Append

Test-NetConnection  -ComputerName  www.example.local  -Port 80  |  Out-File -FilePath $outputFile -Append
```

```
Get-NetIPAddress | Out-File -FilePath $outputFile -Append

Resolve-DnsName www.example.local | Out-File -FilePath $outputFile -Append

Get-NetRoute | Out-File -FilePath $outputFile -Append

Get-NetAdapter | Select-Object Name, Status, LinkSpeed | Out-File -FilePath $outputFile -Append

Get-Counter -Counter "\Network Interface(*)\Bytes Total/sec" | Out-File -FilePath $outputFile -Append

}

& $scriptBlock
```

The following figure displays the values stored in the output text file after executing the diagnostic commands:

```
Destination: www.example.com

Ping Source         Address              Latency BufferSize Status
                                          (ms)    (B)
----  ------        -------              ------- ---------- ------
   1 HELLOITSLIAMWIN... 93.184.216.34          9         32 Success
   2 HELLOITSLIAMWIN... 93.184.216.34          9         32 Success
   3 HELLOITSLIAMWIN... 93.184.216.34         10         32 Success
   4 HELLOITSLIAMWIN... 93.184.216.34         10         32 Success


ComputerName       : www.example.com
RemoteAddress      : 93.184.216.34
RemotePort         : 80
InterfaceAlias     : Ethernet
SourceAddress      : 10.211.55.3
TcpTestSucceeded   : True


IPAddress          : fe80::5574:957b:1002:3e84%9
InterfaceIndex     : 9
InterfaceAlias     : Ethernet
AddressFamily      : IPv6
Type               : Unicast
PrefixLength       : 64
PrefixOrigin       : WellKnown
SuffixOrigin       : Link
AddressState       : Preferred
ValidLifetime      : Infinite ([TimeSpan]::MaxValue)
PreferredLifetime  : Infinite ([TimeSpan]::MaxValue)
```

Figure 12.14: View the diagnostic results text file

By utilizing these PowerShell tools and commands, you can systematically approach network troubleshooting, diagnose the root causes of issues, and take steps toward resolution. Network environments can be complex, and multiple factors might contribute to a problem, so a comprehensive approach is often necessary.

Identifying and remediating security vulnerabilities

Identifying and remediating security vulnerabilities is crucial to maintaining a secure and reliable IT environment. PowerShell offers various cmdlets and scripts that you can use to identify potential security risks and apply necessary remediations. Let us explore how PowerShell can be instrumental in this regard. Security is paramount, and PowerShell provides a powerful platform for automating security checks and responses. PowerShell can effectively manage proactive security with built-in cmdlets for security-related tasks and the ability to interface with Windows security features.

Staying updated with the latest security patches is critical. Using PowerShell, you can check for and install pending Windows updates. This command utilizes the **PSWindowsUpdate** module to find and install available updates automatically:

```
Install-Module PSWindowsUpdate

Import-Module PSWindowsUpdate

Get-WindowsUpdate
```

Analyzing the current state of the Windows Firewall can help identify potential weaknesses. The following command provides an overview of the firewall profiles and their configurations:

```
Get-NetFirewallProfile | `

Select-Object Name, Enabled, DefaultInboundAction, DefaultOutboundAction
```

The following figure displays the current firewall profile details:

Name	Enabled	DefaultInboundAction	DefaultOutboundAction
Domain	True	NotConfigured	NotConfigured
Private	True	NotConfigured	NotConfigured
Public	True	NotConfigured	NotConfigured

Figure 12.15: Displays the network firewall profile details

Windows Firewall has three profiles: **Domain, Private**, and **Public**. Each profile corresponds to a different network type and has its own set of rules and configurations. The computer applies the Domain Profile when connected to a domain. It uses the Private Profile for private or home networks. It activates the Public Profile for public networks like Wi-Fi hotspots.

To review specific firewall rules, you can use the **Get-NetFirewallRule** cmdlet. For example, you can list all enabled inbound rules using the following code:

```
Get-NetFirewallRule -Direction Inbound -Enabled True
```

However, you may only need to view some firewall rules. Instead, you may need to check on specific ones that protect file sharing. You can filter rules based on name, group, or action criteria. For instance, you can execute the following code to find all file-related rules:

```
Get-NetFirewallRule `
    -Group "*File*" | `
Select-Object Name, Action, Enabled, Direction
```

The following figure displays only the current firewall rules in the group **File and Printer Sharing**:

```
Name                                        Action  Enabled  Direction
----                                        ------  -------  ---------
{B6D4AAF3-921E-40C0-AA0E-AC982FF1E61B}      Allow   True     Outbound
{EB66408A-54C7-4100-B66B-AE644A276B4E}      Allow   True     Outbound
```

Figure 12.16: Displays the file-related firewall rules

For troubleshooting or monitoring, you can enable logging of dropped packets or successful connections using the following PowerShell commands:

```
Set-NetFirewallProfile `
    -All `
    -LogFileName "%systemroot%\System32\LogFiles\Firewall\pfirewall.log" `
    -LogAllowed True `
    -LogBlocked True
```

Regularly reviewing firewall configurations is crucial for maintaining security.

Open ports can be entry points for attackers. Use PowerShell to check for listening ports. This command lists all TCP ports on which the computer is listening:

```
Get-NetTCPConnection -State Listen
```

The following figure displays all listening ports:

LocalAddress	LocalPort	RemoteAddress	RemotePort	State
::	49670	::	0	Listen
::	49668	::	0	Listen
::	49667	::	0	Listen
::	49666	::	0	Listen
::	49665	::	0	Listen
::	49664	::	0	Listen
::	7680	::	0	Listen
::	445	::	0	Listen
::	135	::	0	Listen
127.0.0.1	49881	0.0.0.0	0	Listen
0.0.0.0	49670	0.0.0.0	0	Listen
0.0.0.0	49668	0.0.0.0	0	Listen
0.0.0.0	49667	0.0.0.0	0	Listen
0.0.0.0	49666	0.0.0.0	0	Listen
0.0.0.0	49665	0.0.0.0	0	Listen
0.0.0.0	49664	0.0.0.0	0	Listen
127.0.0.1	30631	0.0.0.0	0	Listen
0.0.0.0	5040	0.0.0.0	0	Listen
10.211.55.3	139	0.0.0.0	0	Listen
0.0.0.0	135	0.0.0.0	0	Listen

Figure 12.17: Display all listening ports

You can enforce this command by color coding the TCP ports associated with a process as green and those without an associated process as red:

```
Get-NetTCPConnection | ForEach-Object {
    if ($_.OwningProcess -eq 0) {
        Write-Host $_.LocalAddress $_.LocalPort $_.RemoteAddress $_.RemotePort
        -ForegroundColor Green
    } else {
        Write-Host $_.LocalAddress $_.LocalPort $_.RemoteAddress $_.RemotePort
        -ForegroundColor Red
    }
}
```

The following figure displays all listening ports and colors them either green or red if they have a process assigned to them:

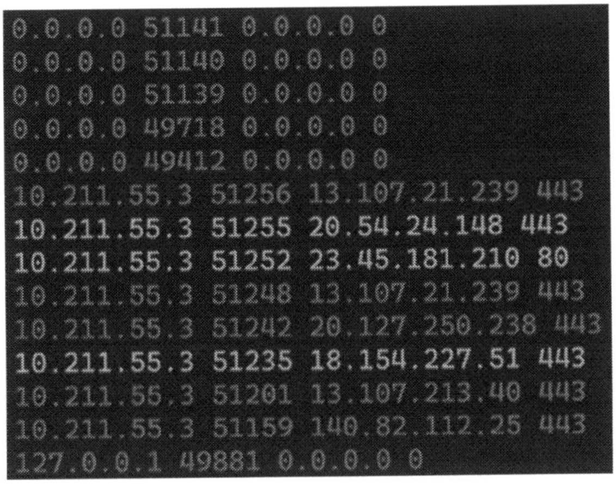

Figure 12.18: Display all listening ports and color code

Automate checks using scheduled PowerShell scripts to ensure ongoing compliance with your security policies. By leveraging these PowerShell commands, you can thoroughly review and manage your Windows Firewall settings, ensuring your network is protected against unauthorized access while allowing legitimate traffic.

Analyzing and filtering event logs

Analyzing and filtering event logs is integral to troubleshooting and optimizing Windows performance. PowerShell provides powerful cmdlets to access, filter, and analyze these logs. Let's explore how you can effectively utilize PowerShell to work with Windows event logs. Event logs in Windows hold a wealth of information about system activities, errors, and operations. With its **Get-EventLog** and **Get-WinEvent** cmdlets, PowerShell offers a flexible approach to accessing and analyzing this data.

Get-EventLog is the older cmdlet primarily used for accessing classic event logs such as **System**, **Application**, and **Security** from older versions of Windows. It is simple to use and sufficient for basic log retrieval tasks, but it cannot access the newer, more complex event logs introduced with later versions of Windows.

Get-WinEvent is a more advanced cmdlet that allows for querying classic and modern event logs, including the newer **Event Trace Log** (ETL) files. It provides more robust filtering options, can handle complex queries with XML, and is generally faster and more flexible than **Get-EventLog**, especially when dealing with large volumes of log data. **Get-WinEvent** is better suited for advanced forensic analysis and is the preferred tool for scripting and automation tasks that require interaction with the Windows Event

Log service on newer Windows platforms. Using either command, you can easily list all available event logs on your system:

`Get-EventLog -List`

`Get-WinEvent -ListLog *`

Retrieving entries from a specific event log requires passing the name of the event log to the command. The following example retrieves 50 events from the system event log:

`Get-WinEvent -LogName System -MaxEvents 50`

The following figure displays fifty system event logs:

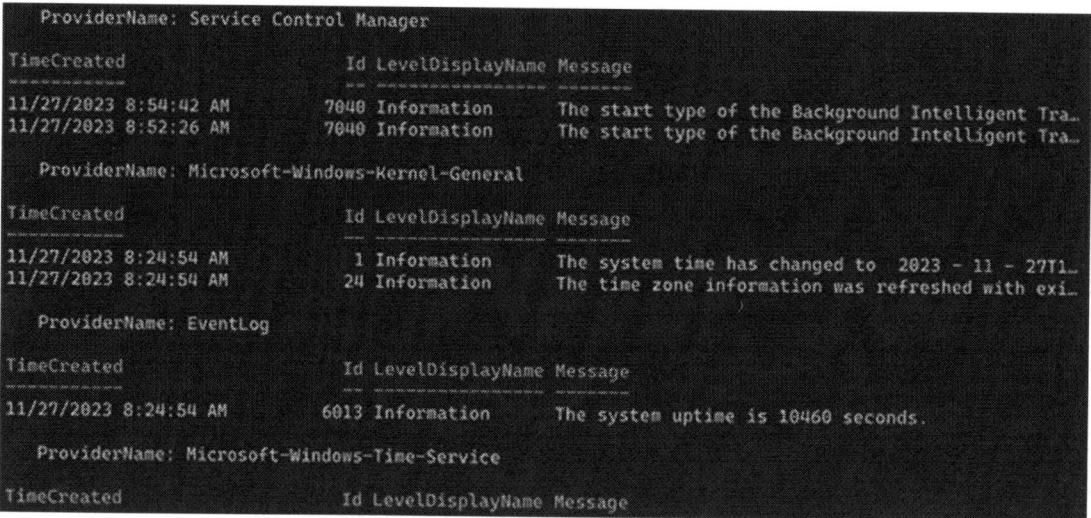

Figure 12.19: Display 50 system event log entries

You can also filter logs within a specific time frame. For example, you can execute the following command to see entries from the last 24 hours of the system log:

```
Get-WinEvent -FilterHashtable @{
    LogName = 'System';StartTime = (Get-Date).AddDays(-1);
}
```

The following figure displays the last 24 hours of entries from the System event log:

```
 ProviderName: Service Control Manager

TimeCreated                    Id LevelDisplayName Message
-----------                    -- ---------------- -------
11/27/2023 8:54:42 AM        7040 Information      The start type of the Background Intelligent Tra...
11/27/2023 8:52:26 AM        7040 Information      The start type of the Background Intelligent Tra...

 ProviderName: Microsoft-Windows-Kernel-General

TimeCreated                    Id LevelDisplayName Message
-----------                    -- ---------------- -------
11/27/2023 8:24:54 AM           1 Information      The system time has changed to  2023 - 11 - 27T1...
11/27/2023 8:24:54 AM          24 Information      The time zone information was refreshed with exi...

 ProviderName: EventLog

TimeCreated                    Id LevelDisplayName Message
-----------                    -- ---------------- -------
11/27/2023 8:24:54 AM        6013 Information      The system uptime is 10460 seconds.

 ProviderName: Microsoft-Windows-Time-Service
```

Figure 12.20: Display system log entries from the last 24 hours

You can filter the entries by event type, such as errors or warnings, or if you know the event's ID:

```
Get-WinEvent -FilterHashtable @{
    LogName = 'System';
    Level = 2;
}

Get-WinEvent -FilterHashtable @{
    LogName = 'System';
    ID = 7001
}
```

You can also combine both queries but must use the **-FilterXml** property this time:

```
$filterXml = @'
<QueryList>
    <Query Id="0" Path="System">
        <Select Path="System">
```

```
            *[System[(Level=2) or (EventID=7001)]]
        </Select>
    </Query>
</QueryList>
'@

Get-WinEvent -FilterXml $filterXml
```

Get-WinEvent enables you to filter events based on various criteria and then extract and analyze the message field, which often includes human-readable descriptions and vital data not present in the basic event metadata. This level of analysis is instrumental for system administrators and security professionals who need to perform root cause analysis and develop strategies to mitigate similar incidents in the future. For a deeper analysis, you can examine the message content of events using this command:

```
Get-WinEvent `
    -LogName Application -MaxEvents 10 | `
Select-Object TimeCreated, Message
```

The following figure returns ten application event log entries but only returns the time created and the message:

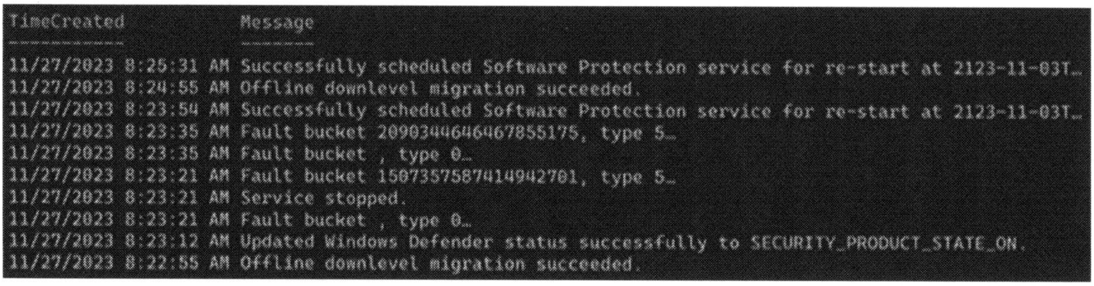

Figure 12.21: Display 10 application event log entries and display the message

For more advanced filtering, especially with large logs, you can use **Get-WinEvent** with various properties. The following example uses a hashtable to filter the System log for errors (Level=2) from the last day:

```
Get-WinEvent `
    -FilterHashtable @{
        LogName='System';
```

```
    Level=2;

    StartTime=(Get-Date).AddDays(-1)}
```

The following figure returns system log entries of type error for the last day:

```
TimeCreated                    Id LevelDisplayName Message
-----------                    -- ---------------- -------
11/27/2023 8:23:54 AM          34 Error            The time service has detected that the system ti…

    ProviderName: Microsoft-Windows-WindowsUpdateClient

TimeCreated                    Id LevelDisplayName Message
-----------                    -- ---------------- -------
11/27/2023 8:23:35 AM          20 Error            Installation Failure: Windows failed to install …
11/27/2023 8:23:21 AM          20 Error            Installation Failure: Windows failed to install …
```

Figure 12.22: Display error log entries for the last day

Create PowerShell scripts to analyze and report on crucial event log data regularly. Automate these scripts using scheduled tasks for ongoing monitoring. Through PowerShell's comprehensive event log cmdlets, you can effectively analyze your system's health and performance, troubleshoot issues, and maintain an audit trail for security and compliance purposes. Regular and automated analysis of event logs can significantly aid in proactive system management.

Challenges in using PowerShell for Windows troubleshooting

Using PowerShell for Windows troubleshooting is incredibly powerful but has challenges and pitfalls. Understanding these can help you avoid common mistakes and use PowerShell more effectively. Let us look at four reasons why it can be challenging and the common pitfalls you may face as you manage your infrastructure.

Handling complex error messages

A common challenge when working with PowerShell is navigating the intricacies of its error messages, which can often be lengthy and convoluted, obscuring the root of the problem. For instance, if a cmdlet encounters a network-related failure, the resulting error message may present an extensive stack trace or cite .NET classes, leading to an information overload that can bewilder even experienced users. To effectively address this, it's advisable to concentrate on the initial lines of the error output, as these typically hold the essential details. Additionally, for a more thorough investigation, you can leverage the command **$Error [0] | Select-Object ***, which displays all the properties of the most recent error, providing greater insight and aiding in the troubleshooting process.

Execution policy restrictions

As a newcomer to PowerShell, it is challenging to execute scripts due to its execution policy. The execution policy is in place to prevent the execution of potentially harmful scripts. You might encounter an error message if you try to run a downloaded script. The execution policy on your system, configured to **Restricted** or **AllSigned**, either prevents any scripts from running or only allows scripts signed by a trusted publisher. To check the current policy settings, you can use the `Get-ExecutionPolicy` cmdlet. For safer script execution, especially for scripts from the internet, you can set the policy to **RemoteSigned** using the `Set-ExecutionPolicy RemoteSigned -Scope CurrentUser` command. It will allow scripts signed by a recognized authority to run while blocking unsigned scripts from unknown sources. This way, you can leverage the powerful scripting capabilities of PowerShell while having an added layer of protection.

Misinterpretation of command outputs

When working with PowerShell, a powerful scripting language that outputs data in an object-oriented format, it can be challenging to interpret the results of its commands. For example, when using the `Get-Service` cmdlet to assess the operational status of services on a Windows system, a service reported as stopped does not necessarily indicate a malfunction. It could be in its default or intended state. To avoid misinterpretations, it is crucial to clearly understand what constitutes a normal state for a given service and apply context-aware analysis while leveraging PowerShell's robust filtering capabilities. To isolate services that are actively running, you can refine the output by appending a filter like `Where-Object {$_.Status -eq 'Running' }`. This approach provides targeted insights into the services' states and ensures a more accurate interpretation of the system's status.

Overlooking security implications

When working with PowerShell scripts, you must be aware of their potential to make system-wide modifications that could unintentionally introduce security vulnerabilities. For example, a script designed to modify firewall configurations or manipulate user accounts may compromise the system's security if not handled carefully. To avoid such risks, it is essential to thoroughly review and test scripts in a controlled environment before executing them in a live setting. It is also vital to fully understand the implications of each change the script will make and to apply the principle of least privilege. Additionally, utilizing PowerShell's built-in logging mechanisms and the `-WhatIf` parameter can add a layer of safety and oversight. The `-WhatIf` parameter simulates the outcome of a script without implementing any changes, allowing you to see potential results before making any modifications.

While PowerShell is a powerful tool for troubleshooting and optimizing Windows systems, it is essential to approach it with an understanding of these common pitfalls. By focusing on clear error interpretation, being aware of execution policies, accurately interpreting command outputs, and considering the security implications of scripts, you can leverage PowerShell more effectively and safely in your troubleshooting and optimization tasks.

Conclusion

Throughout this chapter, you have comprehensively understood how to troubleshoot and optimize performance in Windows environments using PowerShell. We have explored various scenarios, from performance bottlenecks to security, networking, and application compatibility issues. You have seen how you can use PowerShell to diagnose and resolve common challenges in Windows systems and how effectively it analyzes system resources and identifies critical concerns. You have learned how to troubleshoot network connectivity problems and address security vulnerabilities precisely. Additionally, we have demonstrated the power of PowerShell in managing and configuring Windows services, event logs, and system settings, which reinforces its role in enhancing system stability and reliability.

In the next chapter, you will focus on securing PowerShell by understanding execution policies, using AppLocker within Windows, and signing PowerShell scripts.

Join our book's Discord space

Join the book's Discord Workspace for Latest updates, Offers, Tech happenings around the world, New Release and Sessions with the Authors:

https://discord.bpbonline.com

Chapter 13
Miscellaneous PowerShell Capabilities

Introduction

This chapter will guide you through various aspects of PowerShell security. You will learn best practices to enhance the security of this powerful tool. You will gain an understanding of the importance of securing PowerShell environments. It is essential for protecting your systems and data from unauthorized access and malicious activities. You will also delve into PowerShell Execution Policies. You will gain insights into how they govern the execution of scripts and how to configure them for optimal security. You will learn to keep your computer and data secure using PowerShell. It will ensure that your operations are efficient and safeguarded against potential threats. You will review PowerShell Constrained Mode and how it restricts PowerShell's capabilities to prevent misuse.

Additionally, you will learn about employing AppLocker policies, which will help you turn off unauthorized PowerShell scripts. It is a critical measure in securing enterprise environments. You will also learn signing PowerShell scripts and the importance of script integrity and authenticity. Finally, the chapter will offer guidance on the next steps for IT administrators.

Structure

In this chapter, we will cover the following topics:

- Importance of securing PowerShell
- Understanding PowerShell Execution Policies
- Keeping computer and data secure
- Understand PowerShell Constrained Mode
- Using AppLocker policies to disable PowerShell scripts
- Signing PowerShell Scripts for reuse
- Next Steps for the IT administrator

Objectives

By the end of this chapter, you will understand how to secure PowerShell, an essential tool in modern Windows administration. The chapter will guide you through the importance of securing PowerShell and why it is necessary to protect this powerful tool from misuse or malicious exploitation. You will learn about PowerShell Execution Policies and how to configure them to enhance security and control script execution. Additionally, you will learn practical steps to keep your computer and data secure while using PowerShell, ensuring that your administrative tasks do not compromise system integrity or confidentiality. The chapter will also introduce you to PowerShell Constrained Mode and how it can limit PowerShell's capabilities to minimize security risks. You will discover how to leverage AppLocker policies effectively to restrict unauthorized PowerShell scripts, an essential strategy in a secure enterprise environment. You will also understand signing PowerShell scripts for reuse, highlighting the importance of maintaining script integrity and authenticity.

Importance of securing PowerShell

PowerShell is a powerful command-line shell and scripting language deeply integrated into the Windows ecosystem. It simplifies system administration and automates complex tasks. With its ability to access various system components, PowerShell can perform many critical functions, including managing servers and workstations, configuring network settings, and automating routine tasks.

However, PowerShell's advanced capabilities can also attract attackers who can use it for malicious purposes, such as executing harmful scripts, extracting confidential information, or gaining unauthorized access to sensitive systems. Attackers often exploit PowerShell's extensive access to system internals to bypass traditional security measures, making it imperative to secure PowerShell environments.

To secure PowerShell, organizations must follow best practices such as enabling logging and monitoring, limiting administrative privileges, and enforcing strong password policies. Additionally, you can configure PowerShell to run in a constrained mode that restricts the use of potentially harmful commands, mitigating the risk of unauthorized and malicious activity. By taking these steps, organizations can enjoy the benefits of PowerShell while reducing the risk of cyber-attacks.

Understanding PowerShell Execution Policies

PowerShell Execution Policies are fundamental to PowerShell's security model. They provide a mechanism to control the execution of scripts and help prevent the execution of potentially harmful scripts. Understanding these policies is crucial for anyone managing or scripting in PowerShell.

Execution policies are configurations in PowerShell that determine the conditions under which PowerShell loads configuration files and runs scripts. These policies do not prevent the execution of individual cmdlets but control the execution of scripts, including script blocks and PowerShell profiles. PowerShell supports several execution policies:

- **Restricted**: The default policy that does not allow script execution.
- **AllSigned**: Requires that a trusted publisher signs all scripts and configuration files.
- **RemoteSigned**: A trusted publisher must sign all scripts downloaded online.
- **Unrestricted**: Allows all scripts to run but prompts the user before running scripts from the internet.

You can set execution policies at different scopes:

- **MachinePolicy**: Set by Group Policy for all users of the computer.
- **UserPolicy**: Set by Group Policy for the current user.
- **Process**: Only affects the current PowerShell session.
- **CurrentUser**: Affects only the current user.
- **LocalMachine**: Default scope affects all users on the computer.

You can check the current execution policy using the cmdlet:

```
Get-ExecutionPolicy
```

The following figure displays the active policy based on the scope hierarchy:

```
PS C:\PowerShell> Get-ExecutionPolicy
RemoteSigned
```

Figure 13.1: Displays the active execution policy

To change the execution policy, use the **Set-ExecutionPolicy** cmdlet. For example, to set the policy to **RemoteSigned** for the current user:

```
Set-ExecutionPolicy `
    -ExecutionPolicy Unrestricted `
    -Scope CurrentUser
```

The following figure displays setting the current user policy to **Unrestricted**:

```
PS C:\PowerShell> Set-ExecutionPolicy `
>> -ExecutionPolicy Unrestricted `
>> -Scope CurrentUser
PS C:\PowerShell> Get-ExecutionPolicy
Unrestricted
```

Figure 13.2: Set the current user execution policy to unrestricted

To set the execution policy for all users on the machine to **AllSigned**, which requires all scripts to be signed by a trusted publisher:

```
Set-ExecutionPolicy -ExecutionPolicy AllSigned -Scope LocalMachine
```

You can also remove or clear the execution policy set at a specific scope (for example, **CurrentUser**):

```
Set-ExecutionPolicy -ExecutionPolicy Undefined -Scope CurrentUser
```

Remember, modifying execution policies can have security implications, so it is essential to understand the consequences of these changes, especially in a production environment. While execution policies are not security boundaries, they provide a layer of defense by controlling script execution. Administrators should carefully choose an execution policy that balances security with operational needs.

It is important to note that you bypass execution policies. Users with administrative privileges can change or bypass these policies. Administrators can start a new PowerShell session with the execution policy temporarily set to **Bypass** (ignores the execution policy for the session):

```
pwsh -ExecutionPolicy Bypass
```

The following figure displays the current policy after launching PowerShell to bypass the policy:

```
PS C:\PowerShell> Get-ExecutionPolicy
RemoteSigned
PS C:\PowerShell> pwsh -ExecutionPolicy Bypass
PS C:\PowerShell> Get-ExecutionPolicy
Bypass
```

Figure 13.3: Launching PowerShell and bypassing the execution policy

It highlights that execution policies are part of a defense-in-depth strategy but should be one of many security measures relied upon.

In enterprise environments, you can manage execution policies via Group Policy. It ensures consistent policy application across multiple systems and users, enhancing the organization's security posture. When setting the execution policy to **AllSigned** and **RemoteSigned**, you must digitally sign all scripts to add an extra layer. Signing scripts adds a digital signature from a trusted certificate, ensuring the script's source and integrity.

One challenge with execution policies is ensuring compliance and understanding the difference between policy types. Administrators need to communicate and enforce the chosen policy effectively. As a best practice, use execution policies as part of a broader security strategy. Regularly review and update these policies in line with organizational security policies. For most environments, the **RemoteSigned** policy offers a good balance between security and usability.

Keeping computer and data secure

One of the first steps in securing your PowerShell environment is ensuring that your system, including PowerShell itself, is regularly updated with the latest security patches. Use PowerShell to check and install Windows and other Microsoft product updates automatically. You can do it using the **PSWindowsUpdate** module, which adds additional functionality to PowerShell for managing Windows updates. You can install and import this module and then schedule regular updates:

```
Install-Module PSWindowsUpdate

Import-Module PSWindowsUpdate

Get-WindowsUpdate -Install -AcceptAll -AutoReboot
```

In addition to updates, regularly monitor your system's security settings. PowerShell provides cmdlets like **Get-LocalUser** and **Get-LocalGroup** to audit local user accounts and groups, ensuring that only authorized users have the correct level of access. Regularly reviewing user permissions can prevent unauthorized access to sensitive data:

```
Get-LocalUser | `
Select-Object Name, Enabled, LastLogon, `
@{Name="IsAdmin";Expression={$userName = $_.Name
(Get-LocalGroupMember -Group "Administrators" | `
Where-Object { $_.Name -like "*\$userName" }).Count -gt 0}} | `
Format-Table -AutoSize
```

The following figure displays all users and if they are local or domain administrators:

```
Name          Enabled  LastLogon                IsAdmin
----          -------  ---------                -------
_Trainer      True     11/29/2023 8:06:32 PM    True
Guest         False                             False
krbtgt        False                             False
DomainUser1   True                              False
vmDC$         True     11/29/2023 8:01:31 PM    False
```

Figure 13.4: Display all users and show if they are local or domain administrators

To prevent the execution of potentially harmful scripts, configure and enforce appropriate execution policies. The **Set-ExecutionPolicy** cmdlet allows you to define the conditions under which PowerShell loads configuration files and runs scripts. For example, setting the policy to **RemoteSigned** requires that all scripts and configuration files downloaded from the internet are signed by a trusted publisher, thus preventing the execution of untrusted scripts:

```
Set-ExecutionPolicy `
    -ExecutionPolicy RemoteSigned `
    -Scope CurrentUser
```

In addition to setting execution policies, consider signing your PowerShell scripts. Script signing certifies the origin of a script and ensures no one has tampered with it since its signing. You must obtain a code signing certificate from a trusted authority to sign a script. Once you have the certificate, you can sign your scripts using the **Set-AuthenticodeSignature** cmdlet:

```
$cert = @(Get-ChildItem cert:\CurrentUser\My -CodeSigningCert)[0]
```

```
Set-AuthenticodeSignature `
    -FilePath "C:\PowerShell\Script.ps1" `
    -Certificate $cert
```

When running scripts, particularly those that handle sensitive data or make significant system changes, use best practices to avoid accidental data exposure or system modifications. Always test scripts in a non-production environment first and consider using the **-WhatIf** parameter, which shows what would happen if the cmdlet ran without executing any actions.

Use secure strings and PowerShell's built-in encryption capabilities to handle sensitive data, such as passwords or personal information. For example, when you need to store or transmit credentials, use the **ConvertTo-SecureString** and **Get-Credential** cmdlets:

```
$securePassword = ConvertTo-SecureString "PlainTextPassword" `
    -AsPlainText `
    -Force
$credential = New-Object System.Management.Automation.PSCredential ("Username", $securePassword)
```

In summary, keeping your computer and data secure while using PowerShell involves a combination of regular system updates, monitoring security settings, strict execution policies, script signing, and cautious handling of scripts and sensitive data. By adhering to these practices, you can leverage the power of PowerShell while maintaining a strong security posture.

Understanding PowerShell Constrained Mode

System administrators and security professionals must understand PowerShell Constrained Mode. This feature limits PowerShell's capabilities and makes it difficult for malicious scripts or attackers to exploit PowerShell's full functionality. PowerShell Constrained Mode is a security feature that restricts the capabilities of PowerShell to reduce the attack surface that PowerShell might present to an attacker. It primarily affects advanced scripting capabilities and some system interactions, making it a valuable tool in securing systems against threats that might leverage PowerShell for malicious purposes.

Constrained Mode is automatically enabled by PowerShell when it detects that it is running in an environment where system restrictions have been applied, such as AppLocker or

Device Guard. Administrators can also manually enforce Constrained Mode as part of their security strategy. To check if PowerShell is running in Constrained Mode, use:

$ExecutionContext.SessionState.LanguageMode

The following figure displays the current setting for Constrained Mode:

```
PS C:\PowerShell> $ExecutionContext.SessionState.LanguageMode
FullLanguage
```

Figure 13.5: Display the Constrained Mode Setting

Note: If the output is Constrained Language, PowerShell is running in Constrained Mode.

When using Constrained Mode, PowerShell restricts its capabilities in various ways. For example, access to the .NET framework is limited, and many reflective APIs are blocked. It means that complex scripts which rely on these features may function differently than intended. Nevertheless, basic cmdlets and language elements are still operational, enabling the execution of routine administrative tasks.

The primary benefit of the Constrained Mode is enhanced security. Limiting PowerShell's capabilities makes it much harder for attackers to execute complex, malicious scripts or leverage PowerShell for lateral movement and other common attack techniques. It is an effective countermeasure against fileless attacks and advanced persistent threats that utilize PowerShell.

While Constrained Mode can improve security, it may also restrict legitimate administrative scripts. Therefore, before implementing it, testing your existing PowerShell scripts in Constrained Mode is crucial to identify any incompatible ones. Additionally, some third-party management tools that rely on PowerShell may be affected.

Enabling PowerShell Constrained Mode is not done through individual PowerShell commands but through system-wide security settings. Constrained Mode is a security feature that is difficult to bypass and, therefore, does not have a straightforward PowerShell command to turn on or off. Instead, AppLocker or Device Guard usually manages it in enterprise environments.

You can use AppLocker to create a policy restricting PowerShell to Constrained Mode. It requires Group Policy configuration. Here is an example of how you might do it in a broader policy configuration setting, not directly via a PowerShell command:

1. Open the Group Policy Editor (**gpedit.msc**)
2. Navigate to **Computer Configuration | Windows Settings | Security Settings | Application Control Policies | AppLocker**

3. Right-click on **Script Rules** and select **Create New Rule**
4. Under the **Permissions** section, choose **Deny for Everyone**
5. Under **Conditions**, select **Path** and set the **Path** to `%windir%\System32\WindowsPowerShell\v1.0\powershell.exe.`
6. Enable the rule and enforce the policy.

This approach does not directly set Constrained Mode but restricts script execution so that PowerShell automatically switches to Constrained Mode.

Device Guard can also enforce Constrained Mode. It is a more advanced and secure way to manage scripts and applications, usually applied at the enterprise level. You can configure Device Guard policies using the `New-CIPolicy` cmdlet to create a Code Integrity policy. You can set up the policy to enforce script restrictions that trigger Constrained Mode in PowerShell. After creating the policy, you can deploy it via Group Policy or other management tools. This example creates a new policy file based on publisher data, which you can then deploy to enforce restrictions, including triggering Constrained Mode in PowerShell:

```
New-CIPolicy -Level Publisher -FilePath "C:\PowerShell\Policy.xml"
```

> **Note: Creating the policy file can take a while.**

You can also use PowerShell to set the Constrained Mode. However, it does not enforce Constrained Mode system-wide; you can select the language mode in a specific PowerShell session to mimic the constraints:

```
$ExecutionContext.SessionState.LanguageMode = "ConstrainedLanguage"
```

The following figure sets the current PowerShell session to Constrained Mode:

```
PS C:\PowerShell> $ExecutionContext.SessionState.LanguageMode = "ConstrainedLanguage"
PS C:\PowerShell> $ExecutionContext.SessionState.LanguageMode
ConstrainedLanguage
```

Figure 13.6: Set the constrained mode

This command sets the language mode of the current PowerShell session to Constrained Language, which restricts some of the PowerShell features, like Constrained Mode. However, it is important to note that this change is only for the current session and does not provide the same security level as the system-wide Constrained Mode enforced by AppLocker or Device Guard.

Remember to use Constrained Mode as just one aspect of a defense-in-depth strategy and combine it with other security measures like logging, monitoring, and user training. PowerShell Constrained Mode is vital for securing environments against PowerShell-based threats. It effectively reduces the attack surface by restricting PowerShell's advanced features, making it an essential tool in a comprehensive security strategy. However, its impact on legitimate administrative tasks and scripts should be carefully evaluated and tested.

Using AppLocker policies to disable PowerShell scripts

AppLocker is a feature available in some editions of Windows and Windows Server. Group Policy settings enable administrators to specify which users or groups can run organizational applications. AppLocker is an improvement over the Software Restriction Policies, offering greater granularity and more advanced features. AppLocker policies are rules you create to prevent applications from running. These policies can be based on file names, file paths, publishers, or file hash, providing flexibility and precision in defining what is allowed to run on your systems.

PowerShell, a powerful scripting tool, serves both legitimate administrative purposes and malicious activities. In the wrong hands, PowerShell scripts can be tools for executing fileless attacks, exfiltrating data, or gaining unauthorized access to resources. To block unauthorized PowerShell scripts, you can create an AppLocker rule that targets PowerShell executable files. You can use the Group Policy tools to create restrictions and PowerShell.

A common practice is to deny all PowerShell scripts and then create exceptions for known approved scripts. The following creates a policy that prohibits executing the PowerShell 7 (x64) executable for all users:

```
New-AppLockerPolicy `
    -RuleType Path `
    -Path "C:\Program Files\PowerShell\7\pwsh.exe" `
    -Action Deny `
    -User Everyone `
    -OutVariable policy
```

> **Note:** If you are using a 32-bit platform, then the path changes to: C:\Program Files (x86)\PowerShell\7\pwsh.exe.

Using AppLocker to manage PowerShell script execution provides several benefits:
- **Enhanced security:** By controlling which scripts can run, you significantly reduce the risk of using PowerShell as a vector for malware or other security threats.

- **Granular control:** AppLocker allows you to tailor rules based on your organization's needs, allowing specific scripts while blocking others.
- **Audit capabilities:** AppLocker can be configured in audit mode to monitor script usage, helping you understand the impact of potential rules before fully enforcing them.
- **Compliance and standardization:** Enforcing script policies aids in maintaining compliance with internal or external security standards and promotes a standardized environment.

AppLocker is a powerful tool that can help you protect your system from malicious software and unauthorized applications. However, it is crucial to thoroughly test any policies in a controlled environment before deploying them organization-wide. Incorrectly configured policies can block legitimate scripts or applications, which can cause disruptions in your business operations. It is also essential to keep your policies up-to-date and review them regularly to adapt to new security challenges or changes in your IT environment. Doing so can ensure that your systems are safe and secure.

Using AppLocker policies to turn off unauthorized PowerShell scripts is a robust mechanism for enhancing the security of your Windows environments. It is a critical layer in a defense-in-depth strategy, particularly in environments where PowerShell scripting is prevalent.

Signing PowerShell scripts for reuse

Signing PowerShell scripts, you attach a digital signature to the script as a security measure. This process uses cryptographic certificates to verify the author's identity and ensure no one has changed the script since its signing. Signing scripts enhances security, especially under PowerShell policies like **AllSigned** or **RemoteSigned**. These policies mandate that a trusted publisher must sign scripts before execution, safeguarding against unauthorized or malicious script execution.

The most significant benefit of signing PowerShell scripts is increased security. By ensuring they sign scripts, organizations can prevent the execution of unauthorized or tampered scripts, reducing the risk of security breaches. Signed scripts also promote accountability, as the digital signature links a script to a specific individual or entity, helping in audit trials and compliance. In environments where scripts are shared across teams or executed on multiple systems, signing scripts reassures users that the scripts are legitimate and safe to use.

You need a code-signing certificate from a trusted **certificate authority (CA)** to sign a PowerShell script. This certificate can be a self-signed certificate for internal use, or a certificate obtained from an external CA for broader distribution. This command signs **Script.ps1** with the first code signing certificate found in your personal certificate store:

```
$cert = New-SelfSignedCertificate `

    -DnsName "CodeSigningCert" `

    -CertStoreLocation "Cert:\CurrentUser\My" `

    -Type CodeSigningCert


$cert = @(Get-ChildItem cert:\CurrentUser\My -CodeSigningCert)[0]

Set-AuthenticodeSignature `

    -FilePath "C:\PowerShell\Script.ps1" `

    -Certificate $cert
```

This figure displays the output from creating a new self-signed certificate and signing a PowerShell script:

SignerCertificate	Status	StatusMessage	Path
0869B0DD79D680B6691DC96136EF5D580FF819D5	Valid	Signature verified.	Script.ps1

Figure 13.7: Signing a PowerShell Script

Once you sign a script, you can use PowerShell to verify the signature's validity and ensure no one has modified the script. This cmdlet returns information about the script's signature, including the signer's identity and whether the signature is valid:

```
Get-AuthenticodeSignature -FilePath "C:\PowerShell\Script.ps1"
```

Modifying the PowerShell script without resigning will cause an error when validating it.

This figure displays the output from trying to validate the script after it is modified but not resigned:

SignerCertificate	Status	StatusMessage	Path
0869B0DD79D680B6691DC96136EF5D580FF819D5	HashMismatch	The contents of fil...	Script.ps1

Figure 13.8: Checking the Script Signature

While script signing enhances security, it also introduces some complexities. Managing certificates, especially in large environments, can be challenging. Certificates expire, and a process must be in place to renew them without disrupting operations. While easy to create, self-signed certificates are not automatically trusted on other systems, requiring additional configuration to establish trust. Additionally, every time a script is modified, it needs to be re-signed, adding a step to the script maintenance process.

A well-planned strategy to adopt script signing as a standard practice is crucial for organizations. They should establish policies that define when and how to sign scripts, who is authorized to sign them, and how to manage certificates. For scripts that are widely distributed or used in critical environments, it is advisable to use certificates from a recognized CA. You should conduct regular audits and monitoring to ensure adherence to the signing process and promptly address expired or compromised certificates. Signing PowerShell scripts enhances their security and integrity, especially when sharing and reusing scripts is common.

Next steps for the IT administrator

As an IT administrator, you have gained comprehensive knowledge of PowerShell from this book. This knowledge has equipped you to transform your IT environment. Your understanding of PowerShell's capabilities spans from essential command execution to sophisticated scripting techniques, security best practices, and system automation strategies. You have explored the intricacies of PowerShell remoting, the nuances of managing on-premises services, and the critical importance of securing PowerShell environments in an era where cybersecurity is paramount. This journey has not just been about acquiring technical knowledge; it has been about cultivating a mindset that sees PowerShell as a pivotal tool in the IT toolkit. This tool can significantly streamline operations, enhance system reliability, and bolster security. As you embark on the next phase of your professional journey, you are exceptionally positioned to leverage PowerShell to its fullest potential.

Moving forward, you can apply the knowledge you have gained to tackle various challenges and opportunities in your IT landscape. First, identify areas in your current environment where PowerShell can help drive efficiency and resolve long-standing issues. It may involve automating routine tasks, deploying scripts to manage user accounts and services, or implementing monitoring scripts to handle system events proactively. The key is seamlessly integrating PowerShell into your daily operations, transforming theoretical knowledge into practical solutions. Additionally, consider sharing your newfound knowledge with your team to encourage a culture of automation and efficiency. You can conduct training sessions, develop shared script repositories, and collaborate on complex automation projects. It is important to remember that the strength of PowerShell lies not only in its technical capabilities but also in its ability to foster collaboration and knowledge sharing among IT professionals.

It is essential to commit to lifelong learning as PowerShell continues to evolve. Stay engaged with the PowerShell community, participate in forums, attend webinars, and consider contributing to open-source projects. Keep an eye on emerging technologies and how they integrate with PowerShell and be ready to adapt your skills accordingly. Your role as an IT administrator is dynamic and ever-changing. Embracing this change, armed with the powerful toolset that PowerShell offers, will enhance your career and contribute to the success and resilience of your organization. Remember, your journey with PowerShell is continuous, marked by constant growth, adaptation, and a forward-thinking approach to technology and its possibilities.

Conclusion

In this chapter, you have gained a deep and nuanced understanding of the diverse capabilities of PowerShell, particularly in the context of security and script management. You started with the importance of securing PowerShell, a powerful tool that, if left unprotected, could become a vulnerability. You then delved into the realm of PowerShell Execution Policies, comprehending their pivotal role in controlling script execution and bolstering security. Your journey included mastering steps to safeguard both your computer and data while harnessing the power of PowerShell, ensuring your administrative activities are secure and efficient. The exploration of PowerShell Constrained Mode has provided insights into limiting PowerShell's functionality to mitigate risks, an essential aspect in secure scripting environments. You learned about implementing AppLocker policies, an effective strategy to restrict unauthorized PowerShell scripts and enhance organizational security. Overall, this chapter has provided you with vital knowledge and skills, positioning PowerShell as an indispensable tool in your repertoire for managing complex and security-sensitive environments.

Join our book's Discord space

Join the book's Discord Workspace for Latest updates, Offers, Tech happenings around the world, New Release and Sessions with the Authors:

https://discord.bpbonline.com

Index

A

Access Control Lists (ACLs) 59, 229
Active Directory
  configuring 211
  managing 211-216
Active Directory Domain Services
    (AD DS) 211
ActiveDirectory module 26, 61, 210
aliases 57, 58
Alias provider 20
Amazon Web Services (AWS) 28
AppLocker 272
  policies, for disabling PowerShell
    scripts 272, 273
Azure Cloud Shell 8

B

Backup Domain Controllers
    (BDC) 224

bridgehead server 223
built-in PowerShell providers
  existence of certificate, checking
    and importing 23
  new value, adding to
    PATH environment variable 22
  PDF files, finding in
    documents folder 22
  registry entry, creating 22
  using 21, 22
ByPropertyName 73
ByValue 73

C

certificate provider 20
certificates
  managing 230-232
challenges, PowerShell for
    Windows troubleshooting
  command outputs misinterpretation 260

complex error messages handling 259
execution policy restrictions 260
security implications, overlooking 260
child domain controller 223
CimCmdlets module 26
CIM commands 36
cmdlets 55
commands
  aliases 57, 58
  cmdlets 55
  creating, for producing
    multiple outputs 170-175
  discovering, for execution 46-54
  executing, from specific modules 60-63
  existing commands, executing
    within Windows 58-60
  functions 56
  scripts 56
Common Information Model
  (CIM) 17, 26
  reviewing, within PowerShell 40-42
custom objects
  creating 103
  managing 103, 104

D

Database Administrators (DBAs) 4
data filtering
  in pipeline 89-93
Desired State Configuration
  (DSC) 15, 62
DHCP 227
  managing 227, 228
DhcpServer module 210
disk management 238
DNS 226
  managing 226, 227
DnsServer module 26, 210

Docker 8
domain controllers (DC) 222
  managing 222-225
Domain local groups 220
Domain Name Service (DNS) 209
domain naming master 223
do-until loops 148, 157
do-while loops 148, 157
Dynamic Host Configuration Protocol
  (DHCP) 209

E

Enter-PSSession cmdlet 194, 196
ErrorActionPreference 158
error handling 158, 159
  implementing, to control flow 159-166
  non-terminating errors 158
  terminating errors 158
essential requirements, PowerShell
  Arm 10
  Docker 10
  Linux 10
  macOS 10
  Windows 9
event logs
  analyzing 255, 256
  filtering 256-259
execution policies 265-267
Export cmdlets
  using 111, 112
external PowerShell modules
  importing 28-31

F

File Server Resource Manager
  (FSRM) cmdlets 230
file shares
  creating 228, 229

managing 230
FileSystem provider 20
Flexible Single Master Operations (FSMO) roles 223
foreach loops 148
   reviewing 151-154
ForEach-Object command
   reviewing 149-151
for loops 148, 157
Function provider 20
functions 56

G

Get-ADDomain command 214
Get-ADForest command 214
Get-Counter cmdlet 236
Get-EventLog cmdlet 255
Get-GPO cmdlet 215
Get-LocalGroup cmdlet 217
Get-Process command 73
Get-WinEvent cmdlet 255, 258
Global Catalog Server 223, 225
Global groups 220
Google Compute (GC) 28
Group Policy Object (GPO) 215
   managing 215
GroupScope property 220

H

help system
   using 32-35

I

Import cmdlets
   using 112-114
Import-Module command 26
infrastructure master 224

Install-Module cmdlet 29
Integrated Development Environments (IDEs) 54
Internet Information Services (IIS) 15, 233
Invoke-Command cmdlet 204
   for command execution on remote computer 204-208
IT administrator 275, 276

K

Kerberos 189
Key Distribution Center (KDC) 189
Knowledge Consistency Checker (KCC) 223

L

Linux
   remote PowerShell connection 199
   remoting, configuring 193
looping 148
   capabilities 156, 157

M

Microsoft.PowerShell.Core module 26
Microsoft.PowerShell.Management module 26
Microsoft.PowerShell.Utility module 25
Microsoft.WSMan.Management module 26
MSI Package 10

N

NetAdapter module 61
.NET objects 114
   working with, in PowerShell 115-117
NetTCPIP module 60, 61, 211
network connectivity issues
   troubleshooting 247-251

New-PSSession cmdlet 196
New Technology LAN Manager (NTLM) 189

O

object methods
　working with 101, 102
object properties
　working with 100, 101
Organizational Unit (OU) 210
output destinations
　customizing, with conditional statements and loops 180-182

P

parameters
　advanced features 132-137
　creating 127
　data types, using 130-132
　default values, using 130-132
　using 127-130
Parse 87
performance bottlenecks
　diagnosing 242
　resolving 242-247
pipeline operator 72-74
　command execution, that flows into single and multiple pipelines, handling 75-78
piping ability 175
PowerShell 1-4
　current state 2, 3
　essential requirements 9, 10
　execution policies 265-267
　features 4, 5
　for on-premises management 210, 211
　installation options 8
　installing, on non-Windows platform 13-15
　installing, with installable package 10-13
　release dates 2, 3
　securing 264, 265
　users 4
　using, in VSCode 67-69
　versions 2
PowerShell 5.1 2
PowerShell 6+ 3
PowerShell 7+ 2, 8
PowerShell Constrained Mode 269-271
PowerShell for Windows troubleshooting challenges 259
PowerShell functions 122
　advantages 121
　calling 140-142
　combining, into complex scripts 142-145
　creating 120-123
　defining 140
　disadvantages 121
　output, selecting 123-127
　parameters, creating 127, 128
　parameters, using 128-130
　values, passing 137-140
　values, returning 137-140
PowerShell Gallery 15
　using 15, 16
PowerShell modules 18
　importing, from operating system 24-28
　purpose 18, 19
PowerShell objects 96-98
PowerShell output redirection 168
　operators, using 168-170
　output, piping to multiple destinations 175-177
　output, splitting into different files 177-179

results, appending to existing files 179, 180
PowerShell providers 19
  Alias provider 20
  built-in PowerShell providers, using 21, 22
  Certificate provider 20
  Environment provider 20
  FileSystem provider 20
  Function provider 20
  Registry provider 20
  Variable provider 20
PowerShell remoting 186, 187
  configuring, in Linux 193-195
  configuring, in Windows 191-193
  security implications 189-191
  use cases 187
  WinRM, using 188
PowerShell scripts
  disabling, with AppLocker policies 272, 273
  signing, for reuse 273-275
Primary Domain Controller (PDC) Emulator 222, 224
[PSCustomObject] data type
  advantages 105
  disadvantages 105
  using 104-107
PSDiagnostics module 26
Public Key Infrastructure (PKI) 230

R

Read-only Domain Controller (RODC) 223
Registry provider 20
Relative ID (RID) Master 223

remote PowerShell session
  connecting, to Windows and Linux 199-203
Remote Server Administration Tools (RSAT) 213
remote session
  creating, with New-PSSession and Enter-PSSession 196, 197
  using, with New-PSSession and Enter-PSSession 197-199
response object 64
response object types
  array objects 65
  Boolean objects 65
  custom objects 65
  integer objects 65
  string objects 64
return keyword 64
return object 64
Role-Based Access Control (RBAC) 190

S

schema master 223
scripts 56
  examples, with multiple output paths 183, 184
Secure Socket Shell (SSH) 186
Secure Sockets Layer (SSL) 189
Security Identifier (SID) 223
security vulnerabilities
  identifying 252-255
  remediating 252-255
ServerManager 211
server roles and features
  managing 232-234
Set-LocalUser cmdlet 217

Simple Object Access Protocol (SOAP) 186
specific data types
  setting, in PowerShell variables 107-111
SqlServer module 62
Storage module 211
string array 98
  creating 98
  managing 99, 100
switch command
  reviewing 154-156
switch statement 148
system resources
  analyzing 236-241
system security
  maintaining 267-269

T

Tee-Object cmdlet 175
TryParse 86, 87

U

Universal groups 220
user and group management 216-222

V

Variable provider 20
variables
  array variable 79
  creating, in PowerShell 80
  environment variables 79
  global variables 79
  HashTable variables 79
  managing, in PowerShell 80-82
  object variables 79
  passing, between commands 87-89
  PSDrive variables 80
  scalar variables 79
  script variables 79
  using 78-80
variable types
  casting 83-87
  declaring 82, 83
Visual Studio Code (VSCode) 67
  PowerShell, using 67-69

W

WebAdministration 211
while loops 148, 156
Windows
  remote PowerShell connection 199
  remoting, configuring 191
Windows Management Instrumentation (WMI) 17, 36
  classes 38
  namespaces 38
  reviewing, within PowerShell 36-40
Windows Package Manager (Winget) 8
Windows PowerShell Engine 8
Windows Remote Management (WinRM) 185, 188
  role, in PowerShell remoting 188, 189

Z

ZIP Package 10

Printed in Great Britain
by Amazon